Essays on the Poetry
of Trevor Joyce

Essays on the Poetry of Trevor Joyce

edited by

Niamh O'Mahony

Shearsman Books

First published in the United Kingdom in 2015 by
Shearsman Books
50 Westons Hill Drive
Emersons Green
BRISTOL
BS16 7DF

Shearsman Books Ltd Registered Office
30–31 St. James Place, Mangotsfield, Bristol BS16 9JB
(this address not for correspondence)

ISBN 978-1-84861-339-3

ACKNOWLEDGEMENTS
An earlier version of the essay by John Goodby was published in
Études Irlandaises 35.2 (2010). An earlier version of Niamh O'Mahony's
"Bibliography" on Trevor Joyce was published in *Jacket2* on February 3, 2014.
Many thanks to the editors of both journals for permitting the reproduction
of these texts here.

All quotations from the poetry of Trevor Joyce are reproduced by kind
permission of Trevor Joyce and his publishers. The editor would like to
thank the Irish Research Council for helping to fund this project, as well as
the authors of two doctoral dissertations which are quoted in the collection;
thanks to Marcella Edward, author of "Poetry of the Politics of Publishing
in Ireland: Authority in the Writings of Trevor Joyce, 1967-1995," and Julia
Panko, author of "Dead-tree Data: Print Novels, Information Storage, and
Media Transition". Thanks are also due to Fergal Gaynor and Ed Krčma for
permission to quote from Joyce's 2013 essay, "The Phantom Quarry," which
first appeared in *Enclave Review* 8, and to Mary Burger for permission to
quote from her 2000 essay, "Why I Write Narrative" which appeared in
Narrativity 1 in 2000 (The Poetry Centre, San Francisco State University).
Lucy Collins would like to thank Trevor Joyce, Michael Smith and the
National Library of Ireland for permission to quote from the records of New
Writers' Press.

The editor is grateful to Jason Lee for permission to reproduce his
photograph of Joyce on the front cover.

CONTENTS

Preface: Spandrels

Peter Manson

The lyric self is a lonely place, and the life's work of Trevor Joyce can be read as a search for its hidden populace. Translation has been Joyce's primary means of establishing the presence of more than one human consciousness at a time in the same set of words. *The Poems of Sweeny, Peregrine* occupy a position in Joyce's work not unlike that of Ezra Pound's complex early essays in translation ('The Seafarer', *Cathay* and 'Canto 1'). The Pound of 'The Seafarer' was still concerned with the purging of supplemental voices from the history of his text, translating a word meaning "angels" as "English" and rejecting the final lines of the poem as an improvement made by "a monk with literary ambitions" (Ruthven 214). Joyce's *Sweeny*, by contrast, is explicitly "A Working of the Corrupt Irish Text (1966–1976)" and, as a voice in Joyce's 'Trem Neul' has it, "corruption is fertility" (*first dream of fire* 203). I read the incorporation of *Sweeny*'s ten-year gestation into its subtitle as marking a further series of intrapersonal fault-lines in the already heavily sutured and multiply-mediated outcome of this textual relay: Trevor Joyce aged 19 is not Trevor Joyce aged 29 ("With the exception of your neurons / and your muscles, the cells of your / first body are long gone", as another voice in 'Trem Neul' notes) (223). It may be that any honest act of introspection must find the individual divided, and the space of language itself is haunted, for Joyce, by the numberless human lives that have shaped it and been shaped by it. Joyce quotes with approval James Clarence Mangan's description of his own inventive translations as "the antithesis of plagiarism" – if plagiarism is the failure to acknowledge one's sources, then the true plagiarist is the one who imagines his work to have no other source than his own imaginative invention (234). Joyce's writing is that antithesis, a highly sociable matter of workings and versions of prior texts (which themselves are often drawn from folk tradition or popular song), of writings "with" other writers, and of deliberate, exploratory subversions of his own "free" writing, recombining its constituent parts according to predesigned permutational schemata. Joyce has written of the long and ongoing process by which he has come to understand and to imaginatively inhabit the output of his own textual machinery in *Syzygy* – the self in such writing is a destination rather than a point of origin, or, rather, it is a staging-post on a way characterised by perpetual openness to change.[1]

Joyce's last word on the self may well be 'Trem Neul', "an autobiographical essay in prose and verse from which everything personal has been excluded".[2] The self in 'Trem Neul' is defined by the points of intersection of an intricate golden braid of strands of appropriated language, often from scientific or folkloric sources. There are constant shifts of scale and perspective: highly figurative descriptions of neuronal activity in the brain, or the "hive mind" of insects in a termite colony, could equally well be read as the choreography of a complex human dance, or the chaotic gravitational interactions of massive objects in space. With the constant accompaniment of human and avian music, the total effect is both true to experience and extraordinarily moving – I know of nothing else like it.

Joyce's use of formal constraint always carries an emotional charge, and its implications can be disturbing in a way that OuLiPian constraints rarely are. There's an aspect of gleefully violent revenge in an Irish poet's rewriting of the poems of Edmund Spenser (author of 'A View of the Present State of Ireland') in words of one syllable.[3] Joyce has written a remarkable account of his elaboration of a complex mechanism ("the hypersestina") for generating poems from a structural analysis of Botticelli's illustrations for a violently misogynist tale, from Boccaccio, of hell, repetition and social control ('Phantom Quarry').[4] The shared characteristic of most of Joyce's structures and symmetries is that at some point they break down or prove unsymmetrical.[5] Joyce's use of a structure derived from a palindromic musical form in *Syzygy* develops a flaw as soon as words are added to the structure (since a word is not the same thing as a musical note). The original intention with the hypersestina was that the poems generated by it should also function as clues, enabling a committed reader to work backwards and deduce the properties of the original structure for themselves. Joyce has described his own developing need to move onwards and outwards from the seed-words of his generative scheme towards its realisation in actual human language – he came finally to value the resulting swarm of 36-word poems for the poems' own intrinsic properties and to accept that, for the reader, there was no road back to the source. It's the lesson of entropy that you can't unbake a cake, and it's the Universe's overall tendency towards increased disorder that gives time a fixed direction.[6] The breakdown of Joyce's permutational structures implies a transition from cyclic to linear time. Since the hypersestina had its origins in a vision of eternally repeated violence experienced in hell, the escape from that cycle on to the straight road leading to the future is clearly optimistic, but it carries with it the uneasy awareness that not all cycles are hellish. Human life is sustained by the cycles of sleep, breath, menses, brainwave and heartbeat, and one day they all must stop.

The effects of constraint on the perceptible qualities of Joyce's work can be paradoxical. We are used to a poetry whose "measure" is defined by the audible patterning of various surface features of the language, from alternations of stressed and unstressed syllables to rhyme and alliteration. In Joyce, the underlying pattern – whether it's a generative structure like the hypersestina or the *Rome's Wreck* constraint, where each line has exactly eight words, all of one syllable – often can't be heard at all. What we perceive is its upshot, an unusually complex and irregular sonic surface which challenges our inevitable tendency to grasp at any hint of pattern. John Goodby, in his essay in this book, hears *Rome's Wreck* in terms of hexameters, and I remember one listener who commented on Joyce's seven-stress line after hearing a reading of *Rome's Wreck* at the SoundEye festival in Cork. It might be useful to think of Joyce's prosody as a "spandrel", the architectural term borrowed by Stephen Jay Gould and Richard Lewontin to denote a biological characteristic or structure which is not explicitly coded for in an organism's DNA, but which occupies the space "between" other structures which *are* explicitly coded for.[7] Such characteristics do not directly arise from the workings of natural selection but can confer a survival advantage on the organism – Noam Chomsky has suggested that the language faculty itself should be considered a spandrel, arising as a consequence of the growing size and complexity of the human brain. On this view, the remarkable freshness and unpredictability of Joyce's prosody arises by quite different means than a trivial virtuosity of sound-effect: this is a poetry which astonishes because no room has been left for it to do anything else.

Notes

1. 'The Construction of *Syzygy*', online at:
    http://www.drunkenboat.com/db8/oulipo/feature-oulipo/toward/joyce/construct.html (accessed 27 December 2013).
2. Anonymous note on the back cover of the 2001 edition of *with the first dream of fire they hunt the cold*.
3. *Rome's Wreck* by Trevor Joyce, Cusp Books, 2014.

⁴ Joyce's 'Phantom Quarry' essay is available online at http://enclavereview. wordpress.com/er8/.

⁵ Joyce's title *Pentahedron* may be an early signal of this tendency. There are no "regular" pentahedra, since it is impossible to construct a five-sided solid, each of whose faces has the same shape (as the faces of a tetrahedron or octahedron are all equilateral triangles, and those of a cube are all squares). The name "pentahedron" is given to two quite different five-sided solids: a pyramid with a square base, and a triangular prism. These solids are probably not to be read (though I'm tempted) as a shorthand for the span of human history from the pyramids to Sir Isaac Newton.

⁶ In the notes to his poem 'The Turlough' (1995), Joyce mentions the possibility of the Universe eventually halting its expansion and beginning to contract again. In a nice instance of physics imitating art, this cyclic possibility was ruled out in 1998 by the discovery that the expansion of the Universe, far from slowing, was accelerating.

⁷ http://en.wikipedia.org/wiki/Spandrel_(biology)

Works Cited

Joyce, Trevor. *Rome's Wreck. Translated from the English of Edmund Spenser's Ruines of Rome*. Los Angeles, CA: Cusp Books, 2014. Print.

——. 'The Phantom Quarry: Translating a Renaissance Painting into Modern Poetry'. *Enclave Review* 8 (2013): 5–8. Print.

——. 'The Construction of *Syzygy*'. *The Drunken Boat* 8. 2006. Web. 6 Dec. 2012. <http://www.drunkenboat.com/db8/oulipo/feature-oulipo/toward/joyce/construct.html>

——. *with the first dream of fire they hunt the cold: A Body of Work 1966–2000*. 2nd ed. Dublin: New Writers' Press; Exeter: Shearsman Books, 2003. Print.

——. 'Trem Neul'. *with the first dream of fire they hunt the cold: A Body of Work 1966–2000*. 2nd ed. Dublin: New Writers' Press; Exeter: Shearsman Books, 2003. 185–231. Print.

Ruthven, K.K. *A Guide to Ezra Pound's 'Personae'*. 1926. Berkeley, CA: Schafer, 1969. Print.

"Spandrel". *Wikipedia, The Free Encyclopedia*. Wikimedia Foundation, Inc. 29 Dec. 2013. Web. 24 Jan. 2014.

Peter Manson

Introduction

Niamh O'Mahony

It is nearly fifty years since Trevor Joyce published his first collection of poems in Dublin, and the wealth of his writing since 1967 has been alternatively, and often simultaneously, fierce, challenging and familiar. This book is the first collection of essays to discuss Joyce's poetry and the distinguished contribution it makes to the development of Irish literature in the twentieth and twenty-first centuries.

Joyce was born in Dublin in 1947. His mother was born in the Galway Workhouse and his father grew up in south Tipperary, near the Joyce stronghold of East Limerick. The family moved from Mary Street in Dublin city centre to Glasnevin on the north side of the city in the mid-sixties, by which time Joyce was already an avid reader and collector of books. His library began with disintegrating nineteenth-century volumes on classical history, medical textbooks, and the archaeology of Nineveh, and quickly lined the walls of his bedroom, winding its way around the small landing and down the stairs, where his books vied for space with his mother's newspaper collection. It was about this time that Joyce met Michael Smith, which was the beginning of a life-long friendship. Smith was five years older than the poet, and had more experience of printing and publishing which he gained during a period working at a Dublin newspaper. Joyce had already made his first attempts at poetry when he met Smith, but Smith's friendship became a central source of motivation and encouragement for the poet in the following years.

In 1967, Joyce, established New Writers' Press [NWP] with Michael and Irene Smith to provide a publishing outlet for young poets, Irish and international, who were not receiving an audience through the available channels. In Smith's 'Introduction to New Irish Poets' published as a prospectus with Joyce's *Sole Glum Trek*, NWP's first issue, the editors set the parameters of the press as follows:

> Most of the poets whose work will be included in this series are Irish and under thirty. Believing poets should be beyond the herd-instinct, they belong to no school, movement, club or clique. They

are all serious poets – that is, human beings for whom writing poetry is a profoundly central activity, not a mere hobby or ornamental grace.

The essays gathered here offer various perspectives on the experimental nature of NWP publications, and yet it is worth considering Smith and Joyce's agenda for the press as it diverged from their contemporaries in Irish poetry publishing. At the same time that NWP was preparing the first issue of its in-house journal, *The Lace Curtain*, Liam Miller of Dolmen Press was collaborating with Michael and Anne Yeats and Thomas Kinsella on a revival of Cuala Press, originally edited and managed by W.B. Yeats, Lily and Lolly Yeats.[1] Every effort was made to ensure that the new Cuala Press would be as authentic as possible and yet the editors were aware of the difficulties this would create. The first volume to be published by the Press was "inevitably, slow to come to completion" Miller acknowledged, and "it was almost a year before the book, *Reflections*, an unpublished section of the journals of W.B. Yeats, was ready" (100). In the same period that the new Cuala Press prepared one book, NWP published eight of the forty-four publications that appeared in the first ten years of NWP activity.[2] Jorge Luis Borges' *Poems* was published in August 1969, an edition which Joyce believes to be "the first collection anywhere, in English, completely given over to his poetry" (Joyce 'History of a Project' 276). Alongside the Borges collection, NWP also prepared two issues of *The Lace Curtain* during this time, as well as *No Die Cast* by Brian Lynch, *Watches* by Joyce, *Homage to James Thompson (B.V.) at Portobello* by Smith, a translation of *The Hag of Beare* from the Old Irish by Michael Hartnett, *The Flags are Quiet* by Gerard Smyth, *Survival* by Augustus Young and three further collections from Pearse Hutchinson, Leland Bardwell and Macdara Woods. NWP made speed and immediacy their purpose so that the published book became a "cheap, fast, and effective means of getting new poetry before its prospective public". The difference between NWP and the new Cuala Press is compounded by reference to Lynch's *No Die Cast*. In a note to the collection in his NWP checklist, Joyce describes the title of Lynch's book as "the longest meaningful phrase" the editors could "extract from the few letters of display-sized type" they had available – those used for the title of Smith's *Dedications* (288). The innovative quality of NWP publications has been debated but clearly the material production of the press sets Smith and Joyce very much at odds with their peers in nineteen-sixties Ireland. The editors were content to depart from "the legacy of Yeats" which "favoured

Niamh O'Mahony

the book as art-object" in order to publish more poetry faster, and to a wider audience (278).

After *Sole Glum Trek* (1967) and *Watches* (1969), Joyce published two more collections with NWP in the seventies. *Pentahedron* (1972) gathered a range of new poems together with selections from the two earlier collections, and *The Poems of Sweeny, Peregrine* (1976) presented a translation, or "working" of the eighth-century Irish myth of Buile Suibhne. Joyce's father had died in the intervening years, and the poet also had his first brush with university, registering as a mature student at twenty-one to study English and Philosophy at University College Dublin. A lack of funds was primarily to blame for Joyce's repeated deferrals. By 1976, Joyce had withdrawn from active involvement in NWP and was beginning to lose faith in the poetic means he had available in his writing and in its ability to do what he required of it.

NWP now entered what Joyce calls the "second phase of its activity" guided by Smith's correspondence with Brian Coffey ('Irish Terrain' 159). Coffey supported NWP's work and helped Smith recover a generation of poets that Coffey had written and published alongside in the nineteen-thirties such as Denis Devlin, Thomas MacGreevy, Charlie Donnelly and Niall Montgomery. Joyce had worked as a clerk in the Planning Departments of Dublin Corporation and Dublin County Council on and off since 1967, but he soon moved on to a position in the IT sector of P.J. Carroll's, a job secured for him by Montgomery. Over the following years, Joyce set about providing himself with the education he believed necessary for a poet. He read widely in Philosophy, I.T., Politics, Literature, Economics and Chinese and Japanese poetry, even teaching classes on classical Chinese poetry as part of the Ireland China Cultural Society in Dublin.[3] In 1984, Joyce moved to Cork and enrolled to study Mathematical Sciences at University College Cork. Within months of moving to Cork, Joyce founded The Melmoth Press. In a 1984 funding application to the Arts Council, Joyce outlined the purpose of the press as follows: "to sustain the cosmopolitan tradition of writing in Ireland" by publishing "forgotten classics, the neglected work of living masters and the work of emerging writers who show promise of continuing the tradition of Irish avant-garde experiment and innovation" (personal collection). Among the press' projected publications, Joyce listed the selected works of William Dunkin, James Clarence Mangan and Niall Montgomery, as well as a first collection by David Lloyd.[4] The press would also acknowledge the "importance of translation" as a symptom of the "internationalism" characterizing Irish poetry. In 1985, Melmoth Press published two volumes, *Chanterelles* by Brian Coffey and *Selected Poems* by Michael Smith. It wasn't long before the practical difficulties of commissioning, preparing and publishing books at a remove from the Dublin printers and the local impositions of life and work made it impossible for Joyce to continue, and soon both Melmoth Press and NWP went quiet. By this time, Joyce had not published any of his own poetry for nearly ten years, and this period of quietude continued well into the next decade.

Joyce has acknowledged that his was not the self-imposed silence of George Oppen or Paul Valéry and he has spoken about his struggle to write during this time. He remembers poets and peers commenting, 'Trevor Joyce stopped writing', and yet there are boxes of notes which record his efforts to discover a form or language adequate to his needs. In a 2013 interview with Marthine Satris, Joyce explains his aversion to what he saw as a pattern for poets around him in the seventies to "get bogged down and settle on a personal solution or… style and then stick with that as their trademark" (14). Unwilling to settle and unable to write in a way that satisfied him, Joyce chose instead to spend his time seeking out "alternative approaches". Among the various "alternatives" Joyce would discover over the following years, one of the first to emerge was the work of Raymond Roussel, a French poet and novelist whose modernist writings contributed to what would later be named OuLiPo. Soon, Joyce returned to the detective classics of Arthur Conan Doyle and Sax Rohmer he had read as a child, with the protagonists Holmes and Smith deducing from even the most arbitrary item a central clue in identifying the villain. It wasn't long before Joyce read these stories as confirming rather than undermining the hierarchies of "observation, inference and deduction" which had reduced his poetry to "argument, deploration, pleading [and] threats" ("Why I Write Narrative"). Joyce's increasingly specialised knowledge of computer systems and information flow provided a more profitable avenue of exploration, and it was around this time that Joyce first conceived of the three-dimensional structure that would provide a conceptual basis to the 36-word poems that populate *What's in Store.*[5] His experience with information systems benefited him both poetically and professionally, leading him to join Apple as a Business Systems Analyst in 1992. Soon, Joyce encountered John Cage's chaotic and innovative forms for a second time and with the benefit of the intervening years. For Joyce, this second encounter was characterised by "more understanding of how the play of ambient noise across the receptivity of [Cage's] spaces might circumvent"

Niamh O'Mahony

the full extent of authorial intention ("Why I Write Narative"). In Cage, the poet recognised an "alternative approach" to writing which avoided the "exclusions" of the incoherent world that characterised accounts of Sherlock Homes and Fu Manchu, and an ability to "admit what might otherwise not be acknowledged". From here, Joyce could begin to imagine how he might establish the parameters necessary within poetry for the aleatory to intervene. Such "alternative approaches" made a significant contribution to Joyce's return to writing in the mid-nineties, and yet they were, in themselves, not enough to inaugurate this return.

One significant impetus came with J.C.C. Mays' 1990 essay, 'Flourishing and Foul: Six Poets and the Irish Building Industry,' an historically-attuned analysis of Joyce's poetry and the first academic recognition of his writing. The "health or otherwise of Irish poetry is to be measured in what it has chosen to do without," according to Mays, and Joyce is numbered among those poets whose poetry stands outside the parameters provided. Here, Mays aligns Joyce with "James Hogan ('Augustus Young') and Geoff Squires… as the most original poets of their generation" (10). For Joyce, the essay was "ground-breaking," and when one considers the publication of two of Joyce's poems in the same issue, Mays' essay does indeed constitute a significant point in Joyce's return to writing ('Irish Terrain' 162).[6] With Mays' essay supplying a critical imperative, Joyce's encounter with Federico García Lorca's final publication, *Tamarit Poems*, equipped him with a poetic incentive for his return to writing in the early nineties:

> I remember coming across it [*Tamarit Poems*] and thinking it was just marvellous, absolutely gorgeous… [T]here's one poem in it… 'Casida of the Weeping' that just stunned me… I wrote a poem which was my response to it and from that the rest of the book [*stone floods*] just branched out. (Keohane 9)

In 1995, Joyce published *stone floods* with NWP, his first collection in almost two decades, which inaugurated a strikingly prolific period for the poet. At Romana Huk's Assembling Alternatives conference in New Hampshire in 1996, Joyce met Geoffrey Squires, Maurice Scully, Catherine Walsh, Billy Mills and Randolph Healy for the first time.[7] The energy and enthusiasm Joyce gained from this event was reflected in the myriad of publications that followed and the consequences of the conference are "still resonating" in Ireland nearly twenty years later (Joyce 'Irish Terrain' 165).

The immediate effect of Assembling Alternatives was the founding of the 'Cork Poetry Conference' [later the 'SoundEye Festival'] by Catriona Ryan, Matthew Geden and Trevor Joyce the following year in 1997.[8] Ryan and Geden were graduate students in English at University College Cork when Ryan posed the idea for a conference celebrating the thirtieth anniversary of New Writers' Press. Together, she and Geden developed the idea and then met with Joyce to seek his suggestions on poets to invite, contact details and advice.

The Cork Poetry Conference featured readings by Squires, Mills, Healy, Walsh, Scully, and Joyce along with Judy Kravis and Michael Smith, as well as papers on Irish experimental writing by Mills, Joyce and Alex Davis, in acknowledgement of the living tradition of innovation in Irish poetry. In a recent history of the event, Joyce identifies the "primary intent of the festival" being to "provide a forum for poets (and, perhaps, as it turned out, certain strains of poetry) overlooked by other poetry events in Ireland" ('History'). The success of that first year of the conference prompted a second the following year; it soon became less conference-oriented and more of a poetry festival. As the festival became an annual event, it also expanded its range and David Lloyd, Mairéad Byrne, Fanny Howe, Tom Raworth, Keith Tuma, Alison Croggon, Stephen Rodefer and Fergal Gaynor became regular readers at this most international of local festivals. SoundEye is as much about the conversations between guests as it is about the readings, and while the festival has occupied a variety of locations across the city, activity still revolves around Joyce's house in Shandon. Ryan left the city in 1997 and relinquished her involvement with the event, and by 2006 Geden too stepped down from a direct role in the festival. By 2007, Gaynor was assisting Joyce with organisation and in October that year, Lloyd invited Joyce, Gaynor and Mairéad Byrne to attend 'SoundEye West' at the University of Southern California.[9] If 2005 marked a highpoint of the festival as a "nexus of New Writers' Press, the legacy of New Hampshire and [the organisers'] engagement with many other forms of contemporary art," the years that followed did not provide the same opportunities for funding and support. For Joyce, the struggle to "sustain... SoundEye in the financial desert" was eased somewhat by the contribution of James Cummins and Rachel Warriner who took over the organisation of the festival circa 2009. After several years in attendance both as poets and audience members, and arranging readings under the aegis of DEFAULT Press, Cummins and Warriner soon became co-organisers with Joyce and Gaynor, and it is because of their work that the festival continues today.[10] In 2005, Charles Bernstein described SoundEye as "without question… the most innovative and most important literary gathering to take place in Ireland—or just about anywhere else—over the last decade" and having now reached its nineteenth year, SoundEye is one of the most enduring poetry festivals in Ireland.

Joyce published three more chapbooks in the late nineties, and in 2001 his collected works, *with the first dream of fire they hunt the cold: A Body of Work* appeared from Shearsman and NWP.[11] The 2001 collection was followed by *Take Over* and *Undone, Say* in 2003, and by 2007 Joyce had prepared another 300 pages of poetry for publication under the title, *What's in Store*. *Courts of Air and Earth* followed in 2008, gathering together Joyce's translations from Old and Middle Irish including the *Poems of Sweeny, Peregrine* and selections from *Dánta Grádha* and 'Love Songs from a Dead Tongue'. After translating a volume of Finnish dystopian prose poems with Seija Kerttula entitled *Poems of Aregemia* in 2012, Joyce published his next collection, *The Immediate Future* with Runamok Press in 2013. In 2014, *Rome's Wreck* was published by Cusp Books and a further collection entitled *Selected Poems 1967-2014* has just appeared from Shearsman Books.

Much has changed in literary criticism over the past twenty-five years and yet these changes have been slow to influence the critical reception of Joyce's oeuvre. When one considers that Joyce's first collections appeared con-currently with those of Seamus Heaney, Paul Durcan, Derek Mahon, Paul Muldoon, Eavan Boland, Michael Hartnett and Eiléan Ní Chuilleanáin, all poets well-received and much-discussed in Irish Studies, this lack of critical attention is all the more striking. The upswing in Irish Studies in the nineteen-sixties established a critical commitment to Irish writing and culture among an international community of scholars.[12] Timothy J. Meagher attributes the development of the discipline to the "rebirth and reinterpretation of Irish ethnic identity in the 1960s," and this in turn prompted an unprecedented critical interest in Irish poetry (270). Smith took his opportunity in a 1971 essay to inform American and British readers of the redundancy of "that whole body of painstakingly accumulated, mainly useless information called Anglo-Irish Lit. Studies" which granted an "imprimatur" to "Irish poetry of the Yeatsian Dye" (17).[13] Later, Smith explained his difficulty with the discipline, stating that "outside Ireland there is little or no interest in contemporary Irish poetry," so concerned is the scholar of Irish studies "with his Joyce or his Yeats or his Synge" ('Contemporary Situation' 154). While rejecting the "gross process of simplification," "abetted by Anglo-Irish Lit. scholars," that effaced the poetry of Beckett, Devlin, Montgomery, Coffey and MacGreevy," Smith was aware that these scholars emerged both "indigenous and migrant," and the nationalist definition of Irish writing was very much home-grown ('Since Yeats' 18). Smith's affirmation of the value and importance of the "European Irishmen" writing in the thirties also validates that later generation of poets including John Montague, Seamus Heaney, John Jordan, Paul Durcan and Trevor Joyce (20).

If Smith was not concerned to distinguish Joyce's poetry from that of Montague, Heaney or Durcan in this essay, it was because the nationalist trajectory of poetry and criticism he was attacking had yet to exert its full effects on this younger generation of poets. Marcella Edwards' account of poetry and publishing in Ireland in the nineteen-sixties does much to demonstrate the impact of this nationalist imperative on the "new literary renaissance" in Irish writing and the distinctions which would emerge over the following decades (Martin 17).[14] Edwards points to a 1965 essay by the Irish critic, Augustine Martin, which she says tasks writers of the "new literary renaissance" with the responsibility to "express... a national cultural identity freed at last from derivative or petrified attitudes, where the writer assumes a central role in the development of national self-awareness" (68).[15] Here, Martin affirms this new era in Irish writing as challenging the dominance of Joyce and Yeats and their negative appraisals of Ireland and the Irish. A writer must "know his people directly, minutely, omnivorously," Martin says, if the resultant literature is to be "alive and authentic" in its representation of contemporary society (14). Instead of "repudiat[ing] the social and religious pieties of Ireland" as Yeats and Joyce did, Martin encourages the new generation of Irish writers towards a mode of reflection and representation which is "not only for the good of literature but for the good of society" (14). Two years later, Martin would write a positive review of Joyce's *Sole Glum Trek* and the NWP enterprise, an unexpected move perhaps given his 1965 essay, and one that does not reflect the complexity of the situation. For Edwards, Martin's instruction to young writers to absolve themselves of James Joyce's "vision of Ireland" which "is so grievously compelling" is indicative of the "modernising process" affecting "industry, economics and social policy changes" in the nineteen-sixties ("a scheme of echoes" 3). The debates surrounding Irish poetry and publishing at the time "testify to the endurance of certain nationalistic and essentialist tendencies," Edwards says, "and give the lie to the easy assumption of a modernising, let alone a modernist ethos within Irish poetry of the nineteen sixties" (4). The revival of the Yeats family enterprise, Cuala Press, towards the end of this decade serves as evidence of the "regressive poetics" which, for Edwards, manifested an acutely nationalist mode of cultural self-reconstruction in Irish poetry and publishing of the era.

Joyce was vocal in his rejection of what Brian Coffey called the "recognizably Irish quality" of conventional Irish poetry which Coffey said was "bad" for the poet because it exacts one of two effects: "either it refers to the purely physical effects of biological kind and as such says nothing of interest about the poetry, or it sets up a very dubious criterion of a limiting kind almost certainly bound to bias the critical judgement which accepts it" ('Irish Terrain' 159).[16] Joyce's repudiation of the existing parameters of Irish poetry evokes a critical binary of mainstream and avant-garde familiar in the debates surrounding contemporary poetry and which goes some way towards explaining the paucity of critical attention to his work.

The narrative of 'mainstream versus experimental' writing so prevalent in critical accounts of twentieth and twenty-first century poetry in Ireland, Britain, and beyond, has come under scrutiny in recent years from critics on both sides of the divide. Seamus Heaney reflects a seemingly general position when he says that "avant-garde" is "an old-fashioned term by now" because "in literature, nobody can cause bother any more" (Heaney 451). Joyce himself has commented that critical terms such as "innovative" and "experimental" are "boring" when applied to poetry and "don't really matter... anymore" ('Interview' *Jacket2*). Heaney might be correct in his assertion that celebrated contemporary writers rarely provoke the controversy and notoriety that followed Ezra Pound, but while in other contexts some of the most contentious of contemporary schools have been welcomed into the fold of late, there is a long-standing and residual history of opposition in Irish poetry which is readily recognizable in the diverse publishing histories and critical receptions of Heaney and Joyce.[17] Joyce's affiliation with small-press publishing in NWP was prompted, in part, by the anticipated negative response from Dolmen Press to his and Smith's first collections in the sixties. By the time Joyce returned to publishing in the nineties, no presses were actively seeking to publish his work, if indeed they were aware of it. Randolph Healy's Wild Honey Press published *Syzygy* and *Without Asylum* in 1998 with print runs of 228 and 98 respectively, and the remainder of Joyce's work has been published with Shearsman Books, The Gig, and New Writers' Press, with one collection each from Runamok Press and Cusp Books. These are all small presses, some of them very small. For contemporary poets such as Joyce, a commitment to small-press publishing is often interpreted as a personal or political preference on the part of the poet, but the politics of small-press publishing are as particular in Ireland as they are anywhere else, and it is worth noting that even the most recent NWP publications do not resemble the "exquisite," "beautiful objects" published by Punch Press in the US and Crater Press in the UK (Cooke).[18] Working at a "remove [ ] from economic thinking," both presses foster a particular ideological remit for the contemporary late-modernist British poets they publish. Joyce's publishing history provides the clearest example of the restricted opportunities for publishing poetry that does not conform to the conventions provided for Irish writing over the past decades. That Joyce has continued to publish poetry in Ireland and seen his poetry receive critical attention is evidence of the opportunities poetry affords for one to create oneself and one's audience over and against the odds.

It would be unfair to suggest that Joyce and Smith did not contribute to the culture of opposition that they themselves experienced; *The Lace Curtain* featured some rather trenchant editorials over its short span, and several of Joyce's essays bear witness to a very rigid divide between the mainstream and avant-garde communities of poetry. That said, Joyce did not have the benefit of control over, or even access to, the powerful institutions of publishing and criticism that play such a constitutive role in the definition and delimitation of Irish writing. Edna Longley's refusal to consider the existence of traditions of Irish modernism other than the Yeats line, including the line of Brian Coffey, Denis Devlin, Catherine Walsh and Trevor Joyce, goes some way towards demonstrating the divide. "These people are confused" was part of her response to Keith Tuma's question about the possibility of an alternative tradition in Irish modernism at a conference on Post-War Anglo-American Poetic Relations in 1998.[19] Longley elaborates on this perspective in a review of Tuma's *Anthology of Twentieth-Century British and Irish Poetry*. Here, Longley discredits Tuma's inclusion of Joyce, Walsh and Maurice Scully in his *Anthology*, describing them as "poets who feel marginalised by what, in a common paranoid and superior vocabulary, is invariably called the 'mainstream'" (56). It becomes harder to sustain Longley's rejection of this critical opposition when one considers that it wasn't until 2002 that the first essay solely devoted to Joyce's poetry was published.[20] The papers presented at the inaugural SoundEye festival in 1997 offer a variety of responses to this common and deficient critical reception of Joyce's poetry and that of his peers. Joyce,

Davis and Mills each discuss the diverse understandings of and trajectories for the critical analysis of innovative Irish poetry. These essays serve both as a record of a particularly self-conscious moment in the history of Irish writing and as a marker against which to judge the recent developments in Irish poetry criticism.

Joyce's essay, 'The Point of Innovation in Irish Poetry,' constitutes a critical history of the mainstream versus avant-garde divide in Irish poetry and his own position within that history since the nineteen-sixties. Joyce begins by aligning the final poem from *Pentahedron* with the work of Boland and Mahon as exemplifying the "poetry of expression" characteristic of conventional Irish poetry (46). This work is criticised as "merely imitating the images of beauty with which they are already familiar" and submitting "occasionally towards the mess that is the world, only through a sense of guilt… at perpetrating such works of beauty in such a foul environment" (49). The difficulty that such poetry experiences is in "representing" the "reality" of the world and "the irreducible experience of real pain… pressed on us by media" which cannot register in a poetic language "in which all positive terms have been appropriated by advertising" (46). The danger for the poem, then, is that any attempt to represent or respond to the world is "left, once elicited, without possibility of external effect". Joyce is clear that he and Smith certainly conceived as NWP as "alternative to the status quo, but [never]… as eccentric" since to do so "would have been to accede to the claims made by the 'mainstream' for its own centrality" (47). The statement problematises critical attempts to situate Joyce's poetry because it sets NWP activities at a remove from the "'mainstream'" while also undermining the "centrality" of the mainstream as the prevailing form or style.

Joyce has argued for the ill fit between the critical rhetoric of mainstream and avant-garde and the nuances of the Irish context. In his essay published in *Assembling Alternatives,* Joyce emphasises that "there are no second-generation Beats, or Black Mountain, or New York School" in Irish literary history for contemporary poets to "react to" (165). The Celtic Twilight was the sole literary movement to "achieve prominence" in the early twentieth century, on account of its "links with nationalist politics" and the "quality of its major figure, Yeats". Mays describes how James Joyce, Samuel Beckett, and Flann O'Brien were each subject to the phenomenon of "incorporation," assimilated into Irish literary history after the fact of international recognition in a process designed to quash the more incongruous elements of the writer's oeuvre.[21] That each of these writers had to be recovered affirms Joyce's assertion that the majority of Irish writers up until the nineteen-sixties "defined themselves in relation to [The Celtic Twilight]", "either working from within it, as did [Austin] Clarke and, to some extent, Kavanagh, or explicitly opposing it from the outside, as did Beckett and his associates". Mays and Joyce are alert to the lack of a consolidated avant-garde tradition in Irish writing. The recent commitment of Irish poetry to an aesthetics of nation-building means that poets such as Joyce suffer the same exclusion from literary and critical institutions that afflicts avant-garde communities in Europe, but without the benefit of a history of avant-garde poetry to react to or an avant-garde community to join. Alex Davis explains the emergence of a generation of experimental Irish poets in the closing decades of the twentieth-century in terms of "deferred action" as per Hal Foster's *The Return of the Real* (82). That Joyce and his peers constitute an "Irish neo-avant-garde" which has "no immediate or national historical precursor upon which it can act" is not in question for the critic. Rather, Davis is concerned with the "trauma" effected by this poetry which he says "cannot be domesticated as an Irish adjunct to a global (read: North American) neo-avant-garde" while, at the same time it "obdurately refus[es] to conform to the dominant procedures of contemporary Irish poetry" (83). If the lack of critical attention to Joyce's poetry provides one impetus for this book, it also suggests its corollary, that of consolidating the existing critical analysis of Joyce's poetry, and it is here that this collection aims to contribute to Irish poetry criticism.

§

Poetry magazines, "like butterflies," have "all too short a life," Joyce and Smith state in their first issue of *The Lace Curtain*, and while the editors were content that "this brief span" saves magazines from "becom[ing] institutionalised and editorially retrogressive," the consequences for the poet writing are more problematic (Editorial). This book is the first collection of essays on Joyce and is intended to consolidate the critical response to his poetry which got underway nearly thirty years after the publication of his first collection and still resides for the most part in small press magazines, one-off journals and blogs. David Lloyd, Keith Tuma and John Goodby are long-time readers and critics of Joyce's poetry and the essays they contribute here extend and develop the critical reception of Joyce's oeuvre which they themselves helped to establish. Geoffrey Squires and Fanny Howe have both played important roles in Joyce's writing life. Squires was an early contributor to NWP and a compatriot to Joyce in Irish experimental poetry, while Howe's writing has served as inspiration and she herself championed Joyce's poetry. Gaynor's poetry and his work curating and collaborating on artistic performances and festivals in Cork have provided parallels for Joyce's activity. Manson's readings at the SoundEye festival consistently challenge and reinvigorate audiences, while the "lightly-worn scholarship" and "quotidian bathos" of his poetry reflect and provoke Joyce's poetic commitments (Brahic n.p.; Noel-Tod 127). The essays by Marthine Satris, Eric Falci and Jeffrey Twitchell-Waas demonstrate a growing critical interest in Joyce's poetry internationally, and Lucy Collins' contribution bears witness to a renewed commitment in Irish criticism to alternative literary traditions.

Alongside these writers, there are a number of others whose names are not included in the contents page but who must be acknowledged for their importance to Joyce's writing life. In his essay in *Assembling Alternatives*, Joyce states that Mays and Davis are the only two academics "working in English studies in Ireland who have demonstrated in print any interest in or understanding of experimental Irish poetry" (162). Their critical attention and analyses have provided a vital source of enthusiasm and encouragement for the poet, and this is reflected in the many references to and invocations of their criticism over the course of this collection. Nate Dorward, founder and editor of *The Gig* magazine and publishing press, is another individual of crucial importance to Joyce's poetry, and very much outside of the academy. After hearing Joyce read at the 1996 conference in New Hampshire, Dorward got hold of Joyce's recent poetry and soon came to recognise him as "a major writer" (Dorward n.pag.). Dorward took it upon himself to establish *The Gig* magazine to publish the poems Joyce emailed to him. Dorward also co-published *What's In Store* in collaboration with NWP. Alongside Mays, Davis and Dorward, Michael Smith occupied an essential position as fellow-poet, publisher and friend to Joyce. Smith was the first interlocutor for Joyce's poetry for many years, and he continued to publish his poetry and critically-acclaimed translations for many years.

The essays gathered in this collection address the earliest of Joyce's collections right through to his most recent, including *Rome's Wreck*, a collection still forthcoming at the time these essays were being written. *With the first dream of fire they hunt the cold* and *What's in Store* feature across the collection. The essays succeed in demonstrating the range and remit of Joyce's poetry. From the full-length essays on individual poems by Satris, Gaynor and Lloyd to the thematic analyses of Goodby and Twitchell-Waas, the contributors to this collection offer diverse and sometimes conflicting perspectives on Joyce's oeuvre. Howe offers an impressionistic response to various poems and collections combined with a personal recollection of her experience at SoundEye. Squires traces Joyce's negotiations with prosody in an essay which manages to be both genial and declarative. Collins presents a necessary back-history of Joyce's earliest collections from *Sole Glum Trek* and *Watches* through *Pentahedron* and up to *The Poems of Sweeny, Peregrine*. Tuma surveys *What's In Store* asking how and why Joyce determined to gather in one collection the various sections and sequences of that book. These essays ask compelling questions about Joyce's poetry, its place in the history of Irish poetry, and the meaning and definition of the term 'Irish poetry' as it is and might be received.

The authors contributing to this book offer several sets of parameters useful for the growing critical attention directed towards Joyce's poetry; however, as with any collection of essays, not every poem and project is assessed. Beyond this introduction, the *Offsets* project is mentioned only in passing throughout the book, and Joyce's knowledge and use of information systems in his writing merits more focused attention than it receives here. Meanwhile, the critical concern to locate Joyce's poetry as part of the Irish poetry canon, which is perpetuated in this introduction, elides potentially more revealing comparisons of Joyce's poetry with that of his European and American counterparts. So far, criticism has been slower to relinquish the rhetorical and conceptual models it has inherited than Joyce and his poetry have been to demand new approaches to reading and reception. The essays presented in this book are, in effect, catching up on an Irish poet very much in his prime and whose writing continues to outpace its critics.

The editor would like to thank Graham Allen, Alex Davis, Nate Dorward, Keith Tuma and, of course, Trevor Joyce, for their invaluable help with this project.

Notes

[1] Miller outlined the reasons for the revival and the new editors' intentions to remain as faithful as possible to the Press' original aims: "The new Cuala Press books will continue the traditions first set in the original prospectus of 1903... The typographical standards set by Emery Walker will be adhered to. The same typeface, Caslon, in the same size, will be used. The books will be printed at the original handpress used since 1903. The paper, as in the earlier books, will

Niamh O'Mahony

be specially made at Saggart, County Dublin, by the Swiftbrook Mills and bindings, in linen with coloured boards, will also remain unchanged. The publications will include the best new work being written in Ireland, printed with the same craftsmanship that made the Cuala Press famous amongst book collectors everywhere" (99-100).

2 Joyce included a 'Checklist of Publications' by NWP with his essay on the history of the Press in *Modernism and Ireland* edited by Patricia Coughlan and Alex Davis.

3 This work led to Joyce's presentation of a paper at the Europe-China Association Annual Conference at the University of Oxford in 1982 where he spoke alongside Joseph Needham. Joyce's work with the Irish-Chinese Cultural Society prompted an invitation from the Chinese Government for Joyce to join an Irish delegation on a three-week tour of China in September 1983.

4 A collection by Lloyd entitled *Arc & Sill: Poems 1979-2009* was finally published by NWP in collaboration with Shearsman Books in 2012. The fact that a poet such as Lloyd would want his 2012 publication to appear under the aegis of NWP is indicative of its enduring role in Irish poetry, and of the enduring nature of the debates surrounding mainstream and avant-garde in Irish poetry criticism.

5 *Offsets* is archived online at the following address: http://web.archive.org/web/20050209121859/http://www.soundeye.org/offsets/

6 Several more poems were published between 1990 and 1995 in *The Irish Review*, in Michael Smith's 1994 English textbook, *Pathfinder*, and in *The Irish Times*.

7 Assembling Alternatives brought together "five English-speaking comm-unities—the U.S., U.K., Canada, Ireland and Australia—to discuss how national differences have inflected poetic experimentation" and the proceedings were published in 2003 under the conference title.

8 Another major consequence ensuing from the conference is the establishment of Randolph Healy's Wild Honey Press.

9 'SoundEye West' aimed to create an encounter between the Irish poets and California-based poets such as Alfred Arteaga, Jen Hofer, Daniel Tiffany, Gabriela Jauregui (Mexico City) and Fred Moten to discuss the "theory and practice of interlingual and cross-cultural poetics". The SoundEye West schedule of events is available online at: http://dornsife.usc.edu/assets/sites/39/docs/Flyers/2007/flyersoundeye.pdf

10 Sarah Hayden joined as co-organiser with Cummins, Warriner, Gaynor and Joyce in 2013.

11 Re-issued in 2003.

12 The American Conference for Irish Studies (ACIS) was founded in 1960, holding its first conference in 1963, and the International Association for the Study of Irish Literatures followed in 1970. By 1982, ACIS could identify "365 colleges and universities offering Irish Studies courses or programmes" across the United States and Canada, and that number increased to 454 by 1994 (Meagher 270).

[13] The fact that Smith was invited to contribute essays both to the *Denver Quarterly* and to Douglas Dunn's *Two Decades of Irish Writing* might appear to undermine the urgency he felt to present a "Corrected History" of Irish poetry for an American audience. When one considers that Heaney was granted the E.M. Forster Award to travel to the U.S. just four years later in 1975, and became Professor of Poetry at Harvard the following decade, the publication of Smith's essay is revealed as not only unusual but also tokenistic.

[14] Augustine Martin traces the term back to the British-born critic and poet, Robin Skelton.

[15] Edwards' unpublished doctoral thesis, 'Poetry and the Politics of Publishing in Ireland: Authority in the Writings of Trevor Joyce, 1967–1995', offers a detailed history of poetry publishing in Ireland in the nineteen-sixties and the challenge that New Writers' Press presented to that history. Some of that research appeared in an essay co-written with John Goodby entitled '"Glittering Silt": The Poetry of Trevor Joyce and the Myth of Irishness' from 2002.

[16] "Poets work in words," Coffey continued, "and how they work in words is the first object of a critic, not whether they are actually, nearly or remotely Irish" (159).

[17] Conceptual poet and co-editor of the first anthology of conceptual poetry Kenneth Goldsmith was invited to read as part of Michelle Obama's 'Celebration of American Poetry at the White House' in May 2011. Heaney's poetry has attracted more than fifteen critical studies and the same number of major prizes and honours. Joyce is a Fulbright Scholar, a member of Aosdána, and he has been awarded numerous residencies; however the current volume constitutes the first collection of essays on Joyce's poetry.

[18] The differences between the Irish and British contexts for small-press publishing are compounded by the critical penchant for Parker's Crater books published on "a fine textured creamy paper, hand-sewn and with pages ready to cut" which, in the Irish context, explicitly recall "Yeats' legacy" of the "book as art object" which was fostered by Cuala Press and continued by Dolmen Press (Wilson).

[19] Longley's response and the question which prompted it are included as part of a conference report by Keith Tuma which is available online at the following address: http://wings.buffalo.edu/epc/documents/anglo.html

[20] As well as the late date of the essay, it is also significant that the piece was not written by an academic critic but rather by Nate Dorward, Joyce's publisher and friend.

[21] In the rush to incorporate Beckett into the Irish literary canon, several significant issues went unnoticed, that the writer "preferred the [Irish] landscape to the people," "that he preferred to live in France under the Germans than in Ireland under de Valera," and "that the books put in question everything the Irish constitution stands for" (Mays 8).

Works Cited

Brahic, Beverley Bie. 'Beverley Bie Brahic on a new translation of Stéphane Mallarmé.' *Poetry Review* 103.3 (2013). n.pag.

Cooke, Jennifer. '"Public Disorder" and Poetry.' Poetry and Revolution Conference. 27th May 2012. Birkbeck, University of London. Lecture. Web. 20 Mar. 2014. <http://www.bbk.ac.uk/cprc/events/Jennifer_Cooke_-_Poetry_and_Revolution_conference_paper.pdf>

Davis, Alex. '"Deferred Action": Irish Neo-Avant-Garde Poetry.' *Angelaki* 5.1 (2000): 81-93. Print.

Dorward, Nate. 'From An Interview.' Interview by Matt Chambers. *The Gig/ Poetry*. Dec. 2004. Web. 24 Mar. 2014. Archived at: <http://web.archive.org/web/20050419193532/http://www.ndorward.com/poetry/chambers.htm >

Edwards, Marcella. 'Poetry and the Politics of Publishing in Ireland: Authority in the Writings of Trevor Joyce, 1967–1995.' PhD diss., University of Strathclyde, 2003.

——. '"A scheme of echoes": Trevor Joyce, Poetry and Publishing in Ireland in the 1960s.' *Critical Survey* 15.1 (2003): 3-17. Print.

Gilonis, Harry. *For the Birds: Proceedings of the First Cork Conference on New and Experimental Irish Poetry*. Sutton: Mainstream; Dublin: hardPressed, 1998.

Heaney, Seamus. '"An ear to the line": Writing and Reading.' *Stepping Stones: Interviews with Seamus Heaney*. Ed. Dennis O'Driscoll. London: Faber, 2008. 444-460. Print.

Huk, Romana. *Assembling Alternatives: Reading Postmodern Poetries Transnationally*. Middletown, CT: Wesleyan University Press, 2003. Print.

Joyce, Trevor. 'History: A Festival of the Arts of the Word.' Web blog post. *SoundEye*. Wordpress. n.d. Web. 21 Aug. 2014.

——. 'Irish Terrain: Alternate Planes of Cleavage.' *Assembling Alternatives: Reading Postmodern Poetries Transnationally*. Ed. Romana Huk. Middletown, CT: Wesleyan University Press, 2003. 156-168. Print.

——. 'The Point of Innovation in Irish Poetry.' Rpt. in 'Six Poets: Views and Interviews.' Special issue, *The Gig* 2 (2001): 45–50. Ed. Nate Dorward. Willowdale, Ontario: The Gig, 2001. In *For the Birds: Proceedings of the First Cork Conference on New and Experimental Irish Poetry*. Ed. Harry Gilonis. Sutton: Mainstream; Dublin: hardPressed, 1998. 18-24. Print.

——. 'Why I Write Narrative'. *Narrativity* 1. The Poetry Centre, San Francisco State University, Mar. 2000. Web 5 May 2014. <https://www.sfsu.edu/~poetry/narrativity/issue_one/joyce.html>

——. 'New Writers' Press: The History of a Project.' *Modernism and Ireland: The Poetry of the 1930s*. Eds. Patricia Coughlan and Alex Davis. Cork: Cork University Press, 1995. 276-283. Print.

——. 'New Writers' Press: A Checklist of Publications.' *Modernism and Ireland The Poetry of the 1930s*. Eds. Patricia Coughlan and Alex Davis. Cork: Cork University Press, 1995. 284-306. Print.

Joyce, Trevor and Michael Smith. *The Lace Curtain* 1-6. Dublin: New Writers' Press, 1969-1978. Print.

Keohane, Ger. 'Partly for the Shiver.' *Karnival* 5 (2005): 9–10. Print.

Longley, Edna. '"Irish Poetry and 'Internationalism'": Variations on a Critical Theme.' *The Irish Review* 30 (2003): 48-61. Print.

Martin, Augustine. 'Inherited Dissent: the Dilemma of the Irish Writer.' *Studies: An Irish Quarterly Review* 54.213 (1965): 1-20. Print.

Mays, J.C.C. 'Flourishing and Foul: Six Poets and the Irish Building Industry.' *The Irish Review* 8 (1990): 6–11. Print.

Meagher, Timothy J. *The Columbia Guide to Irish American History.* New York, NY: Columbia University Press, 2005. Print.

Miller, Liam. *The Dun Emer, later the Cuala Press.* Dublin: Dolmen Press, 1973. Print.

Noel-Tod, Jeremy. 'In Different Voices: Modernism since the 1960s.' *The Oxford Handbook of Contemporary British and Irish Poetry*. Ed. Peter Robinson. Oxford: Oxford University Press, 2013. 111-129. Print.

O'Mahony, Niamh. 'Finding a Language Use: An Interview with Trevor Joyce.' *Jacket2*. 3 Feb. 2014. Web. 24 Mar. 2014. <https://jacket2.org/interviews/joyce-2011-finding-language-use>

Satris, Marthine. 'Interview with Trevor Joyce.' Spec. issue of *Journal of British and Irish Innovative Poetry* 5.1 (2013): 13-35. Ed. James Cummins and Rachel Warriner. *Gylphi*. Web. 14 Feb. 2014.

Smith, Michael. 'The Contemporary Situation in Irish Poetry.' *Two Decades of Irish Writing*. Ed. Douglas Dunn. Chester Springs, PA: Dufour Editions, 1975. 154-165. Print.

——. 'Irish Poetry Since Yeats: Notes Towards a Corrected History.' *The Denver Quarterly* 5.4 (1971): 1-26. Print.

——. 'Introduction to New Irish Poets.' *Sole Glum Trek* by Trevor Joyce. Dublin: New Writers' Press, 1967. Print.

Wilson, Juliet. '"For the Administration (after Rimbaud)" by Sean Bonney.' *Sabotage Reviews*. 21 June 2011. Web. 29 Mar. 2014.

Textual Voices of Irish History in Trevor Joyce's 'Trem Neul'

Marthine Satris

When the poet Trevor Joyce sat down with me for an interview in 2009, we spoke in the front room of his house in the city of Cork, a room in which every vertical surface that wasn't a window was a bookcase, and every horizontal surface was one too. The bookcases, full of literature and scholarly studies, continued up the stairs and back towards the kitchen. I asked him about the collection, and the poet said, "The shelves and what's on them is far more impressive than my actual knowledge of them. People ask me, *Have you read all these books*, and I say, *No, but I know what's in them*. And that's the thing, I go and I'll touch on things." The image of the poet speaking for hours with me of his life and art while surrounded by sources and references all near to hand and organised according to his own methods is emblematic of Trevor Joyce's poetic practice. He cycles through the reams of language already printed and published, touches on them, in order to create poetry that records his comprehension of the self and the world through a practice of reading that is simultaneously a creative and critical endeavour.

Trevor Joyce's 1999 poem 'Trem Neul' is forty-five pages of interwoven source texts excerpted, adapted and spliced into each other to create a poem that comments on its own act of archiving memory. Each page is composed as an individual piece of the larger work, and each is made of a narrow block of "prose" to the left and apparently "lyric" lines to the right. The words that look like free verse lyrics on the right-hand side of the page are dry, stiff, repetitive and archaic, and they tend to be structured as demands or commands. This construction challenges the reader to puzzle out how he or she might approach and enter a text which is both continuous and fragmented in form and in which the pronouns in a single passage refer to multiple occluded antecedents. The language Joyce chooses to include is not the only information he is conveying – his own processing of the source texts, his *choices*, are equally the substance of the poem. And the smallest decision the poet makes in arranging these source texts reveals his aesthetics and his purpose in writing this poem in the voices of others.

While the poem is a form of expression of the poet at the heart of it, it is also a tool to interrogate how information is organised and transmitted. As Friedrich Kittler has pointed out, "literature (whatever else it may mean to readers) processes, stores, and transmits data" (370), and Joyce, who spent many years as a Business Systems Analyst for Apple, addresses the fraught question in contemporary Ireland of the country's connection to its own past as one of the transmission of data across time. The Celtic Tiger, the term for the recent very prosperous period in Irish history, has been spoken about in the Irish and international press as the teleological conclusion of Ireland's efforts to achieve sovereignty, an ideological point of view rooted in Irish nationalism's assertion of the necessity to recover an authentic Irishness by throwing off the British yoke. While many writers have critiqued this idea of an unbroken connection to the Gaelic past, Joyce is one of the few poets who look to the possibilities of form to represent a history of "breakage and continuity", as Trevor Joyce has called it. Thomas Kinsella has argued that there is a "dual tradition" for Irish writers, an ancient Gaelic and a modern English-language one, and that this division and brokenness has been embedded into Irish literature; he has attempted to resolve the split in Irish poetic tradition through translation, including his masterful rendition of *The Táin* in English. Eavan Boland has represented what she sees as the lack of a private, domestic, or women's history in her lyrics by alternatively acknowledging the vacuum and falteringly attempting to reconstruct this absent past in her lyric poems. The writer most known for creating formal innovation from the history of colonisation in Ireland is of course James Joyce, whose novel *Ulysses* is the record of the shape and movement of the modern city as it is instantiated in 1904 Dublin, then a provincial, colonised capital. The responsiveness to the forces of modernisation that created such an innovative literary representation has seemed to many critics to have waned after the peak of Joyce's and then Beckett's accomplishments, and has been mostly absent from the mainstream of Irish poetry.[1]

'Trem Neul' not only reveals the self-construction of the author through his use of texts, but is also specifically about Joyce's own past: despite the fact that the collage-like structure of the poem seems completely abstracted from the life of the author, it is in many ways a poem whose concept originates in Joyce's personal and family history. Trevor Joyce was born in working-class Dublin to a father descended from the same Cork family that produced the scholars of Irish folksong and place lore Patrick Weston Joyce and Robert Dwyer Joyce. Trevor Joyce and some biographers[2] of

James Joyce also make claims for close family connections between the nineteenth-century scholars and the modernist author. Contrastingly, Trevor Joyce's mother, as he told me in our 2009 interview, did not have a shining family history to look back on, but instead was brought up in an industrial school[3] after being separated from her family in a Gaeltacht (Irish-speaking region) in Galway.[4] If Trevor Joyce's father's story represents the connection of modern Irish people to their history and culture, his mother's represents the fracturing of lives by poverty, the manipulations of a Catholic state and the loss of a native language. In 'Trem Neul', Joyce examines both inheritances. Yet, he turns what could have been a solipsistic examination of family history in less inventive hands into an exploration of how we remember the past. Such a move from the individual to the collective is part of Joyce's reinvention of the connection of the individual to the public in Ireland, the personal to the political, and to do so he uses a form that renounces the lyric focus on expression from a self-contained voice. Joyce's poem is not about the relationship of the poet to the passport he carries; rather, 'Trem Neul' is a web of historical and philosophical influences, some of which directly emerge from his family's history in Connaught, Munster and Dublin, but many of which speak to his concerns as an artist about balancing the organic and the artificial in his creative works, and are drawn from much further afield.

While the Republic of Ireland's fairly staid existence in the last fifty years, especially when compared to the upheaval in Northern Ireland, might not seem likely to stimulate such an immediate need to reinvent forms of representation, the very fact that the state has spent the last one hundred years establishing its sovereignty and its independence from the cultural and political forms of Britain has kept artists and critics aware of the constructed nature of the state now described as the Republic of Ireland. Yet the state has consciously suppressed such a notion: it declared itself the true embodiment of Éire in the 1937 Constitution and, in the preamble of that document, did not emphasise the *new* establishment of Ireland, but rather asserted that the Irish had "regain[ed] the rightful independence of our Nation". Despite this call for a sense of continuity with the past that is the foundation of the Irish state, what it has meant to be Irish has changed over the course of the postcolonial twentieth century as Ireland has reoriented itself politically and economically with regards to Britain, the United States and Europe and reassessed the state's territorial claim over the six counties of Northern Ireland.[5] The rise of the Republic on the world stage in the boom years of the Celtic Tiger (1990s to 2000s) led to a general sense within the Irish public, and especially among its political and business classes, that the country had achieved a final, successful form that validated its sovereignty. Ireland was lauded as a truly postmodern country that had overcome its colonial past and had embraced the global flows of capital. While opening up the country to the abstractions of global finance temporarily buoyed the economy and increased the standard of living in what had long been a very poor country, it has had dire consequences. The unregulated growth and financial gambits that led to a landscape scarred with half-built "ghost estates", bank failures, the ballooning of public debt and a return to high rates of emigration should lead us to question the path of modernisation on which Ireland set itself in recent decades.

When we think of the poetry that accompanied Ireland's rising fortunes, we should note how little of it challenged or critiqued the foundation of the values that led the country to its position as a tax shelter for transnational countries and its focus on growth of all industries over all else. Those poets who have taken on the position of critic or antagonist recently have either done so through irony and vernacular invective, such as Dave Lordan and Brendan Kennelly, or by highlighting individual lives of those whom the Irish Republic has ignored or bulldozed past, as Paula Meehan has done. The majority of the poetry that reached publication at the turn of the twenty-first century, including that of the three poets mentioned above, also remained solidly rooted in the lyric form that has been dominant in Irish and British poetry in the twentieth century, with few formal innovations or stretches away from the goal of self-expression that has been the purview of contemporary poetry. 'Trem Neul' stands apart from this lyric tradition, and its depersonalised structure and content allows it to redirect our attention to the philosophical and structural underpinnings of our understanding of the world. The front-loading of artifice and construction in 'Trem Neul', with its obvious magpie-like appropriation of other texts, is a more nuanced reflection of the constructed state of the post-colonial Republic of Ireland than the contemporary lyric, which, while its content may indict a law or a policy, still maintains an internal coherence that does not acknowledge the similarities between the assertion of the essential voice and the assertions of the essential nationhood of Ireland.

Joyce connects the texts in 'Trem Neul' not in a seamless away, but with edges bleeding and overlapping. Joyce, in an essay on narrative from 2000, says that his goal in 'Trem Neul' was to figure out how one may

> conduct a narrative of change, of loss and recovery, of breakage
> and continuity, without presuming the existence of distinct agents

...The bodies in this plot are not distinct, either from one another or from their ground, they emerge to make themselves, enjoy a transitory closure, and then resolve again into a ground which offers further figures.

While he may be creating a "narrative", it is not one in the sense of being a continuous discursive story, but rather is characterised by dialogism and heteroglossia, which Bakhtin has said are the defining characteristics of the novel and what differentiate it from poetry. In turning away from the univocality that is often a defining characteristic of the contemporary lyric and incorporating so many different levels of discourse, Joyce shows us in 'Trem Neul' that the individual is constructed from its contact with others. The history he is writing asks us to look closely at our acts of selection, through which we define ourselves: which voices do we internalise and which do we prefer to forget?

Joyce's poem argues for an Irishness that always carries the past with it, not as a foundation or assured root, but rather as something unknowable, inaccessible. In one passage of 'Trem Neul', which I have been unable to find in any source text, and which may therefore be the poet's own language, Joyce writes, "This man, this leaping meat, / carries his childhood within him / like a sequestrum" (225). A *sequestrum* is a dead piece of bone that remains in the body, and this statement emphasises both the continuation of the past into the present and the dead but preserved state of that past. While Joyce does not overtly critique the Irish state in this poem, his poem's focus on the role of the mind in constructing what we perceive as reality and meaning gently presses the reader to question the inevitability of the present form of the structures and institutions within which we all operate. Objects and traditions of the past shape the present but have lost meaning along the way, becoming relics whose meaning cannot be recaptured.

Joyce's use of found language in 'Trem Neul' is part of his search in recent years for a way to surprise himself with his own poetry and not lapse into a monotonous, predictable voice. While this inclusion of the non-poetic clearly has precedents in British and American poetry, in Irish poetry such generic grafting is still the preserve of those outside of the poetic mainstream. In our 2009 conversation, Joyce said of the poet Randolph Healy, a friend and frequent attender at the Soundeye Poetry Festival, that he admires Healy's inclusion of scientific language in his poetry: "Look at something like [Healy's long poem] *Arbor Vitae* and just the use of his openness to completely non-poetic language, non-poetic ideas... 'non-poetic' in scare quotes. It's making something from the ground up, just from ordinary language, it's made into poetry." While Healy includes the language of physics, genetics and biology in his poetry, he rarely limits himself to using found language in the way that Joyce frequently has done. Joyce has used constraints throughout his oeuvre, inspired by the historical avant-garde movements Dada and OuLiPo. These movements recognised the benefits of exercising one's mind against restraints in opposition to the openness of free verse, but they wanted to introduce new, inventive constraints rather than the traditional ones of syllable count and rhyme. As Jan Baetans discusses in 'Free Writing, Constrained Writing: The Ideology of Form', the imposition of constraints has been seen by avant-garde writers as a way of demonstrating that what we perceive as "natural speech" is in fact utterly determined by culture. Joyce's choice to limit himself to interfering with and rearranging other texts in order to create the wide-ranging meditation that is 'Trem Neul' connects his work to an international tradition of poetic innovation through limitation.

Such constraints and use of found writing moved from the fringes of early twentieth-century art movements to the centre as American and British modernists used this technique to challenge the Romantic and Victorian trope of sublime inspiration. As Elizabeth Gregory, among others, has noted, the use of quotation in modernist poetry allowed writers to make overt allusions to older – especially classical – literary traditions, to highlight the exhaustion of invention and originality, to ironically juxtapose the reduced circumstances of the present and the grandeur of the past, and to create dialogic texts. These intertextual intersections appear in texts such as Eliot's *The Waste Land* and Marianne Moore's lyrics through the use of quotation marks and notes that guide readers to the poet's source. Quotation became a dominant characteristic of modernist poetry, and so the poems appear as collections of fragments, a formal choice that critics, most notably Marjorie Perloff in *The Futurist Moment*, have connected to the invention of "collage" in the visual arts by Cubists and Futurists in the second decade of the twentieth century, when Picasso and others began to attach textiles, newspaper and other ephemera to their canvases.

A key method shared by those avant-garde artists and poets who compose using found text is that the original context of the quotations or scraps of newspaper is brought into the composition. Collage can therefore assert the materiality of the work of art and its immersion in the mundane world: Perloff asserts that collage is "Cubism transformed by the Futurist (and later Dada) drive to obliterate the distinction between the pictorial field and the 'real' world outside the frame" (77). While this is perhaps more obvious in a physical medium like painting, in which a newspaper cutting contrasts sharply with the oil-painted canvas, it remains true for poetry as well. For instance, Trevor Joyce uses language from Frances Yates' history of memory and mnemonic devices, *The Art of Memory*, in 'Trem Neul', including a statement, lifted from Yates, on page 32 of the poem: "In a taxonomy, for example a zoo- / logical family tree, the structure / arises out of the subject matter, / rather than being arbitrary" (217). By absconding with this sentence, Joyce carries into his poem the discourse of spatiality and organisation of information, infusing a meta-reflection on the form of the poem as a method of organisation and its relationship to other systems of organisation, specifically the categorisation and hierarchism of species.

While I have discussed the qualities of modernist collage that inform 'Trem Neul', in some ways this term does not entirely fit the poem. While the heterogeneity of its material is not disguised, the poem is not utterly disjointed and fragmented either. Part of one's sense of an underlying structure to 'Trem Neul' comes from the fact that it is drawn from a limited corpus of materials, and the poem features multiple selections from the same texts, a fact made clear by the reappearance of a particular metaphor, topic or choice of language. To draw again from the poem itself to address this, an image that occurs multiple times is that of a rope; the image of a rope or braid, with its multiple interwoven strands, intermittent repetition and linear structure, beautifully illustrates both the experience of reading 'Trem Neul' and the work that the poem does in connecting the present to the past, the individual to a collective of voices, and the single work of art to all other uses of language. One instance of Joyce's inclusion of a reference to rope in the poem is the words of fibre artist and sculptor Magdalena Abakanowicz describing her creations. Her statements appear in the left-hand column multiple times, including this description of one her works: "rope sits high like / a petrified organism… Create / forms with it. Divide space with it" (194). Elsewhere in the poem, the form of preservation that is amber is described as a "trans- / lucent topaz-coloured rope coil- / ing gravely down the prehistoric / coniferous trunks", a description whose substance is originally found in White's *Ants and Their Ways*. The significance of "rope" to 'Trem Neul' becomes apparent when one compares the poem to its source text for this last borrowing. White's original sentence reads "The translucent topaz-coloured stream, thus influenced by gravitation, would roll gently down the prehistoric coniferous trunks" (19), and Joyce's deliberate change of *stream* to *rope,* and *roll* to *coil* emphasises the significance of the rope to the poem as a whole. Rope is both movement and solidity, flexibility and strength, a human tool made traditionally from natural materials. Not only does Joyce twine the many strands of his interests together, but 'Trem Neul' continually changes the context of his selected texts, adding new layers of significance to the language he has incorporated each time.

That Joyce altered White's text, and that there even is a source text for the lines about amber, is not readily apparent. Despite the debt owed to the modernists and poets of the historical avant-garde who practised a poetics of collage, Trevor Joyce's 'Trem Neul' has a notable difference: the found texts are not marked with quotation marks or thorough annotations. A brief comment in the notes of *with the first dream of fire they hunt the cold* on 'Trem Neul' lists only some of the authors whose works Joyce manipulates and weaves together:

> [A]lthough it would be pointless to give a complete list, I would like to identify Magdalena Abakanowicz, Judith Campisi, Patrick Weston Joyce, A.R. Luria and 'S', M. MacDonald, Christy Moore, Alain Prochiantz, Tim Robinson and Sir Charles Sherrington as among the more recently sounding, contributing both shell and meat. (240)

Since the poet's intervention is very minor, consisting of changing a few words here and there, Trevor Joyce overall is creating a poem that is a collection of his reading history, allowing the sources primacy. This construction implicitly asserts that not only our language but indeed ourselves are built from the fragments we have absorbed from the world around us, which accords with Mikhail Bakhtin's view of language in the novel. In highlighting the voices of others, Joyce enacts the "ideological becoming of a human being", or the development of a world-view, which Bakhtin has argued occurs through "selectively assimilating the words of others" (532). In this way, drawing together the discourses of science, of colonisation and of Irish history allows us to read 'Trem Neul' as an act of self-construction and self-revelation out of the past. Joyce's focus on texts that either comment on the relation of the present to the past, the mind to the body, or language's relationship to power thereby alert the reader to the way in which each of us has become an archive of ideologies that shape our understanding of the world we inhabit.

Yet the twining structure and the poem's reliance on other texts for the "meat" leave the reader in a conundrum, especially considering the hinting nature of the poet's explanatory note. Joyce alerts the reader to his use of source texts, yet declines to identify them all and indeed labels such an exercise as "pointless" (240). As a reader, then, such hinting seems to indicate that original context is important, as I asserted above, but, over and above that, that the final product of 'Trem Neul' is self-enclosed in terms of determining meaning. Coming to such a conclusion seems to undo Joyce's work of intertextual weaving that so counters the values of New Criticism, which would demand that the poem be final unto itself, read utterly apart from its context. Rejecting this possibility of self-enclosed meaning, I insist that this poem draws strength from the connections it makes across texts, and that the poet does in fact want the reader to embark on a search for the roots of this sprawling poem. Helpfully, Joyce said in our interview that after the 1997 Assembling Alternatives conference, when he finally met other formally innovative poets in Ireland, "I felt as though I actually could construct something as complex as I needed to and that there would be people with patience and interest enough to follow through and decode it, as it were" (15). This phrasing reveals Joyce's vision of poetry as an act of hiding something in plain sight, something that can only be revealed if readers are willing to follow his logic and divine the underlying structure and its significance. It does seem to require the reader to investigate the sources of the texts, but Joyce purposefully offers little more than a few hints as to the sources.

The work of searching out source texts creates the sense that, if only every source could be found, then 'Trem Neul' would become clear, as if the poem were nothing more than notes from greater works. The mostly obscure texts that Joyce uses as his sources for 'Trem Neul' make it unlikely that anyone but the poet himself has read that particular group of books. Yet with the hints that the note provides, seeking the sources of the poem's material becomes part of the reading process. This pushes the reader away from absorption into the work, turning him or her outwards instead. Pound or James Joyce or Eliot could rely on their contemporary readers' familiarity with the common culture of the classics to make sense of their allusions; the same cannot be said today, but now the reader does not need to share the same cultural canon as the author; rather she can rely on communication technologies to access any and all possible volumes. In order to grasp the implications of Trevor Joyce's choice of sources, one must only search the capacious databases of such sites as *Archive.org* or

Google Books. Thanks to the digitisation of out-of-copyright texts by such organisations as Google, Project Gutenberg and the Internet Archive, it is possible for Joyce's readers, wherever they might be, to access a shared library in the cloud.[6]

Discussions of literacy and reading practices arising from the internet have focused on the shortened attention span of readers, the use of hyperlinks to bounce through layers of information, and the overwhelming sea of unedited, possibly suspect, information now available.[7] Additionally, when it comes to the connections between books and the digital, scholars have focused on the technological challenges and possibly worrisome ephemerality of such databases as Early English Books Online (EEBO).[8] More recently, scholars have embraced "culturomics" or "distant reading", harnessing the digitised, OCR-ready books in archives like Google Books and the Internet Archive to create huge datasets from which conclusions about word popularity, the rise of genres, and cultural fascinations can be drawn.[9] Few have yet explored what it means to use the internet and, particularly, the archive of digitised books as part of one's reading practice of a literary text, though some scholars of contemporary experimental fiction and poetry have begun to address this intersection. Julia Panko's reading of the American writer Mark Danielewski's experimental novel *Only Revolutions* in her dissertation, 'Dead-tree Data', is one of the first studies to consider how both author and reader apply digital literacies to a textual object.

Danielewski's experiments with the form of the novel in *Only Revolutions* include adding a stream of phrases and names down the side of each page, forming a "news feed", as Panko calls it, in an allusion to the ticker of information that appears in RSS feeds or on Facebook. Of this form, Panko writes:

> Without an encyclopaedic knowledge of history spanning the events of the two centuries that comprise the book's chronology, such a list cannot immediately be read but instead must be deciphered to reconstruct the full events... The news feed is perhaps best read with the help of an Internet search engine. (28–9)

Knowing, as the reader of a text like *Only Revolutions* or 'Trem Neul' does, that the author's allusions and language are drawn from outside texts, the reader seeks to restore the context of the original language through using the most powerful research tools available: the Google search engine and

Marthine Satris

such sites as Wikipedia. Similar to such paratexts as an introduction or a publisher's imprint, the information about when, where and why the language in 'Trem Neul' was first put into print or first distributed online adds layers of meaning to the selections made by Joyce, as the accumulation of fragments begins to build into a picture of the intellectual and artistic concerns of the author himself.

Panko also points out that *Only Revolutions*, in which masses of information is enclosed within covers while the concepts of the page and linear progression are simultaneously radically rethought, demonstrates that "data sets can become aesthetic objects when mediated and filtered within a closed framework" (37). Panko relates Danielewski's deeply unconventional book, which still bears the subtitle 'A Novel', to the work of American conceptual poets Judith Goldman and Kenneth Goldsmith, noting the authors' shared vision of their function not as originator of art, but rather filterer, condenser, or selector of information. The imposition of constraints, of a form, is what turns the management of information into art in Danielewski's novel, in conceptual poetry and in Joyce's poem.

As mentioned with regard to his insertion of the word "rope", Joyce occasionally alters source texts in 'Trem Neul', differentiating his approach to using constraint in poetry from those conceptual poets who insist on a "non-interventionist" reuse of text. Kenneth Goldsmith's 2000 work *Day*, which consists of Goldsmith's retyping of the 1 September 2000 edition of the *New York Times*, is the example *par excellence* of the school of conceptual poetry, a branch of American poetry for whom the movement of overtly informative, non-poetic information into the sphere of poetry through the transcription and rearrangement of such texts by a poet is the main point. Deriving in some ways from performance art, the emphasis is on the framing of the words in a new context, and that reframing – that *choice* – is claimed as the key creative intervention of conceptual poetry.[10] While there is much affinity with this movement in Joyce's work, 'Trem Neul' differs significantly from conceptual poetry under the rubric that has been defined by the American practitioners of this genre. Goldsmith says of conceptual poems that they turn the reader away from the work towards the generation of new ideas, but the examples he cites in his collection of essays, *Uncreative Writing*, generally turn the reader either self-reflexively inwards or to considering the arbitrary rules of language itself. With regard to the provocative, faux-pirated anthology *Issue 1*, which paired randomly chosen poets' names with computer-generated poems in a PDF freely available for downloading, Goldsmith dismisses the content of the language itself: "[T]here really wasn't much to discuss about the poems – in regard to everything else going on about this gesture, they seemed pretty irrelevant … With one gesture, they had swapped the focus *from content to context*" (emphasis in original) (123). While Goldsmith's attention to reframing texts laudably focuses on the meaning brought to the words through the connotations of their paratextual apparatus and the material context of the language, I find that most of his examples either celebrate the bland mass of language available today or mock its clearly commercial intent by putting them into a poetic form. They make little political intervention other than alerting us to our own behaviour as consumers of language.

In 'Trem Neul', Joyce's arrangements of and meddlings with non-poetic texts do more than simply question generic categorisations, as the more unreadable examples of conceptual poems do. The confluences he has created not only reveal his interests and his reading history, but the words on the page, in addition to their contexts, create a political critique that is more than simply an arch depiction of hypocrisy. When one considers the left-hand side of 'Trem Neul', strong themes of cultural history, loss and the construction of memory emerge from Joyce's manipulations of and extractions from source texts. While the reader may go in many different directions as she follows the ways in which the poem intersects with moments in history and places around the world, the reader who comes to 'Trem Neul' with some knowledge of Irish history can see that Joyce is engaging with questions of how the Irish relate to their past.

As discussed above with regards to conceptual poetry, the language comes to 'Trem Neul' coloured by its prior use. A search for the origins of these words and how they were used before adds connotations that Joyce in fact relies on to create the thematic throughlines of 'Trem Neul'. One example of how contexts do matter is how the import of the right-hand side of 'Trem Neul' changes when one does find the original source. The authors Joyce cites in the note to the poem are used only in the left-hand side of the poem, and he does not refer at all in the note to the sources of the material on the right-hand side. Investigating the sources of information on the right-hand side of the pages by simply copying them out into the box of a search engine reveals that the original texts resound with the traumatic impact of colonisation on the languages of conquered countries, and this information is imperative for understanding 'Trem Neul' as a whole, since it is a poem that reveals the intersections of the private and public in Irish history.

Marthine Satris

The two other critics who have commented on 'Trem Neul', Andrew Duncan in *Jacket* and Dorward in the *Chicago Review*, both noted that the stilted language in the lineated right side of the pages seemed to come from a "phrasebook (rather pre-modern, and probably of Irish)" (Duncan) or "language primer" (Dorward 93). Both assume that they originate in a single source because the sentences have the same halting style throughout. In fact, the right-hand side is drawn from many language primers, phrasebooks and dictionaries, not just one. As my research into phrasebooks made available to search engines demonstrates, Joyce uses phrases from texts that translate into English the languages of those native to the many areas of the globe colonised by the British: the desiccated, utilitarian language is the translation of Maori, Luganda, Tamil, Gaelic, Hausa and Irish-English (Hiberno-English) for future visitors, colonists and missionaries. In no instance in 'Trem Neul' does Joyce provide the original language that these guidebooks, phrasebooks and dictionaries translate, with the exception of that drawn from the Irish-English phrasebook, which is represented in its original phrasing. The authors of each non-Irish text were British missionaries publishing at the turn of the century. The language drawn from the Gaelic dictionary and Irish-English phrasebooks were both written by Patrick S. Dineen; Dineen was a key figure in the Gaelic League, a group essential to the cultural renaissance of the Celtic Revival. The texts on the right-hand side represent a history of global imperialism, hybridity and the erasure and change of native cultures.

The origins of the right-hand side of 'Trem Neul' take what could otherwise have seemed to be a text of personal history and a rumination on practices of organising information and root the poem in the material circumstances of those who bore the burden of British imperialism. If we look at one page of 'Trem Neul', say 217, we find that the left-hand side is composed of a quote from Yates about taxonomy and a selection from Edmund Burke's 1763 *Annual Register* in which Burke details the procedure for preserving and taxidermy. The right-hand side of that same page offers statements about happiness and work ethic copied from the 1902 book *Elements of Luganda Grammar*, written by W.A. Crabtree, a British missionary, to assist European visitors to Uganda, which was a British protectorate at that time. A representation of the page follows:

In a taxonomy, for example a zoo-logical family tree, the structure arises out of the subject matter, rather than being arbitrary. With this in mind, I open the venter, from the lower part of the breast-bone down to the anus, with a pair of fine-pointed scissors, and extract all the contents, such as the intestines, liver, stomach, etc. This cavity I immediately fill with the following mixture of salts and spice, and then bring the lips of the wound together by suture, delicately as it were the finest wed-ding dress, so as to prevent the stuffing from falling out. The gul-let or diamond of the throat must then be filled, from the beak down to where the stomach lay, with the same mixture (but finer ground) which must be forced down a little at a time by the help of a quill or wire. The head I open by breaking through stars near the root of the tongue with the scissors, and after having turned them round three or four times to destroy the structure of the brain, I farce this cavity like-wise with the mixture.

I am at work
  every moment
at times
  I am tired
    but that is nothing
 it is a very
   happy
   work

(217)

Marthine Satris

The juxtapositions of texts both within the left-hand side and in the pairing of left and right halves allows the poet to address the intersection between the physical reality of a body and the language with which we categorise that body, whether human or animal. The left side also draws attention to the processing of that body for scientific purposes, as Burke details how he opens the bird's body and extracts everything internal, replacing it with a "mixture of salts and spice". This selection's left column of text, when read in the context of the entire work, uses the instructional language of scientific discourse to argue that the destabilised chorus of texts that scaffold and fill the poem is in fact a form that has emerged to answer a particular problem: how one might create a poem that attempts both to represent and to understand how the present relates to the past in the particular place that is Ireland. While this is certainly not obvious in a first reading of this page, as one delves deeper into the poem as a whole, this implication rises to the surface. The W.B. Yeats quote that occurs on the poem's title page, "All that is personal soon rots; it must be packed in ice or salt", originated as Yeats' explanation of his choice of formal constraint over free verse. This idea of how one preserves and avoids rot is repurposed by Trevor Joyce to tie together the themes of personal and national history, memory and language. In the text from 'Trem Neul' quoted above, the act of preserving an animal is described in detail. This image of penetration into the body in order to preserve it in a lifelike fashion is drawn from the writing of Edmund Burke, the Irish statesman and writer, and the Burke text serves several purposes: it provides a metaphor for the poet's excavation and preservation of the personal; as a historical document, it turns our attention to the ways in which we hold on to and interpret the past; and, as a specific description of the manipulation of an animal's body, it alerts us to the importance of the material, biological foundation of life. The blend of the structured and organic is a feature throughout 'Trem Neul', implying that one cannot divide the body from the institutions that control it and assign it meaning. The Yates quote primes the reader to consider the relationship of structure and subject in Burke, although that was never the intention of Burke in recording his process for preserving birds. This moment also causes the reader to consider the poem's organisation of information, the relationship between its structure and substance; unlike conceptual poems, both have equal weight in the poem.

The seemingly trite language of the text on the right-hand half of the page clashes with the fluid sophistication of the descriptions with which it shares space. Its grimly grinning work ethic might seem to emit from a speaker shared with the left-hand text, as both speakers are active and working, but the clear difference in rhetoric indicates different authors and purposes. While it might seem to be only a rote recitation asserting the value of work (which of course is still ideological in and of itself), the exercise from which it is extracted finishes with the statement, "In that month there no Europeans arrived [sic]; but now there are many Europeans in the country" (Crabtree 122). The text is evidence of and was instrumental in the expansion of the British Empire, and the seemingly apolitical description of being tired and happy in fact carries with it a history of violence and the subsequent destruction of an indigenous African culture. By not including the original languages which were translated, Joyce shows us that any hope that translations will give the reader access to an original culture as preserved in its language is a false hope. The very words in the title of the poem, 'Trem Neul', are derived from another source that is of great importance to the poem: Patrick Weston Joyce's essay "Some Reminiscences of a Collector of Irish Folk Music", in which the legendary folksong collector recollects how he began collecting and writing down the music of rural Ireland. It is P.W. Joyce's Anglicisation of the Irish phrase "trém néal", meaning "through my dream". The choice to Anglicise the words in P.W. Joyce's idiosyncratic spelling, but not to translate them, echoes the "sequestrum" of the past in the present – visible, preserved without any potential for life.

In a different selection of 'Trem Neul', page 27 (page 223 in *first dream of fire*), the left half of the page asks the reader to reconceive what identity is when we remember the past in a body that is always being reconstructed at the cellular level. However, this universalising gesture occurs on a page full of texts significant to the Irish canon and to Irish culture. This page's use of historical Irish experience and classic Irish texts is unusual for 'Trem Neul' in its use of texts that are all directly about Irish experiences, and not only Irish but specifically rural. It provides an entry into Trevor Joyce's central concern in this long poem, which is, as Dorward has also noted, the interface of the mind and body in the world – and interface mediated by language – and the impact of time upon both body and place. The page reads as follows:

Marthine Satris

With the exception of your neurons and your muscles, the cells of your first body are long gone. All else is new. Evidently, then, the question of what is an individual is a difficult one to settle, and yet a certain round boulder lying on the shore by the landing stage challenges the young men to lift it, and prompts boasts about their fathers or grandfathers who had done so before. The fear of physical failure, of eviction, emigration or the workhouse, must have clung in the night-hours like a cry of despair, satisfying the requirement that images be lively, active, striking, and charged with emotional affects to enter into the storehouse of memory. At the first bend I looked back and she was standing at the door. Years passed; I was in the capital, diligently recalling all my tunes for a noted antiquary, but The Tuning of the Colours had not yet come forward: translated from one place to another it grew old. Bearing its own story within itself, it contributed this to its surroundings, and in cities became an echo of the banished organic world.

Act of mourning
    lamenting
      wailing
    deploring
The form
    of metre
          used in
    deploration
Requiring to be lamented
    :dead

Mildness
smoothness
gentleness

(223)

The justified block of prose on the left is, in order, an assemblage of information about the material body and identity; Tim Robinson's geographical-historical writing about Connemara; Frances Yates' *Art of Memory*; a quote from James Joyce's *Portrait of the Artist as a Young Man*; a slightly altered quote from P.W. Joyce; and a quote about her work in textiles from a contemporary Polish sculptor, Magdalena Abakanowicz. The right-hand side of the page is composed of text drawn from the English definitions of the Irish word *caoin*, which is transliterated as "keen" and means to wail or mourn, and from the definitions of *caoine*, the word that follows *caoin* on the page of Dineen's Irish-English dictionary, a famous text created at the beginning of the twentieth century and still authoritative today.

In the left half of the poem on this page, Joyce connects the statement about biological mutability to the extract from Robinson with a comma and an "and yet", suggesting a contrast between the constantly dissolving and resolving body and Robinson's reflections about the "certain round boulder" and its presence in both the past that he imagines and the moment in which he observes it. This remnant of the past haunts the present in Robinson's text, although the bodies of generations have decayed. The interactions of people with the landscape as represented in the ritual of attempting to lift the boulder are the point at *which the past lingers*. Robinson is a cartographer known for his detailed descriptions and depictions of the Aran Islands and the west coast of Ireland, writing about both their landscapes and their cultural history. These areas are weighted with cultural significance, since they are associated in the classics of modern Irish literature with rural simplicity, cultural authenticity and the Irish language. This discussion of the west coast of Ireland can be seen as part of Joyce's tribute to his mother's experience, both in the source's topic and in the detail Joyce quotes here about the painful consequences of poverty and exclusion from power that were common to Irish peasants and the working poor in the nineteenth and twentieth centuries.

As mentioned earlier, Joyce's transitions between sources are not abrupt, necessarily – they seem always slightly off, but not completely jarring. He smooths the passages' connections, luring us into thinking we are remaining in the guidance of a single consciousness until we realise the topic or speaker has veered far away from where we began, and there simply cannot be a single, guiding speaker with whom we can identify. After Robinson's descriptions of the young men engaging with the landscape and vying with each other, Joyce transitions to another topic, again using a comma to link text from separate sources into a single sentence. He moves from the fears that Robinson describes haunting the men on the shore to a passage that is prescriptive about how to create memorable images: "satisfying the requirement that the images be lively, active, striking, and charged with emotional affects to enter into the storehouse of memory". Without knowing the source of the latter sentence, this transition seems initially to the reader to perhaps be a critique of the artistry that goes into the carefully delineated narrative of a tragic Irish past. Using those words as a search term leads one to the extra knowledge that those words are drawn from Yates' description of Giordano Bruno's innovation of the mnemonic device of associating facts one wants to remember with different rooms in a visualisation of a building. The organisation and retention of information is therefore tied to spatiality, just as Robinson's encounter with the past is keyed by the specific site of the boulder in Connemara. Additionally, the implication, when one considers the context of the text preceding this sentence in the passage that comments on individuality and the relationship of men to the past as symbolised by their interaction with a feature of the landscape, is that information about the past is only selectively retained.

This page begins by citing the fact that, due to cell death and replacement, very little of our born bodies can be found in our adult bodies and suggests that therefore "the question of what is an individual is a difficult one to settle". Like the poem itself, a node in a network of language, culture and the flow of history, the individual is composed of pieces drawn from our interactions with others in the present and in the past. Joyce's destabilisation of the unity of the subject throughout 'Trem Neul' is strongly emphasised in the next lines of the prose passage, which parrot the voices of two other Joyces. The sentence from James Joyce's *A Portrait of the Artist as a Young Man* that follows the *Art of Memory* extract is doubly distancing in that the "I", though written by James Joyce, is spoken by the character of Davin, a good Catholic country boy who is friends with Stephen Dedalus. The next "I" is that of Patrick Weston Joyce. The speakers of both passages are reflecting on a past experience, continuing the page's theme of asking what weight the past carries in the present and how we construct ourselves from the experiences we've absorbed. Davin, in the scene to which Trevor Joyce is making reference, recounts his turn away from the sexual comfort offered by a lonely woman in the Ballyhoura Hills at the border of County Cork and County Limerick. The scene is well known for representing the division James Joyce saw between a real sensuality of rural people and the Catholic Church and the middle class' rejection of sexuality and of the body. It also is significant because of the location, as the character of Stephen Dedalus' father is from County Cork, and the area becomes associated in James Joyce's books with origination, roots and family history, all of which also have resonance for Trevor Joyce, who is currently resident in the city of Cork as well. P.W. Joyce's reminiscences echo Davin's in that there is also an implicit sense of remove from the countryside into the city. Again, in an internal doubling, P.W. Joyce is reminiscing about his own past efforts to recall memories from his rural childhood. Joyce, through the act of reframing classical texts and the touchstones of a traditional conception of Irishness, in particular as it was understood at the time the state was formed, with an unsettling of memory and identity, challenges the idea that there is a continuity with the past. Instead, we see that each retelling of the past is a reinvention of it.

In an unusual chiming for this poem that relies on the reader to create meaning from the paratactical arrangement of many estranged languages and texts from many genres, the right-hand section echoes the "cry of despair" in the extract from Robinson in the left-hand passage. In using the English definitions of *caoin*, Joyce also seems to echo the loss of any organic connection to a past that some of the passages on the left address. Importantly, the Irish words from Dineen's text are never presented. Unlike Ireland's most famous poet, Seamus Heaney, who has striven to identify people, place and language in his *dinnseanchas* poems, which have Irish place names as their titles, such as "Anahorish", Joyce shows us very literally the absence of that connection. The Irish language Dineen had translated was already lost to his Irish readers and his translation was even then an effort to recover the abandoned language. The dictionary entry, like the extracts from the texts by James Joyce and P.W. Joyce, is an early twentieth-century source looking back on interactions with the folk culture of rural Ireland. Even for these texts, such a culture is already a recollection that is being reconstructed in narrative. The translation, rewritten again by Trevor Joyce, is what is left – the sequestrum.

Joyce wrote in a 2001 essay on his poetics that "language arrives already filthy… filthy always with experience, not the world, but heavy with it" (137). The reuse of texts in 'Trem Neul' emphasises that our language comes to us in the present imbued with a palimpsest of politics, history and culture and that any expression of self in a poem must necessarily emerge from that morass of forces as well. Joyce's poem is built from linguistic material, on the left side, that draws attention to the ways in which memory functions, to perceptions of and interactions with space, and to representations of rural Ireland. The multiple languages and experiences of colonisation that are represented in the extracts that make up the right-hand rope of language place Ireland's experience in a global context, refusing to allow a sense of national destiny or exceptionalism. Tying Irish experience to that of other British colonies emphasises the fact that the culture of Ireland is also an adulterated, amalgamated one affected by its inclusion in the global reach of the British Empire.

Joyce's position in relation to the past and the Irish language is not nostalgic, but he does register that there was a loss, and that the ways of life that his ancestors knew are irretrievable. This poem does not only turn to the past, but in its mixture of texts jars the reader to see the connections between the events of the past and the present. His use of turn-of-the-century primers in this 1999 poem emphasises the loss of linguistic diversity that has been a result of the modern era of global imperialism, and which continues as global communication and commercial systems become ever more deeply intertwined. At a moment in which Ireland was capitalising on its position as an English-speaking nation to appeal to US-based multinationals seeking a foothold in Europe, Joyce points out that this immersion in contemporary globalisation has its root in the Republic's history of linguistic loss and cultural change. Rather than the Celtic Tiger being a sign of triumph over a colonial past, it is a result of it. Yet, instead of reacting against the cultural homogenisation that is often feared to accompany American influence by turning to a notion of threatened national purity or authenticity, Joyce highlights the constructed nature of both individual and national identity, both of which are the result of interactions with others, interactions that cannot be erased.

Reading the work of Trevor Joyce means critically reassessing the presentation of Irish experience in the twentieth century, drawing our attention away from violent nationalism as a defining aspect of Irish history, identity and poetry, and instead focusing on trying to critically understand that the present emerges from and interacts with the past, but is not necessarily an inevitable result of it. Both individuals and cultures are made of fragments of the past that have been pulled together into temporary coherence, and such stability is only concrete if its imagined state is not perceived and critiqued. The experience of Ireland's history and present, Joyce demonstrates, can be expressed in forms that seek to replicate the contradictions and gaps within Irishness as it is now, rather than continue to work in a tradition that assumes that identity is something stable, clearly communicable and part of a single national tradition.

Notes

1. See Nolan 169, Grgas 148 and O'Driscoll 49 for examples of this point of view.
2. John Wyse Jackson and Peter Costello's 1998 biography of James Joyce's father, *John Stanislaus Joyce: The Voluminous Life and Genius of James Joyce's Father*, notably makes this claim.
3. These institutions were administered by the Catholic Church both before and after the establishment of the Irish Free State in 1922. They housed and educated impoverished and abandoned children and also acted as reformatories for young convicts. Industrial schools were among the many Church institutions in Ireland that were revealed to have engaged in a multitude of abuses of their young and vulnerable charges by the Ryan Report in 2009.
4. In our interview, Joyce explained that the image that appears at the beginning of 'Trem Neul' is of the farm where his mother spent the first few years of her life.
5. In Articles 2 and 3 of the 1937 Constitution, the Republic had declared that the entire island of Ireland was the national territory, despite the fact that the Anglo-Irish Treaty of 1921 had ceded the six counties of Northern Ireland to Britain. These articles were amended in 1998 to relinquish that absolute claim as part of the Good Friday Agreement.
6. This assumes an audience in the English-speaking West with access to high-speed internet, which is available to far from all the world's inhabitants. However, when one considers where Joyce's work has been published (the UK, Ireland and Canada, or on websites curated by residents of these countries), one can extrapolate that a great majority of the readers of a small press book of poetry would be likely to have the necessary technological infrastructure to access cloud-based data.
7. Some examples of such works are Nicholas Carr, *The Shallows*; Kenneth Goldsmith, *Uncreative Writing*; Jay David Bolter, *Writing Space: Computers, Hypertext, and the Remediation of Print*; and Colin Lankshear and Michele Knobel (eds.), *Digital Literacies: Concepts, Policies and Practices*.
8. Deegan and Sutherland's *Transferred Illusions: Digital Technology and the Forms of Print* is an example of this type of analysis.
9. See the breakthrough 2011 article by Michel et al. on the work of "culturomics" and Franco Moretti's fascinating *Graphs, Maps, and Trees*.
10. Craig Dworkin's introduction to *Against Expression: An Anthology of Conceptual Writing* has become a key text that articulates the contemporary approach to the use of found texts. He writes of the poets selected for the anthology: "They replace making with choosing, fabrication with arrangement, and production with transcription. In these ways, previously written language comes to be seen and understood in a new light" (xliv). Two meanings are present continuously: that of the language in its original context, and the critique of the information as it was originally present that the reframing forces upon the

reader. As a corollary to this, Judith Goldman, writing of conceptual poetry's apparently objective, non-interventionist approach to found texts, has said that "the textual readymade, over against this would be self-effacing documentary effect, also draws attention to its work of mediation, its re-siting and medium translation of the text it captures" (n. pag.). As Kenneth Jeong has pointed out, after Derrida's and Barthes' unravelling of the originary position of the author, there can be little difference seen between those who profess to originally create language and those who manipulate the published words of others, which is part of the impetus behind the drive to curate rather than create.

Works Cited

Archambeau, Robert. 'Not Heaney, Healy: Questions, Answers and Explorations at the Edge of Irish Writing', *Readme* 1 (1999): N.d. Web. 20 Dec. 2010.

Baetens, Jan. 'Free Writing, Constrained Writing: The Ideology of Form', *Poetics Today* 18.1 (1997): 1–14. *JSTOR*. Web. 18 July 2010.

Bakhtin, Mikhail. 'From "Discourse in the Novel"', *The Dialogic Imagination: Four Essays*. Ed. Michael Holquist. Trans. Caryl Emerson and Michael Holquist. Austin, TX: University of Texas Press, 1981. Rpt. in *The Critical Tradition: Classic Texts and Contemporary Trends*. 2nd ed. Ed. David Richter. Boston, MA: Bedford, 1998. 530–539. Print.

Bornstein, George. *Material Modernism*. Cambridge: Cambridge University Press, 2001. Print.

Crabtree, William. *Elements of Luganda, Together with Exercises and Grammar*. London: Society for Promoting Christian Knowledge, 1902. *Open Library*. Web. 22 Apr. 2012.

Davis, Alex. 'The Irish Modernists and Their Legacy', *The Cambridge Companion to Contemporary Irish Poetry*. Cambridge: Cambridge University Press, 2003. 76–93. Print.

Deegan, Marilyn and Kathryn Sutherland. *Transferred Illusions: Digital Technology and the Forms of Print*. Farnham: Ashgate, 2009. Print.

Dorward, Nate. 'On Trevor Joyce', *Chicago Review* 48.4 (2002/2003): 82–96. Print.

Duncan, Andrew. 'Pale angel exuvial who can mix it with the chicken'. Rev. of *with the first dream of fire they hunt the cold: A Body of Work 1966–2000*, by Trevor Joyce. *Jacket* 20, Dec. 2002. Web. 7 Apr. 2012. <http://jacketmagazine.com/20/dunc-r-joyc.html>

Dworkin, Craig. 'The Fate of Echo', *Against Expression: An Anthology of Conceptual Writing*. Eds. Craig Dworkin and Kenneth Goldsmith. Evanston, IL: Northwestern University Press, 2010. xxiii–liv. Print.

Goldman, Judith. 'Re-thinking "Non-retinal Literature": Citation, 'Radical Mimesis', and Phenomenologies of Reading in Conceptual Writing', *Postmodern Culture* 22.1 (2011): n. pag. *Project MUSE*. Web. 4 Aug. 2012.

Goldsmith, Kenneth. *Uncreative Writing*. New York, NY: Columbia University Press, 2011. Print.

Gregory, Elizabeth. *Quotation and Modern American Poetry: "'Imaginary Gardens with Real Toads'"*. Houston, TX: Rice University Press, 1996. Print.

Grgas, Stipe. 'Contemporary Poetry at a Tangent.' *Sub-Versions: Trans-National Readings of Modern Irish Literature*. Ed. Ciaran Ross. New York, NY: Rodopi, 2010. 145–160. Print.

Harvey, David. *The Condition of Postmodernity: An Inquiry into the Origins of Cultural Change*. Oxford: Blackwell, 1989. Print.

Joyce, Trevor. 'Interrogate the Thrush: Another Name for Something Else.' *Vectors: New Poetics*. Ed. Robert Archambeau. Lincoln, NE: Writers Club Press, 2001. 136–169. Google Book Search. Web. 4 Apr. 2012.

———. 'Trem Neul.' *with the first dream of fire they hunt the cold: A Body of Work 1966–2000*. 2nd ed. Dublin: New Writers' Press; Exeter: Shearsman Books, 2003. 185–231. Print.

———. 'Why I Write Narrative'. *Narrativity* 1. The Poetry Centre, San Francisco State University, Mar. 2000. Web. 5 Apr. 2012. <http://www.sfsu.edu/~poetry/narrativity/issueone.html>

Kittler, Friedrich A. *Discourse Networks 1800/1900*. Trans. Michael Metteer and Chris Cullens. Redwood City, CA: Stanford University Press, 1990. Print.

Lloyd, David. *Anomalous States: Irish Writing and the Post-Colonial Moment*. Durham, NC: Duke University Press, 1993. Print.

McGann, Jerome. *The Textual Condition*. Princeton, NJ: Princeton University Press, 1991. Print.

Michel, Jean-Baptiste, et al. 'Quantitative analysis of culture using millions of digitized books.' *Science* 331.6014 (2011): 176–182. *PubMed*. Web. 25 Oct. 2012.

Nolan, Emer. 'Modernism and the Irish Revival.' *The Cambridge Companion to Modern Irish Culture*. Eds. Joe Cleary and Claire Connolly. Cambridge: Cambridge University Press, 2005. 157–172. Print.

O'Driscoll, Dennis. 'Foreign Relations: Irish and International Poetry.' *Poetry in Contemporary Irish Literature*. Ed. Michael Kenneally. Gerrards Cross: Colin Smythe, 1995. 48–60. Print.

O'Toole, Fintan. *Ship of Fools: How Stupidity and Corruption Sank the Celtic Tiger*. London: Faber; Philadelphia, PA: PublicAffairs-Perseus, 2010. Print.

Panko, Julia. 'Dead-tree Data: Print Novels, Information Storage, and Media Transition, 1910/2010.' Dissertation UC Santa Barbara, 2012. Print.

Perloff, Marjorie. *The Futurist Moment: Avant-Garde, Avant-Guerre, and the Language of Rupture*. Chicago, IL: University of Chicago Press, 1986. Print.

Robinson, Tim. *Setting Foot on the Shores of Connemara & Other Writings*. Dublin: Lilliput, 1996. Print.

Yates, Frances. *The Art of Memory*. Chicago: University of Chicago Press, 1966. Print.

Marthine Satris

Still Man:
The Human as Unvoiced in the Poetry of Trevor Joyce

Fergal Gaynor

'…and he that will / …about must, and about must go'
(Donne, *Satire 3*)

What's in Store, Trevor Joyce's 2007 collection, is arranged symmetrically about a central block, giving the impression that it could be folded on to itself, like a hinge, perhaps, with a central pin. At the edge of each wing are translations (or, better, "versions") from "dead tongues"; that is, from extinct, threatened or minority languages like the Turkic Tatar, the Finno-Ugric Votyak, and Middle and Early Modern Irish. Moving towards the centre from either edge a pattern becomes apparent – a group of 36-word poems alternates with the generally longer products of various poetic projects: e.g. selections from Joyce's contributions to *OffSets*, an internet-based collaborative work; the three-part, stanzaic 'Saws'; 'Capital Accounts', workings from the Chinese; etc. At the centre is 'Outcry' – again based on the Chinese, this time that of the poet Ruan Ji – but not the dead centre. The sequence wraps around a block of nine-and-a-half pages of justified, bold, sans serif, for the most part unpunctuated text: 'STILLSMAN'. The visual effect of changing the book's formatting is matched by the idiom of the poem itself: it is a dense prose collage, not impenetrable, but certainly obstructive. The arrangement of the book calls attention to this resistant work, as a core *about* which it folds, and the formatting of 'STILLSMAN' calls attention to the resistant character of this core. Despite this resistance, or rather in tandem with it – resistance to being "broken open", to showing its interior, delivering up its terms of recognition, in short, to revealing what it is *about* – I am going to argue that 'STILLSMAN', the work signalled as the core of *What's in Store*, has in its turn its own core, albeit one that, significantly, tells us nothing.

In terms of the culture of modern Irish poetry, in which, to use J.C.C. Mays' terminology, a persistent alternative strain based on a "modernist" "I-it" relationship to the poem can be discriminated from a mainstream of "I-thou" poetry, that is, poetry concerned with readerly identifications – the poet answering perceived needs in the reading market with a well-crafted product – 'STILLSMAN' seems to flaunt its inaccessibility, parade a lack of concern for its prospective readership.[1] Instead of acknowledging a model in which, in Mays' description, "words are pitched towards communication and seek confirmation through the approval of those who hear them", the poem blocks communication from the outset (6.3.2). As such, it is always likely to be understood as a work showing off its "alternative" credentials, to use the identifier preferred by Mays to "modernist" and "experimental", etc., in 2000, and reaffirmed by John Goodby as applicable to the work of Joyce, Walsh, Scully, Ó Tuairisc, etc., in the recent *Oxford Handbook of Modern Irish Poetry* (2012). And so it was understood in its chief treatment in the mass press – an *Irish Times* review of *What's in Store* of 2008, titled: "Process, Product and a Peacock" (B10). The word "peacock" in the title set the tone for an account of Joyce's collection as a "blockbuster" exercise in exclusivist display, with the "hard on the eye", "Copperplate Gothic typeface" of 'STILLSMAN' being dismissively compared to the "easy on the ear" versions from minority languages, which suggest "the archaic character of folksong disarmingly and directly". The identifiable quality of folksong ("archaic") is effectively communicated ("directly") with audience responsiveness in mind ("disarmingly"). Elsewhere, again very much along the lines of Mays' analysis, Joyce's versions from the Irish are saved from their failure to "renovate familiar cadences" – that is, provide the reader with recognised Irish-language poetry pleasures – by being 'consummately turned'; that is, by their character as crafted products. The review unabashedly reiterates the accepted terms of reader-oriented modern Irish poetry and consequently finds work like 'STILLSMAN' (where Joyce endeavours to be something other than the "accomplished lyric poet and gifted maker of versions" for whom the review reserves praise) to be affectedly, and needlessly, "troublesome".

The trouble with all this – and the troubling aspect of this argument on the threshold of public attention, an argument that judges purely in terms of a single, synchronic model of Irish writing, for which the reader-oriented "modern Irish poetry" is exemplary – is that it gives no time to the working of a poem like 'STILLSMAN', that it fails to take thought of the possibility that matters of "accessibility" and "inaccessibility" prompted by the poem's form might in fact be worked through, questioned and deepened by the poem. In short, the trouble with all of this is that it is unthoughtful, rash even, which is ironic considering the fact that much of what the international reader expects from modern Irish poetry is a place of slowed temporalities suitable for a contemplative mood, more or less lost elsewhere in the global-capitalist world (if not quite a "small cabin… of clay and wattles made", perhaps a comfortable whitewashed cottage by the Atlantic) (Yeats 39).

That Joyce might be thinking about matters of "access" is clear even from the book that opens his second phase of writing in 1995, *stone floods*.[2] Not far from the centre of that collection, and next to 'Tohu-bohu', with its references to the troubling conceptions of meaning and language of the Gnostic heresies –

> ringed round with tokens
>
> protocols addresses
> codes conventions empty forms (*first dream of fire* 118)

– ''93/4' might almost have been written by a poet wishing to place himself in the mainstream of Irish writing, the idiom presents so many "familiar cadences" (Fryatt B10). The poem's first word contains the first-person pronoun ("I've got no means of knowing for sure") and the conventional "you" of the personal lyric is there by the second line: "if you can hear the knocking of the bells". The lyric "I-you" idiom is not the same as the reader-oriented "I-you" poem, as Celan's tortuous interrogation of the former idiom makes clear, but the personal lyric form remains a staple of reader-oriented poetry – economically conjuring an intimate space of communicating subjectivities. The sense of intimacy of

> but do my dear friend remember
> to feed the fire I built
> to counteract the streaming flood
> inside your walls the spreading rot (120)

and the poem's unemphatic resolution of the "I-you" address in its last lines with the "we" of

> let's together each
> again make free
> for the time being (122)

is unproblematically related to the idiom of, say, Seamus Heaney's

No treaty
I foresee will salve completely your tracked
And stretchmarked body, the big pain
That leaves you raw, like opened ground, again. ('Act of Union' 127)

where the poem's resonance depends on the failure to resolve the initial
distance opened by the I-you address, or Paula Meehan's

These hot midsummer nights I whisper
assignations, trysts, heather beds
I'd like to lay you down in, remote beaches
we could escape to, watch
bonfire sparks mix with stars ('Pillow Talk' 32)

which, initially at least, before introducing the complicating theme of a
second, uncanny "I", lays out the personal idiom and its dynamic in the
simplest way possible. In this respect ''93/4' is unabashedly "accessible".
But then, that is exactly what it is, *an access* to the collection as a whole. The
hint has already been there in the "streaming flood" of damp in the "dear
friend['s]" house, drawing into the poem the "floods" of the collection's
title, and the rains, courses and floods that appear (and disappear)
throughout the collection after the early, Heraclitean 'Fast Rivers' (8–9).[3]
''93/4' presents the poet unpacking his library and, in the process, more
or less lays out a programme for the book, almost in the manner of a
showman:

for your pleasure I arrange

Dickinson and Dogen
Lorca and Tao Qian
with other esoterica
and miscellaneous pots and pans (121)

And before its simply resolved ending ''93/4' furnishes an image of the
operation of a kind of "meaning" (I'll return to this word shortly) that
can be sensed at work throughout the collection. It is introduced into
the poem, hospitably, as a kind of hallucination or vision, brought on in
conventional fashion by a little narrative of burning essential oils:

Fergal Gaynor

...complex vapours
above the steady flame

that in the column of the lamp
burns almost enclosed
aware the unfinished buddha
at the shut summit

of the terraced worlds
sees the rough suns tumble out
where the furious high god
hurls his net (122)

This image of the Hindu god Indra casting a net of jewelled intersections, in which each jewel reflects every other jewel simultaneously (as *stone floods*' notes expand upon "and each jewelled node / glitters with every other / as they fall" [237]), corresponds to a working of connectivity throughout the collection, the instances of freezing, melting, flowing and metamorphosing in each, relatively short (compared to 'STILLSMAN' at least), and for the most part lyric form, reflecting and linking with similar instances within others, generating a dynamic against the resolutional movement of each individual piece, towards a supra-individual systematisation.[4] As the poem suggests, however, this operative connectivity is "effortless exactly": it not only threatens to prise apart the closed forms of *meaningful* resolution of the individual poems, but it corresponds to systematic workings that fail to recognise the human terms in which meaning is made. The poems themselves contain descriptions of these processes of connection that leak through and dissolve the bounds of human categories:

Circuits and gates collapse
in sand ('The Turlough' 96)

cuckoos in due course again turn raptor
swallows become oysters seashells hatch geese ('Chimaera' 111)

Gorged on vermilion, his peers sweated
bright death, transfused the rockveins to their own. ('Cold Course' 106)

I'll return to what I'll call provisionally this "metaphysics" of inhuman process when discussing 'STILLSMAN'; at this juncture it is only important to recognise that the image of the divine net does indeed provide a conceptual access to the working of a system discernible throughout *stone floods*, part of a role – to provide access to the collection as a whole – that "93/4" plays in general. This it does in three ways: by employing a reader-oriented idiom; by rehearsing many of the themes of the other poems in the collection; and by providing an image for a conceptuality, of connectivity between isolated parts, at work throughout the collection as a whole.

If this is what it means to be accessible in Joyce's work (and clearly we are dealing with a way of thinking about poetry that extends beyond the bounds of each individual poem or sequence), what does it mean to be "inaccessible"? In a certain way, the image of Indra's net prefigures work produced after *stone floods* – 'The Net' that catches and reassembles the elements of 'The Drift' in 1998's *Syzygy* being an obvious example – something that suggests a relation between "93/4"s other image, that of the "unfinished buddha / at the shut summit", and 'STILLSMAN'. The notes again elaborate on this image:

> The immense monument of Borobodur, in Java, contains the im-
> ages of many buddhas. Those near the base are clearly visible in
> the open while those at the penultimate level as one ascends the
> world-mountain are almost hidden in great bell-shaped lattices
> of stone, or stupas. The single stupa which stands at the highest
> point is completely closed, and inside it was found by its restorers
> an image of the buddha, whose rudimentary unfinished form is
> generally taken to indicate the only partial presence in our realm
> of a supreme buddha. (*first dream of fire* 236-7)

The totally enclosed image of the buddha is a striking figure of an inaccessible artwork: invisible, placed at the "summit" of a world-mountain which the votive / viewer must "ascend" – it is assumed, with difficulty, going about and about – encountering other images of the buddha on the way which, clearly, are not intended as ends in themselves. The dynamic of the description of the ultimate buddha, though, is interesting: we are given its meaning – the tenor for which its "unfinished form" is the vehicle – it is "generally taken to indicate the only partial presence in our realm of a supreme buddha", etc., – but we are robbed in the process of the working of this meaning. We know that the "shut summit" contains an unfinished buddha because the restorers have, at least temporarily, dismantled the topmost stupa and revealed what was intended to be hidden. The figure, in short, plays accessibility and inaccessibility against each other, leaving us with a meaning (the partial presence of the supreme buddha) which both allows us to gain a greater grasp on what the inaccessible is, and removes it from us again. We are left with a question – what is this image about (and about)? – which has grown in specificity and indeed (partial) presence, but which in doing so has separated itself off, paradoxically, within our terms of meaning.

To descend the "world-mountain" again, it is worthwhile looking at *N11: A Musing*'s account of the "I-thou" and "I-it" models of poetry in its application to this question of inaccessibility. Mays summarises that "reception-oriented writing thrives on recognition and reciprocal understanding" (6.3.1), thus echoing an earlier comment on "a thriving protest-industry of writing by Irish women": "it tends to work within the framework it protests against, that is, not to question the grounds of conventional recognition" (5.4.4). The important word here is "recognition", in particular "conventional recognition": that the poem should represent something that too quickly, almost immediately in fact, should receive its completing response in its readership, either because of the poem's restriction to wholly familiar forms and subject matter or because of its attunement to and involvement in its audience's desires and expectations. The moment of recognition may be delayed, played with, made a puzzle of (often the badge of the "postmodern"), but once it arrives it closes with a satisfying snap.[5] "The danger is in the neatness of identifications", as Mays later quotes Beckett (6.6.1), thus repeating an insight of modernism in general independent of matters of experimentation, progressiveness, originality or politics, though necessarily entangled in such matters once it attempts to practically resist the pressure towards such neatness.[6] And what the poetry of neat identification is incapable of doing is precisely to "[question] the grounds of recognition", or, perhaps better, in the light of the violence and upheaval experienced since the years of modernism's early twentieth-century formulations, to acknowledge the factual questioning of the same grounds. Unless the reader-oriented poet works on the assumption that the reduced "grounds of conventional recognition" in his or her community of well-meaning readers is somehow safely detached from the general, that they are an essentially comfortable island of right opinion, then the question must arise as to whether their work represents an insulation or escape from reality. As the framing argument of Mays' *N11* also warns, however, the mere "keeping ahead", the performance of an "ever-renewing escape act", of the terms of recognition by a poetic vanguard is always likely to lead to new territories for recognitive colonisation, not to mention a form of immediate recognition in itself (how do you know "new stuff" when you hear it? By certain effects? By unconventional media? By its references? By its politics?) (4.1.3). A poetry based on the *questioning* of the grounds, however – which would be more than the adoption of a position of anxiety or vulnerability within the terms of recognition – would necessarily place pressure on the circuit from representation to recognition, and such a poetry by its very nature would put to work matters of accessibility and inaccessibility, making entry a conscious, reflective matter, à la "93/4'. The obstructive form of 'STILLSMAN' begins such a process of reflection from the opposite direction, a process which is continued *within* the poem: to a great extent it is a work "about" obstructions to meaning, failures of communication, the change beyond recognition of language and meanings.

§

All that said, there is a certain bravado about the formatting of 'STILLSMAN', which is to say that it shows some spirit in its public appearance, despite its distance from the fashion. The same kind of spirit is to be found in that "tart lyricism" that is often characteristic of Joyce's style – there is a sharpness to the language, playful but pointed, even when dealing with moving or emotional subject matter, or rather, *especially* when dealing with emotional subject matter.[7] What's at stake here is that resistance to sentimentality forefronted by Fanny Howe in her foreword to Joyce's 2008 collection of versions from the Middle and Early Modern Irish, *Courts of Air and Earth*.[8] Sentiment – a form of feeling that has taken on the quality of currency through its overuse, to be exchanged in a particular situation between a particular agent and client as easily as in any other – is the safest and most universal of poetic goods for the market of easy recognition. Since the representative–recognitive circuit is an interaction between human beings, the danger always exists that it become a "market in affects" once the distance between participants is collapsed by the immediacy of recognition.[9] Another of the long pieces in *What's in Store*, "Capital Accounts", touches on the subject in its account of the place of prostitution in the economy of the capital in question:

while hit-men
make
their contracts
in full light

and fat cats
in hand-
tooled footware
deal strict cash,

till all are drawn
down the same side-street
to the hookers'
sweet emporium.

•

The hookers
in the darkening
put on
flash stuff,

and then with purest voices
sing
familiar
sentimental airs; (262–3)

"Sweetness" is the essential quality of the prostitutes' "emporium", and there is a sense in which sugar – industrially refined, dissolving on the tongue, an extractable essence – is the sentimental currency in question. *What's in Store*, in fact, opens with the Tatar –

The truth
I dreamed
I craved
sweet fruit. (3)

– and its suspicion of certainties, and their "sweet" satisfactions. Joyce's idiom, by contrast, could then be associated with that foodstuff more usually treated as currency, salt.[10] The long poem 'Trem Neul' (1999) is prefaced by a line from Yeats – "All that is personal soon rots; it must be packed in ice or salt" – that sets the action of salt against the "corruption" and "honeying", in Hamlet's words, of the merely personal and sentimental (Yeats 213).[11] But salt is appropriate as a metaphor for Joyce's language in other ways: it is inorganic, a mineral, and thus associated with the non-human elemental processes already noted in *stone floods*; and like those processes it works its own changes, not a slow dissolution into sweetness within the organic cell, but a corrosion through surfaces and casings that simultaneously tautens, hardens, petrifies.

It is also hardly surprising that a writer who has opened himself to developments in international music and visual art, not to mention poetry, of the last hundred years or so should show an awareness of graphic and typographic possibilities, and the same acquaintance with twentieth-century innovation is reflected in the poem's collage form. To pin down the particular character of that collage form, and its sources, is not, however, straightforward. It is not Poundian collage; that is, collage in the tradition that passes through Charles Olson's theorisation in "Projective Verse". It is not a "field", in other words – it lacks the distances between elements of a "field" poem, the capacity for bright individual moments to be held separately but in a tense, measured relation with their neighbours, and chiming with causally unrelated elements elsewhere in the space of the poem – nor does it have the personal, occasional marks of the "process poem". 'STILLSMAN' is crowded, segments of found text pressing on each other, jostling for space, and in doing so, often penetrating, interrupting or overwriting the sense of the adjoining segments. The lack of punctuation amplifies the disruptive effect of the resultant pressure – the only punctuation, apart from the piece's beginning and ending, being a division into twelve stages, denoted by the relevant number inserted without formatting into the general press of the text. So, in "stage two", we can extract the following passage:

SWITCH THE LETTER Q & C BY
AN EXACT OBSERVATION OF WHICH PARTICULARS IT MAY
BE POSSIBLE TO MAKE A STATUE SPEAK SOME WORDS
AND YET THIS FRAUGHT INCAPACITY FRIGHTENS THE
PATIENT C BOUND SO NARROW IN A TANGLE OF MUSCLE
NEAR THE HEART THE NUT SHAPED SYRINX PITEOUSLY TO
CHAUNGE HIR SHAPE[.][12] (144)

Fergal Gaynor

Five different texts are involved here. "SWITCH THE LETTER Q & C" is the end of a segment that belongs to a philosophical text that appears to be quoted only once (which Joyce tells me was authored by "the Right Reverend John Wilkins"). "BY AN EXACT OBSERVATION OF WHICH PARTICULARS IT MAY BE POSSIBLE TO MAKE A STATUE SPEAK SOME WORDS" is from a text on technologies of speech, that is quoted a handful of times across the poem (four times?). "AND YET THIS FRAUGHT INCAPACITY FRIGHTENS THE PATIENT C" is from a long late-nineteenth-century account of a communicative disorder (referred to as "agraphia" in the text), which is one of the three "master texts" of 'STILLSMAN' and about which I will have much to say shortly. "BOUND SO NARROW IN A TANGLE OF MUSCLE NEAR THE HEART THE NUT SHAPED SYRINX" is from another "master text", appearing quite frequently, a modern piece on birdsong (from an issue of *New Scientist*, according to Joyce). "PITEOUSLY TO CHAUNGE HIR SHAPE" is from Ovid's *Metamorphoses* (in Golding's translation, I am told by Joyce).[13] However, to separate out these passages is to risk losing the effect of the text as published, and the working of the poem. The interference of the agraphia narrative with the "C" of "SWITCH THE LETTER Q & C" (is C the same "PATIENT C" a little afterwards?), and the disturbance of that same agraphia passage by the assertion that C (the patient) can, as a letter, be simply 'switched' with another, Q, are lost. In addition, the core of the technologies of speech segment – "IT MAY BE POSSIBLE TO MAKE A STATUE SPEAK SOME WORDS" – is fractured at its joint with the text preceding – "BY AN EXACT OBSERVATION OF WHICH PARTICULARS" – since the particulars in question may at once be the switching of the letters Q and C, or some other "particulars", offstage, as it were, in the original technologies of speech source. And so on: patient C is frightened by a "FRAUGHT INCAPACITY" that somehow is also related to the ability of an automaton to speak, and the "BOUND SO NARROW" that seems to promise a description of the individual's emotional condition rapidly reveals itself as an intrusion by another text (related to birdsong), which "metamorphoses" into Ovid (the story of Syrinx, as it happens, thus resonating and interfering with the birdsong passages and various references to music). The effect is of geological crush – various strata convulsed by extreme pressures, pressed into each other's horizontal extension, fragmented at the edges, buckling and shifting away from their original positions and vectors while remaining, just about, recognisable as strata – that is, lines moving according to a logic of resolution and closure.

Such a collage form is more closely related to anglophone "experimental poetry", to the work of those poets influenced by the Language movement in the seventies and eighties in the US, for instance, but there is a distinct difference. When Charles Bernstein talks in 'Semblance' of "shifting the contexts in which even a fairly 'standard' sentence finds itself" (he refers at this point to the "prose-format work of Barrett Watten"), after which

> the seriality of the ordering of sentences within a paragraph [displacing] from its habitual surrounding the projected representational fixation that the sentence conveys (116)

he is thinking of a poetry which has lifted itself away from any "conventional expository or narrational paragraph structure" – but this is something that is maintained, if only for the sake of the performance of its violation, in 'STILLSMAN' (116). 'STILLSMAN' progresses, as a disease or a disorder progresses; which is *not* to say that it has the disclosive structure of traditional tragedy – towards a bringing of all the elements of a catastrophic situation into full light – either. If anything, the movement is one of closure, beginning with the conventional light of ordinary perception and proceeding by way of various destructive, inhuman processes towards the extinction of that light, leaving us with barren permutation; the "poetry", "music", "embodiment", "resonance" and "tragedy" adhering conventionally to the themes of the poem become

SONET NOTES STONE TONES ONSET [.] (152)

And the result is clearly different: for Language poetry "a perceptual vividness is intensified for each sentence" (Bernstein 116); for 'STILLSMAN' there are no such delimited, bright "cuts" or flashes; the burdened line moves inexorably on, often brightly coloured, but always within the surrounding, thickening murk. The fact of the matter is that 'STILLSMAN' feels somehow more related to art from the thirties to the fifties – that is, in the shadow of totalitarianism – than to the movements since sixties counterculture. It feels late modernist and Old World, rather than New World and making claim to some postmodernist, changed field of experience. Unlike the poetry of Maurice Scully, for instance, I don't think "experimental poetry", in the post-sixties sense, has had much influence on the evolution of Joyce's style. My guess, from hearing Joyce in conversation, is that the experience of contemporary poets experimenting with non-lyrical forms at the Assembling Alternatives conference in New Hampshire in 1996 did inspire him to devise his own collages and assemblages,[14] but the sensibility behind these new forms had already been cultivated by an interest in art, in late and fringe Dada, surrealist and absurdist modes – Klee, Schwitters (as poet and collagist), Lorca, Ernst (particularly of the *Une Semaine de Bonté*), Kafka, *Finnegans Wake*, Borges, Beckett, Joseph Cornell's boxes. It was then alerted to new constructive possibilities by Joyce's exposure to the development of programming systems as an employee of the tobacco company P.J. Carroll and then of Apple computers, an anachronistic combination not untypical of Irish culture.[15] There are many other ingredients in the mix, especially if we are talking of Joyce's poetry as a whole (one could talk about a mannered "Dublin gothic" tradition, the influence of Chinese poetry cannot be ignored, "folk" elements are frequently employed, etc.), but the resultant idiom feels most like an intensified post-surrealism; that is, an art of irrational or violent conjunction, but one in which the operation of dream or somatic logic has been replaced by a more materialistic, conceptual awareness. "The chance meeting of a sewing-machine and an umbrella on a dissecting table", perhaps, but with the dissecting table furnished by Roman Jakobson, the sewing-machine set up as a cybernetic system and the resultant stitches resembling the isorhythm of Guillaume de Machaut (Lautréamont 161). It has often been labelled "Oulipian" as a result, but, although there are certain crossovers (a liking for writing "under constraint" for instance) and affinities, I think it just happens that Joyce has arrived in an adjoining territory – it is not a matter of influence.

It is natural, when put in these terms, that readers (apart, clearly, from Fanny Howe, if the Foreword is anything to go by) should miss the fact that Joyce's poetry is not simply a matter of play of intelligence, or "heartless", in Howes' terms: 'STILLSMAN', for instance, harshly unsentimental as it is, is nevertheless emotionally charged. A reading or performance of the poem can be a harrowing experience.[16] This is closely bound up with the agraphia "master text" mentioned above. Having moved about the presentation, and then the form, of the poem, it becomes impossible now not to acknowledge this point of access to a possible interior – the fact that 'STILLSMAN' does include a narrative, and a straightforward one at that – that there is a recession granted by the recognisable terms of the unfolding of a story. That the slow, grinding movement of texts of 'STILLSMAN' might be *about* something, specifically about what is revealed in the agraphia narrative, was taken for granted by the *Irish Times* review: 'STILLSMAN' is a "story of bourgeois neurosis and decline" (a story appropriate to its form, which is that of a "visiting card run amok"). Newspaper reviews are about delineation – of giving a clear, recognisable character to artworks, which is part of the process of persuading a readership that a piece should or should not be placed within the space of public attention – and doing so in a tight space – but even so, this is severe economy. The pressure towards contemporary recognition is so strong that the gradual destruction and eventual death of an individual, the C of the agraphia narrative, can only be viewed as the characteristic predicament of an unsympathetic historical class. The review is not wholly wrong, however. When the less rash, more perceptive reviews by Michael S. Begnal in *Freeverse* and Stephen Vincent in *Galatea Resurrects* come down, as reviews do, to the question of what 'STILLSMAN' is about – "the indeterminacy of language"; and "the transience of beauty" and the "liberation" from that transience through "song", respectively – they reflect recognisable features of the poem but fail to register the importance of the plain narrative, and in doing so risk realigning 'STILLSMAN' as either a poetic transcription of post-structuralist theory or an act of lyric resistance. 'STILLSMAN' works in the way it does, a way which carries a difficult emotional charge, because it grants us a story to draw us into the crucible, or better, "still" of mutually interfering texts and registers; that is, through a process in twelve parts that eventually leads to the closure of the same story, not in terms of resolution, but as a possible way of making meaning out of the process undergone. This process undergone is reflected in the third of the collage's "master narratives", which also gives us the twelve-part structure, that of distilling whiskey, and this inhuman movement through time and transformation competes with the other form of such organised movement – the story – even in the poem's title: both the "still man" that c becomes in section twelve –

THE CONSUMED C QUITE STILL / QUITE GONE QUITE PATIENT YET (152)

(one of the poem's most important segments) – and the man overseeing operations in the whiskey still. The overlap between the two, moreover, is figured in two excerpts from the traditional ballad "John Barleycorn", in which the living source of whiskey, barley, is anthropomorphised and put through a mythic process of death and transformation. The passages

BEFORE THAT FALL WHEN THEY PLOUGHED HIM DOWN (143)

and

CUT WITH A SOLEMN OATH (143)

Fergal Gaynor

figuratively bond the story of c to the "MISHMASH" (stage six) of the process of making whiskey and of the working of the crowded texts.[17]

So what is the story of c? In stage one we are introduced to a "PATIENT ONE", only referred to, in the manner of medical casebooks, by an abbreviation of his name: Oscar C (the form recalls the heroes of Kafka's novels and stories). He is a "BRIGHT SHARP MAN" with none of the major male vices of the age (being neither alcoholic or syphilitic). We are told that he is happily married, and that bound up with this happiness is his sharing of a love of music with his wife. In advance of the agraphia theme we are further told that his eyesight is very sharp, and that he has never suffered from neurological problems – not even a migraine. The stage ends with the grim

AND THE TASK OF TRANSLATION BEGAN (143)

from the whiskey source. But before it the fragment

AS MME C RELATED (143)

alerts us to the fact that throughout the narrative we will always deal with reported speech – that Oscar C, or merely c, though the centre of the narrative, is also peculiarly distant. His loss of ability to make meaningful speech or signs is accompanied from the outset by the mediation of his presence in the text.

Stage two begins with the familiar narrative phrase "ONE DAY", taken from another mythical source (other than the story of "John Barleycorn", that is), the ancient Irish narrative of the *Destruction of Da Derga's Hostel*. Here the "ONSET" of c's disorder occurs, related at two removes, through the medical recorder and through c's wife:

HER HUSBAND ABRUPTLY ENDURED SEVERAL SHARP STROKES [.]
(144)

C experiences physical ailments and finds he can no longer read, though he can write and speak normally. He turns to the medical profession for help or advice, initially to an eye specialist who recommends him to consult the author of the report, presumably a neurologist of some kind. There is both a perfunctory and a basic quality to the act of consulting a doctor – it is what one does, systematically, either confidently or anxiously, applying in a certain situation to the official administrator of such situations, but it is also the act of one individual in trouble seeking the aid of another – a simple human interaction that seems only to be able to enter the experience of 'STILLSMAN' at a deep, figurative remove, through the aforementioned *Da Derga* source:

ONE WENT IN SEARCH OF LIVING WATER FOR HIS KING (150)

corresponding to the later

AND CRIED ALOUD WHO BRINGS DRINK TO A KING DOES WELL [,] (152)

the king in question having also been afflicted by a physical disorder, in his case an "INSUFFERABLE THIRST". It becomes clear, however, that the idiom of the medical reporter is quite detached from such matters of "DOING WELL" – it maintains a clinical distance throughout, which, when tart phrases like

HIS SCRIPT AND SPEECH STAYED UP TO SCRATCH (144)

appear, verges on the cruel, despite, or perhaps because of its belonging to matters of institutional and social functionality. A diagnosis is made – that C has a case of "MARKED AGRAPHIA" – and the remainder of the stage recounts C's struggles with the tests of his perceptual faculties, eventually ending with the consultant's observations on C's emotional condition:

THIS FRAUGHT INCAPACITY FRIGHTENS THE PATIENT [,] (144)

[HE] THINKS HE HAS GONE MAD [.] (144)

This latter statement is as close as C gets to expressing himself directly, a commentless observation included in such a way that it seems to belong to the same category as the neurological symptoms that follow:

HE KNOWS THE SIGNS THAT HE CAN T NAME ARE LETTERS AND WHILE STUMBLING CAN TELL [,] (144) etc.

Stage three, which is relatively short, begins to recount C's attempts at continuing with his habitual life while afflicted, which in stage four leads to an elaboration of the details of the agraphia:

Fergal Gaynor

AFTER A SPELLING LESSON OF 15 MINUTES HE IS FINALLY ABLE TO
READ THE TITLE BUT IN ORDER TO RECALL THE LETTERS [ETC.]
(146)

These passages, as they are mediated by the medical reporter, read simultaneously as the struggle of an individual, perhaps still in the hope of controlling or overcoming his disability, and the account of what may function as a series of experiments capable of revealing further scientific knowledge of the agraphic phenomenon. In the latter terms C is merely a case study, the human equivalent of a "GUINEA-PIG". Stage five begins along the same lines but quickly makes clear that any hope of C having experienced the worst of his condition, and of being able to control it, are illusory: further destruction of his faculties is registered. The agraphia narrative, a large chunk of which had ended stage five, takes a while to appear in stage six; when it does, C appears to be trying to regain control of his faculties at a lower level, performing exercises of an elementary school kind – addition and the recognition of letters. However, he cannot take refuge even in these rudimentary functions: he fails a test designed to see if he can recognise numbers made up of multiple digits. The consequent sense of exposure, and the approaching full catastrophe, is figured again in an excerpt from the *Da Derga* text, which closes this stage:

COLD WIND ACROSS A DANGEROUS EDGE NIGHT FOR DESTROY-
ING A KING [.] (147)

Prior to this, a new textual source has entered the melee, Zbigniew Herbert's version of the myth of Marsyas, again a musician. The cruelty of the god Apollo, who flays Marsyas alive for having the temerity to challenge him in a musical contest, has traditionally led to artists registering the disturbing inhumanity of the story, Titian's famous painting of the scene bringing out the strange combination of divine impassivity and pain. The same registration of pain, violent to the point of breaking the poem's frame, occurs in the excerpt from the Herbert poem with the sudden appearance of "A SINGLE VOWEL": "AAA" (147).

Stage seven takes the action out of the clinic and into C's daily life and we learn that C has lived with the disorder for four years, thus bringing about an easing of the tension in the narrative (which had come to a certain climax in stage six). It is probably the descriptions of C's domestic life in this stage that led to the dismissive treatment of the story in the *Irish Times* review: they go for walks, look at paintings in gallery windows, play music and cards together in the evenings, and generally maintain a pre-World War I leisured middle-class existence. It would take great callousness, however, or a fervent antagonism to this now almost extinct class not to feel some relief at this temporary respite in c's destructive process, or to sense that this lifestyle, in c's case at least, is no more than a kind of a defence erected against the impinging chaos, the "MISHMASH". The struggle underlying this lifestyle is again made clear in the opening of stage eight, a significant segment to which I will return shortly –

SO AGAIN AND AGAIN C TRIES (148)

– which effort and its failure naturally leads to c becoming "AGITATED". Our awareness of emotional anguish increases as the account, with the impassivity of the flayers in Titian's *Apollo and Marsyas*, informs us that c has been taking steps towards an attempt at suicide, a jarring turn of events that has been prepared for by a kind of alarm call taken from the *Da Derga* source, a dog barking whose name (or is it an onomatapoeic representation of the barking sound?) resembles that of Oscar C, and who had already appeared just before the crisis in stage six:

IT IS HEARD AGAIN THE CRY OF OSSAR OSSAR THE HOUND [.] (149)

The *Da Derga* narrative appears again near the stage's end, this time giving full expression to the sense of catastrophe:

DECLARATIONS OF WAR A PEOPLE DESTROYED THE RUIN OF A LODG-
ING MEN WOUNDED [etc.] (149)

Stage nine begins with a cool reference to the preceding as a "PERIOD OF AGITATION", then portrays a disquieting scene in which c mimics the act of strangling himself and his wife, before recounting a retreat into a final refuge, that of music, where he appears to exercise still a certain mastery, the excerpts concerned surrounded by birdsong segments. The stage's final line,

THE FIERCE UPSHOT MAKES THE SPIRIT SAFE [,] (149)

intimates that events are coming to an end and transposes the movement of the text into an inhuman, empty register: that of the whiskey-making process. Stage ten continues the theme of c's refuge in musical mastery, but, *pace* Stephen Vincent, it is clear that the disaster/process has yet to run its full course, and c begins to lose his ability to communicate, to make meaningful verbal or graphic signs of any kind, and is reduced to mimicry and gestures. In any case, we might have noted by this stage that the references to birdsong, rather than granting any sense of lyric transcendence, have served to amplify the cold quality of the agraphia narrative by obliquely giving a sense of the small-scale cruelty involved in learning the mechanics of the birdsong's production. And we may note as well, from stage ten, that the fruit of these scientific labours has been the capacity to regard the

SYRINX AS MACHINE RATHER THAN AS AGENT [.] (150)

Stage eleven glibly describes this struggle to maintain contact with the outside world with a connoisseur's appreciation:

HIS MIMIC IS EXTREMELY EXPRESSIVE AND HIS PANTOMIME VERY ARRESTING [.][18] (151)

When an example is given at length of this "PANTOMIME", the effect is far from simply aesthetic, as c's pathetic desperation is all too evident. We have been prepared for this by another excerpt from Golding's Ovid:

WHICH MADE A STILL AND MOURNING NOYSE [.] (151)

And so we reach the final stage. The agraphia narrative appears twice in stage twelve, which is dominated by inhuman registers and ends, as previously stated, with empty permutation. The second appearance is hardly recognisable –

BUT THIS BROUGHT ON A FURTHER VISITATION (152)

– extending the narrative into a meaningless temporal continuum, as c, the subject of possible visitation, is already dead:

FOUND ON THE MORNING OF JANUARY 16TH 1892 THE CONSUMED C QUITE STILL QUITE GONE QUITE PATIENT YET [.] (152)

The terms of c's death, how he is described at the end of the process, are significant: he is "QUITE STILL" – that is, motionless – but also silent. Then again he has always been in some sense silent, in that he has never been able to articulate, and thus come to terms with, his situation in the clinician's narrative – unless it has been in those moments of outburst and pain, the "AAA" from Herbert's poem and a later "HA HA HA THIRST", lifted from a piece by Messiaen, which may be direct expressions of a condition, but are hardly articulate. He is, of course, also now "STILL" – that is, silent – in the sense that the process of his loss of communicative ability is now complete. The "YET" of "QUITE PATIENT YET" is interesting. It suggests that not only was C's status always that of a "patient", one that was merely the "SUBJECT" of medical activity, but that for such a subject death brings about no fundamental change in condition. "PATIENT" also clearly refers to the quality "patience", but in this context the connotations are hardly those of Christian or Victorian virtue, rather the etymological relation to "passion" and suffering ("long-suffering", perhaps) are to the fore, and that overlap with the medical usage, "the recipient of active measures", who must "suffer" the action, rather than one who acts on others. C, that denamed one, insofar as he has been a subject, has been the subject of action: appalling natural active processes, and the detached, dehumanised recording and testing activity of the clinician. He is "YET PATIENT", in fact he is now the perfect patient, because he may not now, as an inanimate body, even struggle against his circumstances.

Considering the centrality of the agraphia narrative, stage twelve could be thought of in terms of C's afterlife, an afterlife without transcendence or "MAKING OF THE SPIRIT SAFE" beyond the material result of the whiskey-making process; that is, without a narrative continuing into a non-material realm. It introduces two pieces of natural philosophy taken, apparently, from a Chinese Taoist source. Both are concerned with the tendencies to metamorphosis of organic substances, of bodies in particular:

IN SEEDS
ARE GERMS THAT HAPPENING IN WATER BECOME FILAMENTS OR BETWEEN WATER AND EARTH ARE SLIME OR WHEN THEY FIGURE IN EXALTED SITES MARK A PROFOUND MUTABILITY (151)

and

SO THE MUTABILITY IS RECOVERED FROM FINE TILTH AS CROW S FOOT ITS ROOTS LARVAE ITS LEAVES BUTTERFLIES AND THIS THE BODY [.] (152)

Fergal Gaynor

Evident here is what I referred to earlier as Joyce's "metaphysics", a kind of cosmological image and lexicon that seems characteristic of his work. We might describe it as follows: we, as human beings (though Joycean gods and angels seem to have similar habits), are given to making systems, by which we enclose and organise the stuff of our environment – universe, land, animals, plants and people. The systems range from (grammatical) language to the walls and economic structures by which we build societies. We do this because we are prone to change and decay, which appears to be the one certainty in the universe; but also because it gives us power, puts us, like the Great Wall-enclosed First Emperor, in the position of the divine. From within our systems, which is where we almost always are, the non-systematic appears as a chaos continually threatening our limits. The point at which this chaos actually irrupts, when metamorphosis and decay (mutability) reassert themselves, overthrowing human systems and transgressing categories, is the point at which an elemental character to the universe appears, and much of Joyce's poetry seems in pursuit of this. It is not only struck by the beauty of the elemental but it relishes its inhuman, caustic action, which attacks and removes the sweet, sentimental currency of the closed human systems and their economies, hardening it and revealing its material basis. The point before the return of full mutability, after the appearance of the elemental, sees the jacks, knaves and card-carrying courtiers of the economies become subject to the unmediated laws of system-building, become automata – in short, material systems themselves, forms of technology. But there are not only large systems, there are little systems too, and it is here that power as a theme comes into play. The singing birds too are incapable of resisting their reduction to "TECHNOLOGY", material systems to be manipulated and reproduced artificially. Big systems exert power over little systems – in doing so, they identify with the non-human, with the inevitable action of the elemental. But if the action of the elemental on the big systems is in many ways celebrated, the elemental-like action of the powerful on the little systems (more often than not, bodies of various kinds) is always shown to contain measures of cruelty – it is one thing to be non-human, another to be inhuman. The indictment not only extends to the rulers, tyrants and big men of the human world, but to those other, less direct agents of power, inventing and applying systems: surveyors, engineers, experimenters, grammarians, taxonomists, etc.

This is a rough enough précis of the Joycean cosmology, but I think it sufficient to convey that most recognisable characteristic of Joycean poetry, what on first impressions it seems to be *about*: a kind of tart revenge on those great structures that wield power over the small by means of an invocation of the elemental, the whole taking place against a melancholy backdrop of universal change and decay. Indeed, a sense of this appears already in the first public impression of Joyce's work: a review by Eavan Boland in 1967 of a reading by the nineteen-year-old Joyce which, though laudatory in the main, found itself repelled by the relentless imagery of a fallen world:

> he can also manage to invade an imaginative world of decay without adopting its listlessness. All the same, I look forward to a decrease in the number of dead rats and sewers which at the moment populate his work. (6)

The problem with this apprehension of recognisable content, of concentration on what Joyce's poetry is about, no matter how faithful, is that it can at best register the jarring, modernist tonality of the language. A split occurs, in other words, between what is conveyed and the stylistic and formal mode of conveyance. It does not, in short, register what the language is *about*, in the sense of being "about a business" of some kind. For instance, 'STILLSMAN''s point of access, its essential primary narrative, works only in conjunction with the action of the texts about it, and here the "MISHMASH" extends also to the matter of accessibility and recognition. The main movement of the agraphia narrative, as we have noted, is premised on c's "AGAIN AND AGAIN TRYING" to come to terms with his new position within things, to control and articulate the scrambled elements of experience. In narrative terms this effort is sometimes successful, sometimes frustrated, and proceeds in stages of increasing difficulty (about and about) before the eventual closure with c's death. In terms of the full working of language, this effort by c extends out, through even the formatting and omission of punctuation, to include our effort at reading, at making sense, narrative and syntactic, of the whole affair. Passages like the following are exemplary:

ORGAN WHICH CONCEALS ITSELF BY
CHANNELS DEEP BELOW THE NECK SO THAT WHEN
READING AN EYE CHART C CAN IDENTIFY NO LETTER
THOUGH HE CLAIMS PERFECTLY TO DISCERN THE SYRINX
LYING LOW WITHIN THE BODY AND INSTINCTIVELY HE
SKETCHES THE SHAPES OF THE LETTERS WITH HIS HAND

Fergal Gaynor

BUT CAN T UTTER EVEN ONE OF THEIR NAMES FOR BIRDS
DON T BREATHE LIKE YOU AND I HAVING INSTEAD AIR
SACS TO PUMP AIR THROUGH THE LUNGS WHERE A
SMOKELESS HEAT [.] (144)

If I divide this passage into the five segments (*more or less* discrete – it becomes evident across the poem that the sources have sometimes been "TAMPERED WITH"), I lose much of the interference effect of the language. If I, perhaps in a spirit of utopian egalitarianism, ignore the segmentation, and furthermore resist the recognisable access provided by the ongoing agraphia narrative, treating all units of language as I can make them out as equals, the poem quickly atomises and becomes incoherent. If I accept the access granted by the agraphia narrative but then extrapolate an essential image of the poem's world (cosmos perhaps) from that narrative and its presentation, I lose the poem's dynamic, how it is happening lingually. Where I am left is within the poem, with C, trying to "READ", "IDENTIFY", "DISCERN", "INSTINCTIVELY SKETCHING". And what I find is that I grasp at moments of punctuation, of causal movement, of the delineation of objects of perception, only to find that resolution is robbed, distorted. "SO THAT", for instance, joins itself before and after, disrupting both. The "ORGAN THAT CONCEALS ITSELF " – could it have something to do with reading? It is unlikely, since there are clearly birdsong passages weaving in and out here, but it frustrates the movement towards resolution of the description of the bird's organ, confuses singing and reading somehow, before returning us to C's effort at reading, but with a half-remembered sense that the problem lies somehow with the concealment of an organ. "DISCERN" promises a resolution, but the line skips to another source, and we are back with the "organ", the syrinx again, itself carrying Ovidian associations that can only have confusing connotations for the anatomical item. "FOR" obviously joins a birdsong and agraphia segment, but what is it grammatically? A conjunction introducing an explanation that offers and derails our attempt at finding an explanation for the situation, but simultaneously a preposition, "NAMES FOR BIRDS"? The point of access brings us within a carefully articulated dissonance that continues to move, continues to hold out hope of closure (as resolution), itself articulated in platforms or stages, before simply stopping with C's death, the possibilities of further reading and interpretation closed down, leaving us with a frighteningly empty resonance. The movement is both conceptually challenging and emotionally disturbing: our efforts at reading and understanding are steeped, turned, dried, mashed, heated – as it were – alongside the "passion" of c's efforts at halting the slide of his own capacity to read and understand. We are given no distance from c's destruction but are forced to undergo every stage in all its detail – what could be called a "compassion" were it not for the absence of "feeling", that is, withdrawal to an appropriate distance for reflection or response, within the poem. What we have instead is a "co-passion", an emotional process that cannot claim to lift c out of his experience into an economy of appropriate emotional response.

We are almost at the end, or the top, to reintroduce the image of the "unfinished buddha at the shut summit", but I would cautiously continue, beyond the turnings of the poem, and propose one last parsing of what the poem is *about*. *What's in Store* is "about" 'STILLSMAN', and 'STILLSMAN' is "about" its making of a particular experience of closure of communicative meaning, but this experience ultimately has its subject. It is not an authoritative subject by any means, or the familiar lyric subject of Irish poetry, it is a subject as "one who is subjected", one who suffers what happens; it is whoever c is. As such it is "unfinished": like the buddha, in a stupa closed by the working of 'STILLSMAN', it is not entirely in the realm of the poem. How could it be in terms of the cosmological scheme that we earlier sketched? The disempowered one is simply not recognised as anything other than an object of power within its grammars and technical systems. But it is there in the working of the poem, albeit as someone untongued, both denied direct speech by the idiom of the medical report and finally made "STILL", silent, dead. As such, c is of the same family as those other tongues in Joyce's poetry that become extinct, or under threat – the people speaking and singing Tocharian, Votyak, the "Dead Tongue" of Middle-Irish – not to mention all those who have added phrases like "De Iron Trote" and "A Black Swap" to oral tradition – a remainder, those left behind, who did not or could not identify inhumanly with the big systems of power in which language too is enmeshed. 'STILLSMAN' presents us – that is, provides us necessarily incompletely and "inarticulately" – with a point still human in a largely inhuman moving universe.[19]

> The causeway comes round
> again round
> again round
> again
>
> leave it (*first dream of fire* 133).

Fergal Gaynor

Notes

1 Perceived needs: Mays lists "old certainties, clear voices, identifiable subject-matter" among these needs of the international readership, looking to Ireland as "a special poetic case". Mays' account of the "two kinds of writing" is drawn from the work of German editor and theorist Klaus Hurlebusch and comes with the caveat "the distinction between reception-oriented and production-oriented writing is crude but useful" (6.3.1).

2 Between 1967 and 1976 Joyce produced the major collections *Sole Glum Trek*, *Pentahedron* and *The Poems of Sweeny, Peregrine*. There followed a hiatus of nearly twenty years before the appearance of *stone floods*. His poetry has appeared more or less regularly, though often in small press publications, since then.

3 There are a number of other reflections in ''93/4' of elements of the collection as a whole: the scented oils appear again in 'Golden Master'; "dull O'Laoghaire" corresponds to another dead and lamented Gaelic nobleman in 'Cry Help'; the star that is also a computer language, Algol, echoes the final, completed stage of computer software development, the "Golden Master"; and so on.

4 One could also point to the connections between instances of bureaucratic orders, worldly and celestial, and the angels/pigeons (the identification is made in both 'Tohu-bohu' and 'The Course of Nature') that deliver their demands (bills, decrees, etc.). The poems that make up *stone floods* are perhaps better described, in Eric Falci's terms, as "counterlyrics" (4).

5 Mays' thumbnail – "Never mind the cloth, feel the width, every piece is different. Paul Muldoon makes a career from changing the width of the cloth before our very eyes" – characterises Muldoon's work in terms of "postmodernist" conjuring (6.5.1).

6 'Dante... Bruno. Vico... Joyce' (1). Beckett's perception of the neatness as necessarily being a "danger", however, is not universal in modernist art – it has also been treated at times as an opportunity. Joyce's *Ulysses*, for instance, revels in the freedom afforded the author in manipulating the dead, literal, clichéd and empty languages dominated by the reflex of pure recognition, as indeed, with a more aggressive, absurdist take, does Beckett, in *Watt*, for instance, and in the dialogue of his character-based plays. The important thing is that the "neatness of identifications" is not inhabited, or exploited from the inside.

7 "Tart lyricism", a precise phrase, comes ironically from the advertising blurb for *What's in Store*. See, for instance, <http://www.spdbooks.org/Producte/9780973587531/what39s-in-store.aspx> (accessed 19 Mar. 2013).

8 "They are wild things, ravaged, and empty of all sentimentality, but all heart. I think the key to their force is that they are based in syntax and sound. They move word by word, rather than by phrasing, and so it is the relationship between the words that holds the stanzas (heartbeats) together, not a rush of sentiment" (7). Howe ups the stakes by her use of the word "heart", surrounded, as it is, by a thick layer of mass-produced meanings.

9 The opening of one of Joyce's 36-word poems: "let's have / a market in affects" (Joyce, *What's in Store* 91).

10 *Pace* my earlier reference to the "precise" "tart lyricism".

11 "Stewed in corruption, honeying and making love" (*Hamlet* 3.4 85). Hamlet's psychologically fraught phrase contains something of the sweet smell of decay, and its family resemblance to oversentimental intimacy, but it should be noted that "honey" is associated in *stone flood's* 'Cold Course' with a counter-process of dehumanising preservation.

12 The lineation of 'STILLSMAN' is not exactly as it appears in the text of the poem in *first dream of fire*. The poet advised that the block prose paragraph format is more important than reproducing the exact layout of words and lines in the collection.

13 I am indebted to Trevor Joyce for making clear how many source texts are involved in 'STILLSMAN', and for identifying most of them.

14 It was not until 1996, at the Assembling Alternatives conference at the University of New Hampshire, that Trevor Joyce – whose earliest work appeared in the late 1960s – met for the first time the poets of the 1980s. The importance of this conference, in leading to the Cork International Poetry Festival (later SoundEye) and in opening up the lines of communication and influence between Irish "alternative poets", is well documented.

15 Joyce first began to work with computers, at Carroll's, in 1976/7 (email to me 26 March 2013).

16 I have had the good fortune to perform the poem on a number of occasions, in a version made by Joyce for three voices. This version started as an *Art/not art* project with Joyce (*Art/not art* being an art-interventionist group initiated by the visual artist Dobz O'Brien and Fergal Gaynor in Glasgow in 2000). Joyce, O'Brien and I performed the piece at a fringe event of Limerick's Ev+a (as it was then called) Festival in 2007. As a homage to the late John Latham, there was an attempt at eating the script at the performance's close. In 2008 this version was performed again in Santa Cruz and Los Angeles' *Beyond Baroque*, with Marja Gaynor substituting for O'Brien. Despite this history, and the fact that a version of 'STILLSMAN' printed as a single block on a large white, weather-insulated banner formed part of Simon Cutts' *Vinyl Project* in 2005, the poem is not an "installation or performance" piece, as the *Irish Times* review claimed. It first appeared in printed form in *Undone, Say*, a chapbook published by The Gig in 2003.

17 The process recalls a similar affair among the notes to *Syzygy*, gleaned from Mary Douglas' *Purity and Danger*, "of pulverizing, dissolving and rotting" that "awaits any physical things that have been recognised as dirt. In the end, all identity is gone" (Joyce, *first dream of fire* 238).

18 His "intelligence", apparently, is unimpaired, but we have come to expect by this point that every fortification occupied on C's retreat from the disorder is simply being prepared for further destruction by the narrative.

[19] The poem 'Proceeds of a Black Swap' appears in *first dream of fire* (161), 'De Iron Trote' in *What's in Store* (233).

Works Cited

Beckett, Samuel. 'Dante... Bruno. Vico... Joyce.' *Our Exagmination Round his Factification for Incamination of Work in Progress*. Eds. Samuel Beckett et al. Paris: Shakespeare & Co., 1929. Print.

Begnal, Michael S. 'Polar / cold / marks terminus.' *Freeverse* (2008). Web. 1 Mar. 2013.

Bernstein, Charles. 'Semblance.' *The L=A=N=G=U=A=G=E Book*. Eds. Bruce Andrew and Charles Bernstein. Carbondale, IL: Southern Illinois University Press, 1984. Print.

Boland, Eavan. 'Evening of Poetry.' *Irish Times*, 31 Aug. 1967, 6. Print.

Falci, Eric. *Continuity and Change in Irish Poetry: 1966–2010*. Cambridge: Cambridge University Press, 2012. Print.

Fryatt, Kit. 'Process, Product, and a Peacock.' *Irish Times*, 19 Apr. 2008, B10. Print.

Goodby, John. '"Current, Historical, Mythical, or Spook?": Irish Modernist and Experimental Poetry.' *Súitear Na n-Aingeal/Angel Exhaust* (1999) 17: 51–60. Print.

Heaney, Seamus. 'Act of Union.' *Opened Ground*. London: Faber, 1998. 127. Print.

Howe, Fanny. 'Foreword'. *Courts of Air and Earth*. Foreword by Fanny Howe; afterword by Máire Herbert. Exeter: Shearsman Books, 2008. 7. Print.

Joyce, Trevor. *What's in Store: Poems 2000–2007*. Dublin: New Writers' Press; Willowdale, ON: The Gig, 2007. Print.

—. 'STILLSMAN.' *What's in Store: Poems 2000–2007*. Dublin: New Writers' Press; Willowdale, ON: The Gig, 2007. 142–152. Print.

—. *with the first dream of fire they hunt the cold: A Body of Work 1966–2000*. 2nd ed. Dublin: New Writers' Press; Exeter: Shearsman Books, 2003. Print.

—. *stone floods*. Dublin: New Writers' Press, 1995. Print.

Lautréamont, Comte de. *Man Ray*. By Arturo Schwarz. London: Thames and Hudson, 1977. 161. Print.

Mays, J.C.C. *N11: A Musing. A Lecture Given at the 3rd Cork Poetry Conference 2000*. Little Critic No. 18. Clonmel: Coracle, 2006. Print. (Originally published by the Coelacanth Press and distributed at the conference.)

Meehan, Paula. 'Pillow Talk.' *Pillow Talk*. Oldcastle, Co. Meath: Gallery Press, 1994. 32. Print.

Tiziano Vecelli. *The Punishment of Marsyas* (1550–1576). Painting. Archdiocesan Museum, Kroměříž.

Vincent, Stephen. '*What's in Store* by Trevor Joyce.' *Galatea Resurrects*, 31 Mar. 2008. 9. Web. 1 Mar. 2013.

Yeats, W. B. *The Collected Works of W.B. Yeats.* Ed. Richard J. Finneran. 2nd ed. Vol. 2. New York, NY: Simon & Schuster, 1997. Print.

Snifting and Snurting
The Impurity of Diction in Trevor Joyce's *What's in Store*

Keith Tuma

What's in Store (2007) often reminds its reader of the vanity of human wishes, without ignoring for too many pages what it sets out in the translated folk songs that open the book: "what lies / in store" for us is death. *What's in Store* has continuities that are not only tonal and thematic but also formal, thanks especially to the 36-word poems that Joyce at first planned to join up in a "hyper-sestina" (*What's in Store* 312). But for all of its continuities *What's in Store* is more various than Joyce's volume of collected poems published six years earlier when it comes to the diction of the poetry on view. With regard to its diction this store is almost a warehouse.

Writing about Joyce's earlier work as collected in *with the first dream of fire they hunt the cold* (2001) I suggested some years ago that his poems use a more "restricted" diction than the poems of many of his peers. I was thinking about poets who are often identified as part of an avant-garde or alternative or experimental writing, and I was especially thinking of poets beyond Ireland. The statement appears in my essay about Joyce's 'DARK SENSES PARALLEL STREETS', which was published in Nate Dorward's *Removed for Further Study: The Poetry of Tom Raworth* (2003).[1] Joyce used Raworth's poem 'Dark Senses' to build his poem, incorporating Raworth's poem in his own; my essay offers passing commentary about the poem's two columns as they distinguish the work of the two poets. My remarks about Joyce's diction as typically more restricted or limited than Raworth's – I should have said more conventionally "poetic" – eventually came to his attention. 'De Iron Trote' in *What's in Store* offers his response, working with found text to shape a lively, humorous prose and poetry diptych about the craft of putting words to song (the prose section) and what is required for success in doing that (the verse section). Words used in the poem including "snurting" and "snifting," together with the title 'De Iron Trote' which names Cork's Eye, Ear, and Throat Hospital in the local idiom, work to put to rest my claim that Joyce's diction hovers around an archetypal image-kit of bones and stones, stars and fire, and so on. Snurting and snifting are comical *as* words; that's part of the point of using them in the poem. Having said this I will hope for a poem from Joyce using these words to remind readers of the brevity of life and the foolishness of their plans for it. But the case is closed for now: 'De Iron Trote' shows readers that Joyce is a poet who *can* wear wild ties, to use an image he uses in the poem, at least in his poetry.

In making my claim about Joyce's diction in that essay I was remembering Donald Davie's *Purity of Diction in English Verse* (1952), which draws a distinction between poets for whom anything goes when it comes to the language that can be used in poetry and those for whom a stronger sense of poetic decorum means distinguishing between words that do and do not belong in a particular poem or genre of poetry. Even to think about diction is the beginning of a strategy for limiting it. Davie argues that this thinking is something too few modern poets have done, though his key distinctions contrast the "chaste" diction of Oliver Goldsmith's poems and the more anything goes diction of Hopkins and Shakespeare. Other poets, Wordsworth and Cowper among them, enter into Davie's argument, and so does Irish poetry by way of Synge and Yeats when he writes, "[T]he poet's choice of diction is determined in part… by the structure and the prevailing ideologies of his society" (10).

Davie's book was important in its time and continues to reward reading however much the axes it grinds seem old now. I mention it here only to offer context for the claim I made in my essay, which I am not prepared to abandon, as far as it concerns Joyce's poetry before *What's in Store*. It still makes sense to describe Joyce's earlier work as being of a piece, or of several pieces, when it comes to its diction. Davie discusses Synge's writing as "making a diction out of the talk of Irish peasantry," and contrasts that diction with the "courtly-humanist" or "bourgeois-pious" diction of other poets (9). Joyce's diction is not tied to ideological agendas, I think, but there are two or three poetic traditions that have been important to it and which are more or less distinctive in their image-kits. The writing of European post-symbolist poets, perhaps especially Georg Trakl, clearly influenced the poems of *Pentahedron* (1972). Andrew Duncan has written about the many images of dead birds in that book, and together with the dead birds scattered across an urban wasteland corroded moons and other images out of the post-symbolist catalogue establish the book's mood.[2] More important than the post-symbolists as they figure in *Pentahedron* is Joyce's engagement with folk song. Joyce's ancestor P. W. Joyce collected folk songs. While *Syzygy* (1998) and some of the other poems in the back half of *first dream of fire* were made using procedures that have a late modernist pedigree, the images and language of folk song and folk poetry are important to them. They make up a significant part of the matter that has been reshaped by experimental procedures.

The history of Irish writing includes many corruptions of text and problems of transmission; Joyce's version of the Sweeny story, *The Poems of Sweeny, Peregrine: A Working of the Corrupt Irish Text* (1976) acknowledges this. Twinned translations in the Shearsman book *Courts of Air and Earth* (2008) render the same poem in contrasting idioms, the one demotic and the other more traditionally "literary", also suggesting that there is hybridity and diversity in Irish poetry going back almost to its beginning. Purity cannot be the right word to describe any poetry by Joyce if we consider that history and his knowledge of it, but I will hold out for "restricted" as indicating a range of diction that reflects focused engagement with specific sources and the kind of thoughtfulness about poetic diction that Davie recommended.

Joyce's diction in his earlier poems is restricted in the sense that key words and images recur but also in the sense that they count as "poetic," which only means that the words and tropes and images on call are familiar from the poetry and song of the past. This does not mean that they are not used in the present; on the contrary they are widely used especially in what counts as popular and folk poetry. What I am saying is as true of 'Trem Neul', which includes prose, as it is of *Syzygy*, which is entirely in lines. I cannot imagine Joyce in his middle years writing a poem like Raworth's 'Sixty Words I've Never Used Before' from *Meadow* (1999), where the point is to use the oddest words one can find. If you argue that that poem is a one-off for Raworth, I will reply that I also cannot imagine Joyce's poetry taking on board the administrative and art-theoretical language – the language of academics and intellectuals – that one finds in Raworth's *Eternal Sections* (1993) where it is presented in fragments or cut up and repurposed. Or I should say that before *What's in Store* was published I would have been unable to imagine finding something like that in a Joyce poem. I am a little more able to imagine it now.

The poems in *What's in Store* are more diverse in their diction than the poems in the earlier book. I need to admit that I am talking about my impressions of them; I have not made a systematic study of word frequency in the poems. But I can try to explain what accounts for my impressions by citing a few poems from a cluster of poems in the book about women and relationships. The connection in subject matter or theme is loose, since some of the poems comment on particular behaviour while others are more broadly about desire and love, or about acknowledging the memory of love or its loss. However arbitrary my grouping turns out to be, I think that these are poems that will serve to make my point: I mean the poems between 'Saws' and 'Action Sequence'.

'Saws' is a poem about a broken or failed relationship. It has three sections each with five five-line stanzas, quintains. The discourse of this complex poem comes to a kind of resolution in the poem's final stanza, which opens with a direct address to the "you" introduced earlier in the work. "Have you forgotten", the poem asks, and then it insists that, whatever the circumstances that have intervened between and separated poet and lover, the poet will forget nothing. The past is "indelible" and will "lodge at heart in dream through fright." This is not a comforting thought if the phrase is cut like this – the poem runs it directly into another phrase, which arguably softens it a little. Joyce means, perhaps, that fears return processed in dreams and that these dreams preserve the past. The poem elsewhere is also not comforting in its thoughts about passion and sex ("touch") though it is tender by Joyce's standards. 'Saws' are of course "sayings".[3] The diction of 'Saws' is restricted in the manner of the poems in the latter half of *first dream of fire*.

Some ten pages after 'Saws' in *What's in Store* comes 'Action Sequence', a poem that would be much harder to imagine having a place in that earlier book because its language is all over the place and misses the hints of the poetic and archaic that we find in 'Saws'. 'Action Sequence' expresses the poet's bemused disappointment with films about love and breakups, about women and sex, or alternatively it might be about a breakup, about a love life that has been a little too much like an action sequence in a movie and which has seen a lover disappear into the sunset in the west, leaving for America.

In between 'Saws' and 'Action Sequence' are seven of the 36-word poems that thread *What's in Store* together, plus an odd, hardboiled sonnet in short lines and without rhyme beginning "Drink hard, girls" and offering advice that is close to the advice women get in the pop classic 'Diamonds Are a Girl's Best Friend'. There is also an ecstatic lyric quatrain titled 'Hoofing It', an invitation to dance or fuck that really is all about its vocabulary, demonstrating among other things Joyce's extensive knowledge of footwear (I take it that a pun about prosody is part of it):

Hoofing It
o my belle saboteuse of fur mukluks and pac boots,

o sweet stiletto, astragalus mine galoshed;
swish me in jodhpurs, chukka me, granny me thighways,
then your sesamoid swivel to this zygoma's bliss (58)

In terms of its diction 'Hoofing It' is as close to the poetry of Clark Coolidge
as Joyce is likely to get. This longtime reader of Joyce's poetry had his head
jerked around in first coming upon the poem after the aforementioned
sonnet, which closes with these lines: "A doll doesn't last / If she can't seem
to please" (57). One doesn't hear women called "dolls" in poetry much
anymore, not outside of efforts to mimic or send up film noir, unless one
finds the word in a translated folk song. But this sonnet, which rhymes
"pearls" with "curls" and "trees" with "devotees" in its middle stanza, is only
as archaic as a 1960s pop song. "Hoofing It" is a different kind of poem
altogether, almost Sitwellian.

So too are the 36-worders very different poems. At least five of them
between 'Saws' and 'Action Sequence' refer to a "she" or "her" or offer
advice to women or express curiosity or befuddlement concerning their
behaviour. The first of these after noting the presence of an attractive
woman remarks on her unnatural posture before averring that "if it gazes
/ long / unblinking / at the / dark / then / it's not / real" (50) which is
either an ugly way of using the pronoun "it" to refer to a woman or, more
likely, a comment on the way that men including the speaker of the poem
project unrealistic images of women. Another 36-worder begins "i grieve /
for her / hair // gold //glistening" (52) and goes on to express displeasure
at the damage a woman is doing to her face in crying. Another, like 'Saws',
ends in direct address – "don't go" – after suggesting that "excess of seeing"
has turned the woman's "eyes / to milk" (53). These are powerful lyrics all,
blunt and judgmental, and their diction is yet again different from what
one finds in 'Saws' and 'Sonnet' and 'Hoofing It' and 'Action Sequence'.
The 36-worders are sometimes, perhaps often, aphoristic; they suggest a
highly literate, sceptical observer. They are as comfortable with statement
as with image: "a very / ugly / effect /may result / from comb / ining two /
different / tones / of the same / colour" (55).

But now it is time to juxtapose 'Saws' and 'Action Sequence' to show
how different they are. I will start with 'Saws', quoting the entirety of its
first section:

flame has a skin of cold
light sets limit to the dark

so name me then
the outside rind of memory
the clothes love wears

•

rock in the streambed
fluid thats your element is absence
complex with vortices and currents
bears cold against the bone
still hand reaches grips itself

•

silence vexed
touch when presence would suffice
anatomizing scrutiny
break the made whole
care gathers mute blind here

•

faulting crowd from fend
touch impairs the waist the small
the shoulder prompts the touch
as instruments diminish even to the heart
needs must intents persist

•

spontaneously sight unseen
in the intervals between
where venture hunts its gain
beasts may become familiar
and grow tame (47)

I need a little more of the poem to make my case, so at the risk of letting the poem do all of the talking here is the second stanza of the second section followed by the first and third stanzas of the third:

Keith Tuma

chance set of winds you
fixed deck of bones you
my chambered and mined
my furnished with tables
my table of cases of tides

•

mirrors eclipses departures
loss instantaneous or slow
barren doubling
death is all we see awake
and sleeping only sleep

•

no cage is found for wind and rain
so older than desire that stirs the hand
prior to relief to grief to nerve and nerves
what by the heart
is hidden hidden is (47-49)

The last phrase in the last stanza I quote here seems broken across the line to fill out the form and slow down the reader. The last two lines in the stanza above it (two stanzas above it in the poem itself) risk venturing a memorable phrase, and indeed the phrase, like the last phrase in the next stanza, should be memorable since it is taken from a translation of fragments attributed to Heraclitus.[4] 'Saws' as a whole is written in what I might as well call the high style, though the compression of the syntax and the modularity of the lines and stanzas prevents it from floating off like a balloon. "Flame" and "light" and "rock" and "bone" and "touch" and "wind and rain" are the kind of nouns that led me in the earlier essay to call this diction archetypal, but it is hard in the end to talk about diction apart from syntax and rhythm. "Wind and rain" suggests Thomas Hardy and border ballads but equally 'Wagon Wheel' by Old Crow Medicine Show. Familiarity or use in a range of contexts is what makes this or any diction seem "poetic."

Echoes of the canonical and the archaic come often in 'Saws'. The third line of the first stanza suggests the language of riddles, riddles being one root of lyric, as Andrew Welsh reminds us.[5] In that same stanza a metaphor that has love wearing clothes similarly reaches into the past. The phrase "venture hunts its gain" even with its pun on "nothing ventured, nothing gained" and the use of "beasts" to stand for (probably) sexual appetite all suggest the high style. Modernist poetry from Pound forward can accommodate archaic language and older styles, and Pound's influence also partly explains the poem's compression of syntax. The line "care gathers mute blind here" might be paraphrased as "care is present but mute and blind here" or, without personification, as "care exists but has little purpose here," though the sense of the stanza as a whole is that one would be better off gathering the pieces of a broken whole rather than allowing for their dispersal.

With this diction and this syntax a reader finding the poem on the web would be forgiven for thinking it was written 50 or even 100 years ago. There *is* one stanza that mentions "data". There is also the line "you claim with care your personal effects" which Joyce's future biographers will suggest refers to his American girlfriend at that time; the poem is dedicated to her. But the personal histories and contexts for the poem have been largely sidelined, after the fashion of a modernist impersonality. Bunting's work also comes to mind.

It is consistency of register that distinguishes 'Saws' from 'Action Sequence', which is all over the map:

Great gals gone west
into millions of sunsets,
claiming *absence*
my presence is,
strangeness my grace,
as whackers and knackers,
sad slackers, court packers,
sundry vatic pragmatics
are with axes and tumbrils,
old agues and age,
all adroitly despatched,
amid armies of leggings
and earrings of ice, there
there is felt a nice
nostalgia for ambiguity.

One thing's for sure – the
sub-basement deportment
department's not there
for your bloody idle amusement.
Mother Teresa, Peggy Sue?
They're all deported, Helen too.
The dominant is melancholy,
and not by subs or doms
or four-letter bombs can I be
comforted. "Entertainment"
you call it? Yes, and "God
will provide." Sure! We'll all
sleep easy on the other side. (59)

I don't know another poem by a poet who travels with the avant-garde that uses the words "gals", with or without the cornball western motif, and whether that motif relates to the movies or instead to the movement of an American woman once based in Cork and now headed back to the United States. For some readers the word will irk, surely, as will the idea of an Irish poet using the tired imagery of sunsets to suggest endings, or it would if the lines immediately following in italics did not clash so violently with the poem's cornball opening. The italics cite a phrase, the most famous lines, from Fulke Greville's *Caelica* (1633), a poem with language a lot closer to the language of 'Saws' than to "great gals gone west," with its heavy alliteration. Then we are on to spasms of rhyming suggesting skeltonics or even Dr. Seuss. 'Action Sequence' rhymes heavily and does another thing that few Joyce poems have done—names persons, Mother Teresa on the one hand and Peggy Sue on the other, presumably the Peggy Sue of the Buddy Holly song. Here they are named somewhat after the fashion of several famous poems by Villon.

What is the poem about? It might be about loneliness and unhappiness on the dating scene, to use the most banal terms, or it could be about movies that do not satisfy the speaker because they are superficial or only amusing and do not reach to the core of the human heart, in the same way that a cliché about the afterlife means to comfort but rarely does.

It helps to know that 'Action Sequence' emerged from Joyce's work with *OffSets*, an online collaborative project that he initiated via a poetics listserv. Some of the language in the poem owes to other poets and ultimately to web searches, Joyce letting many voices in. It is quite a different thing to let in the voice of others working beside you in a collaborative writing exercise than it is to work with material selected from a published text dating back a century or two or with a poem in another language, and I don't want to represent 'Action Sequence' as typical of a new direction in his writing. 'Saws' is still more typical of Joyce's poetry even in the period covered by *What's in Store*. But it is worth thinking about the weirder moments that 'Action Sequence' and the other poems I have mentioned here represent. At least for me it was easier before *What's in Store* to think that the intensity of Joyce's renderings of folk song and older poetries had to do with his poetry belonging to a more bardic tradition. The poetry has other resources now.

Notes

[1] See 'Collaborating with 'Dark Senses', in *Removed for Further Study: The Poetry of Tom Raworth* edited by Nate Dorward.

[2] See Duncan's 'Pale angel exuvial who can mix it with the chicken' published in *Jacket* 20.

[3] The design of some saws (meaning the tool, in this case) as they feature alternating sets of teeth is also relevant, Joyce writes. The poem features a series of binaries and lines and stanzas that alternate "to mime argument, reconciliation, and argument resumed." Email to the author 20 February 2014.

[4] Joyce hopes that the palindromic quality of some of the fragments attributed to Heraclitus is emphasised by his line breaks. Email to the author 20 February 2014.

[5] See Welsh's 1987 publication entitled *Roots of Lyric: Primitive Poetry and Modern Poetics*.

Works Cited

Davie, Donald. *Purity of Diction in English Verse*. London: Chatto & Windus, 1952. Print.

Duncan, Andrew. 'Pale angel exuvial who can mix it with the chicken'. Rev. of *with the first dream of fire they hunt the cold: A Body of Work 1966-2000* by Trevor Joyce. *Jacket* 20 Dec. 2002. Web. 3 Jan. 2014. <http://jacketmagazine. com/20/dunc-r-joyc.html>

Greville, Fulke. 'Caelica'. *Five Courtier Poets of the English Renaissance*. Ed. Robert Bender. New York, NY: Washington Square, 1967. 484-561. Print.

Joyce, Trevor. *Pentahedron*. Dublin: New Writers' Press, 1972. Print.

——. *The Poems of Sweeny, Peregrine: A Working of the Corrupt Irish Text*. Dublin: New Writers' Press, 1976. Print.

——. *Syzygy.* Bray, Co. Wicklow: Wild Honey Press, 1998. Print.

——. 'Trem Neul'. *with the first dream of fire they hunt the cold: A Body of Work 1966–2000.* 2nd ed. Dublin: New Writers' Press; Exeter: Shearsman Books, 2003. 185–231. Print.

—— et al. *Offsets: an on-line, on-going poem with many authors.* Internet Archive. Jan.-Mar. 2004. Web. 3 Jan. 2014. <http://web.archive.org/web/20050210005541/http://www.soundeye.org/offsets1/index.htm>

——. 'De Iron Trote.' *What's in Store: Poems 2000–2007.* Dublin: New Writers' Press; Willowdale, ON: The Gig, 2007. 233. Print.

——. *Courts of Air and Earth.* Foreword by Fanny Howe; afterword by Máire Herbert. Exeter: Shearsman Books, 2008. Print.

Raworth, Tom. 'Sixty Words I've Never Used Before'. *Meadow.* Sausalito: Post-Apollo, 1999. 10-12. Print.

——. *Eternal Sections.* Los Angeles: Sun and Moon, 1993. Print.

Tuma, Keith. 'Collaborating with "Dark Senses"'. *Removed for Further Study: The Poetry of Tom Raworth.* Ed. Nate Dorward. Special issue of *The Gig* 13/14. Willowdale, ON: The Gig, 2003. 207-216. Print.

Welsh, Andrew. *Roots of Lyric: Primitive Poetry and Modern Poetics.* Princeton, NJ: Princeton University Press, 1987. Print.

Joyce's Prosody

Geoffrey Squires

> and so you find me here
> living disgraced in Ros Bearaigh;
> the life God gave
> seems somehow dislocated. ('Sweeny' *first dream of fire* 17)

There are precisely ten iambic pentameters in the whole of Joyce's *Sweeny*. This is one measure of the prosodic innovation or, to the normative ear, dislocation of the poem. It may be that some of this comes through from the Irish, which has not only its own, different metres but a dissimilar syntax. However, the aural dislocation characterises much of Joyce's subsequent work and makes him, to my mind, one of the most interesting modern Irish poets in terms of rhythm, foot and line. Indeed the whole technical array of rhythmic analysis, involving not only disyllabic, trisyllabic but even tetrasyllabic feet, does not quite capture the nature of Joyce's prosody: there are consecutive stressed syllables stamped in, little runs of the unstressed, unexpected halts, lines that come up short. Nor is this quite "voice": it is not somehow personal, but rather an exploration of the aural qualities of English rhythms to which he and thus the reader submits and which leaves one feeling that one has been through something of a linguistic workout. But the first thing to say is that, to enjoy Joyce's verse, you need an ear.

§

> my soft co-occupant of woods. ('Sweeny' 36)

It was this line that first alerted me to something fresh and original in Joyce's writing. Irish poetry is not, whatever its faults, short on lyricism, but the juxtaposition of the lyrical "soft" and dryly legal "co-occupant" suggested something new that was not content to abide within the usual registers. There are incursions of technical, scientific and formal administrative language, a raiding of public domains. And Joyce is not averse to trawling the dictionary: in *Sweeny* alone we encounter energumen, quincunx, anfractuous and aviform. There is a scholastic side to him, a pleasure in the arcane and out-of-the-way, a testament to his wide reading. But in *Sweeny* this element is balanced by a powerful evocation of the physical. To read the poem is to have one's senses turned up (life is loud in the glade) and there is a pervasive awareness of the body, here and often elsewhere in pain, torn, fractured, ill, a sense which in some later work becomes pathological. There is a self, but it is a long way from the self of the personal lyric, remembering, describing and reflecting on its experiences. The Sweeny figure is, for the moment, emblematic of the fugitive, marginalised, conflicted, withdrawn poet: "you do not wish to know me" (I). Would that some other poets said the same.

§

Vertical rivers reverse
stone floods
the karst domain
each sink turns source ('The Turlough' *first dream of fire* 95)

The near twenty-year gap between *Pentahedron* and *stone floods* may help to account for the much greater prosodic variety of the second. Whereas the writing in the first is largely contained and low key, reflecting the dismal urban landscape it describes, the second ranges from the quiet personal lyric ("You are reading this book" 92) through the bouncy and funny 'Verses with a Refrain from a Solicitor's Letter' to the tart comment of 'Parting Words' ("If there's going to be a general resurrection / count me out" 105). However, in 'The Turlough' (quoted above in the epigraph) and 'Lines in Fall' we also encounter for the first time the short, dense line that was to become a key feature of Joyce's poetry. The line-break becomes important as a restraining device (think strait-jacket) which creates a compact, condensed, complex and sometimes contradictory verse, which in 'The Turlough' deals with reversal, the re-winding or running back of events, a theme we will find taken up again in Joyce's work, with its preoccupation with time and causality. It is worth noting here that, unlike the majority of poets, Joyce studied both arts and science/mathematics to undergraduate level, and there is something of the scientist's observation of phenomena here, an objectivity which must be distinguished from poetic "objectivism". This sometimes appears as a certain coldness, detachment or distancing from people and things, which is all the more striking given the dominance in Irish poetry of the subjective, personal lyric. In *stone floods* there are still examples of the latter as well, but, as time goes on, it would diminish and virtually disappear from the *oeuvre*. Leaving what? No wonder that some readers find Joyce difficult to get to grips with, because the usual personal, experiential core seems not to be there. Joyce the person, the autobiographical coat-hanger, is missing from the wardrobe when we open the door.

This brief discussion of the short line does not do justice to the prosodic variety of *stone floods*, and indeed what is striking is the assurance with which Joyce deploys a range of different metres, forms and styles in the book, including some very long lines. However, nothing in it hinted at the radical break that was to come three years later with *Syzygy*.

§

when the thieving
that was well advanced faltered
the imperial presence surveyed
the ordered territories
and declared in measured words
nothing there is savage any more

('The Drift' first dream of fire 138)

Syzygy marks the entrance into Joyce's work of formalism. This is not to say that there were not formalist elements and tendencies in his earlier writing, but this is the first time that a whole poem is designed according to an overt formal structure, in this case the difference and relationship between the two parts, 'The Drift' and 'The Net'. Joyce's preoccupation with form and forms has continued up until the present day, drawing variously on linguistic and musical analogies. However, the concern with pattern, substitution and permutation can also be described in mathematical terms and it is perhaps no accident that the scientifically trained poet has been so interested in these, an interest shared by some modern French writers in a country where mathematics is a paradigmatic discipline and has had much closer links with literature than in the English-speaking world.

But the question is: what effect does this have on his prosody? It is too easy to concentrate on the formal innovations of *Syzygy* and forget to look at and listen to what is actually happening at word level, and here there is an interesting development: the incursion of prose, or more precisely prose patterns and rhythms. The passage from 'The Drift' quoted above could easily be transcribed as a continuous prose sentence, and indeed that is also true of the opening of the poem ("and then there is this sound / that starts with a scarcely audible / rustling inside gold…" 136). This prose element derives partly from the incorporation of prose passages or narratives, found text, which may come from a wide variety of sources (often disparate, historical or arcane), but it also seems to result in passages which are not so derived. The question is why: why does Joyce at this juncture want to draw on and in these extraneous elements which shift the patterns and rhythms of his writing, at least in part, from the "poetic" to the "prosaic" (I use these words grossly). The answer lies in what he does with them. Such passages are disaggregated, chopped up as if on little pieces of paper, displaced, reordered, substituted, permutated, while still preserving normal syntax. The result is thus a combination of syntactic coherence and semantic incoherence (though the "incoherence" throws up its own coherences). To read *Syzygy* is to experience a kind of lapidary disjunction: it all flows, but in unpredictable directions; it is both ordered and random.

The incursion of prose patterns and rhythms brings with it a further shift away from the personal subject, the "I" that lies at the heart of the traditional lyric, towards a range of public registers. We can no longer talk about Joyce's "voice": rather we enter a world of contrasting, cross-cutting discourses which straddle historical periods, cultures, domains of thought and activity. The authorial agent survives only as the arbiter and organiser of these various elements: a kind of poetic "hidden hand".

All this makes *Syzygy* the first of Joyce's identifiably modernist works and as such it began to get him an international reputation that went well beyond the relatively small congregation of people in Ireland who knew and valued his work. The label has stuck, and Joyce could now be pigeon-holed as an "avant-garde" or "experimental" writer who lay outside the "mainstream". This was a double-edged development, opening up access to and membership of a cosmopolitan network while alienating him from his immediate peers and audience. In truth, Joyce had belonged to a literary minority in his native land ever since the early days of New Writers' Press and *The Lace Curtain*, but one unfortunate effect was that his "workings" from the Irish were largely ignored by both the national and international readership. However, I would argue that there is actually more continuity between such "workings" and his later modernist work than between the earlier, quasi-realist Dublin poems and where he was eventually to go. The common element is translation, in the loosest sense of the word: the taking of a source or text and the reshaping and reusing of it in a different form or context. Indeed it might not be too far from the truth to describe most of Joyce's work as "workings". And because such workings involve transposition, they always raise questions about the relationships between the original and destination prosody, the influence of sometimes hidden patterns, rhythms and forms. But if Joyce had been pigeon-holed, he was still a restless bird. Unlike some poets who find a style that works and then stick with it, he displayed a chronic inability to stay put. Where would he fly next?

§

He had from the beginning an inner and an outer sphere with a north pole and south pole, an ecliptic, the equator, twenty-four positions of the sun during the year, twenty-eight lunar stations, the sun, moon, the five planets, the inner and outer stars, from which, the head being clearly distinguished, and in it the eyes, swollen out to a great extent, it was only by degrees that they diminished and collapsed. The whole was moved by water-power and placed in an upper room of the palace.

('Hopeful Monsters', *first dream of fire* 146)[1]

The prose rhythms which first really entered Joyce's work in *Syzygy* continued and developed after that. As the above quotation exemplifies, sentences become longer, more complex, replete with subordinate clauses which variously explain, amplify or qualify the main clause. There are frequent lists of things, objects, phenomena or procedures and narratives of events. The subject matter is sometimes historical, sometimes scientific or proto-scientific, or has to do with bureaucracy and public administration. The tone is dry, analytical, objective, detached, often with an overlay of archaism.

Prose seems to have come like a liberation to Joyce, allowing him to access and draw in linguistic registers which lie far distant from the personal lyric. The question of what he is doing with these registers and why he draws on them goes well beyond this analysis of prosody, but one can see the range of his writing broadening all the time. Prose of one kind or another plays an important part not only in *Hopeful Monsters* (1998) but in 'Trem Neul' (1999). Even some of the shorter poems of that period, such as 'The Fishers Fished' or 'Proceeds of a Black Swap', can be read as broken prose rather than in terms of the verse rhythms of the work before *Syzygy*.

However, that Joyce's development was anything but unilinear is shown by one of the most remarkable of the poems of that period, or indeed any: 'Without Asylum'. This poem, which deals with Joyce's recurrent theme of reversed time/causality is written in the tight quatrains that characterise some of his earlier work. There is frequent use of enjambement, the sense running over each time into the next line. The combination of short lines and over-running sense produces a poetry of remarkable density and intensity, with striking images such as

> sound
> is severed from the dog's throat (184)

and climaxes in lines which constitute a kind of reference point for the whole of Joyce's writing:

> one sees at last displayed
> an armoured beast whose
> head a growth of flame
> in the shadow of the ripening
>
> clocks the river sames
> destroys itself the jug
> absconds leaving to the grasp
> only a sustained bewilderment
>
> like dice spinning (184)

This is not Mallarmé's dice, signifying chance or randomness, a core theme of modernism, but visual incomprehension, an inability to make sense of what we actually see. Joyce's work is now preoccupied with what seems like a manic rationality, a desperate attempt at order, whether orderly cognition, the observed orders of science or the imposed order of public administration. The breakdown of these exemplifies the ultimate failure of rationality, and the terror and chaos that ensue.

§

By the end of *with the first dream of fire they hunt the cold*, hereafter *first dream of fire*, Joyce had developed an impressive prosodic range, from the rhythmic inventiveness of *Sweeny*, through the earlier, tight short-line poems to the prose or prose-like expansiveness of *Syzygy* and 'Hopeful Monsters'. Many of these elements can be found again in the successor volume, *What's in Store* (2007). Where *first dream of fire* begins with a long translation from the Irish, *What's in Store* ends with one. (Joyce's "workings" of the Irish are brought together in a subsequent volume, *Courts of Air and Earth* [2008]). 'Love Songs from a Dead Tongue' (*What's in Store*) reads rather differently from *Sweeny*, primarily because it is a different kind of poem, or rather group of poems, forming a long lament by a queen for her husband killed in battle. It is rhythmically less lively and inventive than *Sweeny*, more sustained, regular, emphatic. This is achieved in two main ways. First, the poem is entirely in unrhymed quatrains and in some parts the first word is repeated on its own right at the end (Grief in the king-fort / grief). Secondly, although the lines vary a lot in terms of length and rhythm, the stress is often front-loaded, driving the poem forward:

> Empty, a fort
> stands forewarning to others;
> such desolation in a palace
> just one trick among life's many. (291)

It is in fact difficult to analyse the rhythm of such lines in terms of the binary distinction between stressed and unstressed syllables and the combinations of these that form "feet". Often the rhythms seem flattened, the syllables equalised, so that the final line here could be read in terms of five more or less equal stresses. Perhaps at this point we see the influence of Joyce's prose on his verse.

There are also "workings" from other languages, including Chinese, which by now had become important to Joyce, prose pieces and a variety of verse forms. However, amidst all this variety, two things in particular catch the eye as new: the very short lines of many poems and the block of capitalised text of 'STILLSMAN'. Each of these deserves comment. To take an example of the first almost at random:

> barbarians
> are bad
> at walls
>
> ours keep
> them out

hordes
break
like a river
against
our bastions
and then
flow on

sweet
orchards
gentle
hounds
we have

the hands
of slaves
draw us
sweet
water
up (133)

In his endnotes, Joyce explains: "The many thirty-six-word poems scattered throughout this volume spring from an attempt to write a large work under rigorous constraints" and goes on to relate them to his original idea of a three-dimensional sestina (312). This development can thus be seen as a continuation of Joyce's interest in formalism, which first manifested itself in *Syzygy*. His notes refer to the Oulipian idea of self-imposed constraints, but technical virtuosity also has a long history (some would say pathology) in Irish poetry. Aspiring medieval bards reputedly had to compose fiendishly difficult metres lying in cold water with heavy stones on their chests and one exemplary poem uses a different metre in each stanza, including the name of that metre (Stifter 307–309). Was Joyce perhaps yearning for a stone on his chest? Whatever the reason, it is clear that he was at this stage looking for something new in terms of prosody, though how successful he was is another matter. In the above example, the layout if anything seems to dilute the effect, although the ending is nice. However, the poem on the following page makes much better use of the form:

successively
each emperor's
doubles were
assassinated

then
himself

therefore
this stratagem

our latest
emperor
was chosen
secretly

no-one
informed
not even
the elect

it worked

somewhere
he lives
obscurely
on

quite
unaware
he is
a god (134)

This is taut, pithy and funny and draws out Joyce's capacity for economy and dry understatement ("it worked") and in the final lines the enormity of the idea contrasts with the simplicity of the statement. However, in the main I am less impressed by these 36-ers. The problem is that they do not allow much scope to do things, to exercise the skills that Joyce had already developed in his previous work, to deploy his imagination and maintain his intensity. Their net effect is to weaken the volume and isolate some of the other fine poems that appear among them.

§

I STILL THE HEART BEATS AS THE FIRST LIGHT
BROACHES THE HORIZON HUNDREDS OF BIRDS STRIKE
UP THEIR TINY BODIES FILLING THE AIR WITH FF
MELODIES CUT WITH A SOLEMN OATH RECALL THE
PATIENT ONE OSCAR C THOUGH A BED FULL OF BONES
HAD ALWAYS ENJOYED EXCELLENT HEALTH PRESENTING
NEVER BUT THE SHALLOWEST OF MALADIES AND BEING
NEITHER ALCOHOLIC NOR SYPHILITIC GREW INTO A
BRIGHT SHARP MAN POSSESSING THE THREE GIFTS OF
HEARING SEEING AND OF JUDGEMENT ('STILLSMAN' 143)

'STILLSMAN' is a different matter. Originally printed on several large panels measuring about seven feet by five, as part of the Vinyl Project referred to in the endnotes, it was, for one thing, a quite new departure for Joyce in terms of visual presentation. The panels formed walls of text which combined the effects of size and detail: one saw the thing as a whole, but one could also zero in on the text at any point. The effect was stunning in the precise sense of the word: language as impact.

To put it simply, 'STILLSMAN' is about a man who keeps songbirds who has a stroke. The stroke affects his linguistic capacities, in contrast with the birds who continue to sing. (He and his wife also used to make music together.) Language thus becomes an issue: one might distinguish between poets who see words as a problem and those who see language as the problem. In parallel, the physiological production of birdsong is examined in clinical detail. Put thus baldly, 'STILLSMAN' does not seem remarkable. Its impact comes from the driving force of its prose. Although the numbers one through twelve appear in the text, it reads as a single piece and even the short opening extract quoted above gives some sense of its relentless momentum (although to my mind the final part veers off at a tangent). The use and development of prose which has figured at various points in Joyce's earlier work here comes to a climax. The narrative, if one can call it that, is diverted at various points by sudden intrusions of other phrases or references which call up wider themes of history, war, chaos and corruption. The tone is largely objective and analytical, sometimes lyrical, sometimes humorous. The syntax is not complex and does not often resort to the back-tracking relative or qualifying clauses one finds in *Syzygy*; instead, it simply runs on, one phrase or sentence following another in a virtually unbroken sequence, linked by little words such as "as" (in its various senses) "and", "since" and "so". The piece is a tour de force and, perhaps more than any other, draws together the various qualities which have earlier been emerging in Joyce's writing. In particular, it allows free rein to his imagination in bringing together the sensory and the cognitive:

> BUT STILL THE NAMES OF LETTERS REMAIN LOST TO HIM AS HE SAYS THE A IS AN EASEL Z IS A SERPENT AND P A BUCKLE THOUGH THIS WILL NOT APPEAR QUITE SO FARFETCHED GIVEN HOW CERTAIN INARTICULATE SOUNDS DO RESEMBLE PARTICULAR LETTERS AS THE TREMBLING OF WATER IS LIKE THE LETTER L THE QUENCHING OF HOT THINGS THE LETTER Z THE JIRKING OF A SWITCH THE LETTER Q & C BY AN EXACT OBSERVATION OF WHICH PARTICULARS IT MAY BE POSSIBLE TO MAKE A STATUE SPEAK SOME WORDS ('STILLSMAN' 144)

The tension is created by the disjunction between the normal syntax of observation, argument and reasoning and the bizarre content, relationships and results of that reasoning. Unlike some modernists, Joyce never attacks syntax itself, only semantics. As noted before, the structure of his prose embodies logic and rationality; it is its content that is irrational.

§

By sampling Joyce's prosodies – and the plural is needed – I hope I have shown that this offers one way into his writing. A much fuller and more rigorous treatment would be needed to explore this facet of his work properly, and it would also need to be extended to cover other areas. For example, I have not attempted to address the aural side of his work, his use of rhyme or assonance. This is partly because I do not feel it to be as central as his rhythms, lines and verse forms; also, he tends to read quickly, and there is often little chance to absorb sound rather than sense (and sometimes even not much time to get hold of the latter).

But by sampling his work over the years, I hope I have managed to show just what a restless, innovative and inventive writer he is. Where others may find or develop a style that suits them, and which then becomes their recognisable voice or signature, Joyce is continually on the move.

Geoffrey Squires

This makes it difficult to evaluate him, to pin down the nature of his achievement, but I for one would happily accept that problem in return for the spread he puts on the table.

Notes

[1] The lineation of 'Hopeful Monsters' and 'STILLSMAN' is not exactly as it appears in the text of the poem in *first dream of fire*. Joyce has said that the block prose paragraph format is more important than reproducing the exact layout of words and lines in the collection in both of these poems.

Works Cited

Joyce, Trevor. *What's in Store: Poems 2000–2007*. Dublin: New Writers' Press; Willowdale, ON: The Gig, 2007. Print.

—. 'STILLSMAN.' *What's in Store: Poems 2000–2007*. Dublin: New Writers' Press; Willowdale, ON: The Gig, 2007. 142–152. Print.

—. 'The Poems of Sweeny, Peregrine.' *with the first dream of fire they hunt the cold: A Body of Work 1966–2000*. 2nd ed. Dublin: New Writers' Press; Exeter: Shearsman Books, 2003. 9-44. Print.

—. *Syzygy*. Bray, Co. Wicklow: Wild Honey Press, 1998. Print.

—. 'stone floods.' *with the first dream of fire they hunt the cold: A Body of Work 1966–2000*. 2nd ed. Dublin: New Writers' Press; Exeter: Shearsman Books, 2003. 91-133. Print.

—. *The Poems of Sweeny, Peregrine: A Working of the Corrupt Irish Text*. Dublin: New Writers' Press, 1976. Print.

Stifter, D. *Sengoídelc*. Syracuse, NY: Syracuse University Press, 2006. Print.

Through my Dream: Trevor Joyce's Translations

JOHN GOODBY

Translation is a condition of being for anglophone Irish poetry; for over two hundred years Irish poets have been drawn to translation, both internal and external; internally, from the Irish language, in the attempt to establish a relationship with the broken past; externally, from other languages, in order to circumvent English hegemony and a marginal geographical location. However, while there is a wide range in the motives (and linguistic abilities) behind translation, most poets translate in the manner of their own original work, which is that of most Irish poetry: namely, in the voice of a singular, coherent lyric "I", empirically grounded, expressing itself in language which is largely transparent. Stylistic liberties may be taken by this self, but its integrity is never in doubt.

Translation studies calls this "naturalised" or "domesticated" translation; the source text is recreated in the target language so that it reads as if it had been written by a native speaker, and with a fluency which elides its translated status (Munday 146–148). As against this, however, there is the "literal" or "foreignising" approach to translation, which foregrounds the otherness of the source text by, for example, carrying non-idiomatic syntactical structures and lexis across into the target language.[1] This kind of translation is far rarer, and is associated with avant-garde poetry, which was until recently largely marginalised by mainstream poetic discourse. Nevertheless, the "foreignising" mode is the one in which Irish poetry translation has had some of its most distinctive successes, including as it does Brian Coffey's inventive rendering of Mallarmé's *Un Coup de dés n'abolira jamais le hasard* (*Dice Thrown Never Will Annul Chance*) (1965) and the work of the greatest translator of the nineteenth century, James Clarence Mangan (who invented the "originals" of some of his "translations"). As David Lloyd has argued, Mangan's translations are "proto-Modernist", and translation, given a keener edge by the translated Irish condition, is one reason for the strength of Irish modernism.[2]

Translation is central to modernist poetics more generally, of course. For Ezra Pound, its chief practitioner, it was not so much a vehicle for personal expression as a way of constructing a transcultural, timeless "tradition"; and, insofar as this was Pound's chief aim as a writer, it was an integral part of his own poetic practice, haunting all his "original" work. Pound's example informs the translations of the 1930s Irish modernist poets, one of whom, Samuel Beckett, has been, with Mangan, a major influence on the leading contemporary Irish neo-modernist poet Trevor Joyce, whose poetic evolution has also been complexly bound up with translation activity.[3] In what follows I will discuss the role of translation in Joyce's work, drawing on the distinction between "domesticating" and "foreignising" forms. I begin with his version of the Middle Irish *Buile Suibhne* (*The Poems of Sweeny, Peregrine: A Working of the Corrupt Irish text*) (1976), which I see as a source for his mature practice as a poet. This is first apparent in his collection *stone floods* (1995), which uses translated Irish, Chinese and Japanese material. I will then examine Joyce's use of translated folk materials in 'Trem Neul' (1999), and his return to Irish translation in *What's in Store* (2007) and *Courts of Air and Earth* (2008), as well as Central European folksong in the first of these. Finally I discuss *Rome's Wreck* (written 2009), in which Joyce translates from one form of English into another.[4]

Buile Suibhne (The Poems of Sweeny, Peregrine)

Joyce's own earliest poems, collected in *Pentahedron* (1972), are dense lyrics owing something to a reading of Trakl and Vallejo, and perhaps to unpublished early translations of Celan; they are set in an inner-city Dublin of constraining walls, river, hoardings, monuments, a milieu replete with death and decay, and articulate an anxiety concerning the ability of language to represent external reality so profound that it became a dead-end. In an essay published in 1998, Joyce partly explained his writer's block and publication hiatus (which also had to do with personal circumstances and a climate hostile to experiment) by pointing out the similarities between his early poems and mainstream Irish "poetry of expression" (46). This poetry, he argued, suffered from the problems of "representing" the "reality" of twentieth-century history, one exacerbated in modern times by the electronic media overload of images of suffering which demanded an "outraged response, but le[ft] that response... without possibility of external effect". Mainstream poetry tended to reflect this anguished yet passive relationship, able to respond only by guiltily nudging its familiar images of beauty towards the "bulk dead". It was therefore condemned merely to "[state] forcibly the horror of its own privileged futility", to risk arrogating suffering to the individual lyric ego, while offering only an archaic beauty as compensation (45). Thus, to believe that "language and poetic form are ideally neutral vessels into which the poetic sense may be poured, shuttles to bear towards the reader the burden of an already formed meaning" was to reject invention and resistance, and succumb to the dominant discourses of the corporate, government and military spheres (46).

The difficulty of overcoming the impasse created by these dilemmas may be gauged from the twenty-three year gap between *Pentahedron* and *stone floods*. However, *Sweeny, Peregrine*, the composition of which overlapped with that of the lyrics of *Pentahedron*, shows Joyce discovering poetic strategies which were to eventually lead him out of this dead-end. The *Buile Suibhne* describes the fate of Sweeny, king of Dal Ariadha; insulting Saint Ronan, he is cursed and becomes a *gealt*, or bird-man, living in woods and wild places, unable to re-establish social or familial bonds, until he is finally killed by a swineherd. The work, in prose interspersed with lyrics, contains several dramatic episodes, although much of its appeal lies in its evocation of the harsh yet beautiful natural world in which Sweeny is forced to subsist. Joyce's version can be usefully contrasted with Seamus Heaney's better-known *Sweeney Astray* (1983), in order to explain its significance for his later work. First, unlike Heaney, Joyce eschews many of the opportunities the original affords for drama. Second, whereas Heaney views Sweeny romantically, as "a figure of the artist, displaced, guilty, assuaging himself by his utterance", Joyce manages to distance Sweeny's sufferings.[5] Joyce's subtitle, "A Working of the Corrupt Irish Text", indicates the manner in which he does so; namely, by foregrounding the provisionality of his version and highlighting the irresolvable cruxes, gaps and interpolations of the original. Joyce treats these as a kind of proto-modernist disjunctiveness, expressive in a manner beyond that of an individual subjectivity – "[the lacunae] have at least the virtue of reinforcing the sense of Sweeny's stress and distress", he notes (*first dream of fire* 234). Some verse from the original becomes prose in Joyce's version, while some prose mutates to verse. More, in his most radical break with the original, he heightens this quality by separating the prose and Sweeny's lyrics into two sections, one of prose narrative the second a suite of twenty-two lyrics, dropping some material in the original entirely. The main effect is to make the verse a first-person lament by Sweeny, while the prose purports to be an external and objective account.

Following one of Joyce's favourite authors of the time, Flann O'Brien (whose version of the *Buile Suibhne* appears in *At Swim-Two-Birds*), the prose section problematises the narrative in postmodern fashion; for example, Sweeny tells the Man of the Woods his life story, up to and including his own death, "as it is set down hereinafter" – that is, Sweeny foresees and narrates his own fate to a character who is just about to die (*first dream of fire* 14). Who, then, is telling the tale we are reading? Even more disorienting is the retrospective moment, at the end of the prose section, when we learn that "it is uncertain" how far the tale's scribe, Moling, might have "emend[ed] [this] strange and confused history" and how far later "editors and critics [may] have conspired with him", asking "May we, then, conclude just this: that, after all, we have not here these words which Sweeny, between flight and fall, spoke to the Man of the Wood?" (16). The resultant narrative seems to exist in a limbo between some originary, pure *ur*-text and this denial. Joyce's lyrics convey Sweeny's pain and the starkly beautiful landscape as effectively as Heaney does:

> IX
> In summertime the blue-grey herons stand
> rigid above sharp waters.
>
> In wintertime the wolfpacks
> thread the snow-glens with their spoor,
> and with their moaning they thread the long wind.
>
> I hear their snow-blurred howling
> as I cross the iron lakes
> and crack the frost from my beard. (25)

But while they are clearly in Sweeny's voice, coming after the prose, they also concentrate the work's disjunctive effects: "the life God gave / seems somehow dislocated" (17), as the first poem notes. Since we are told that this is a retelling of material already worked over, of twice-told, uncertain status, Sweeny's voice is never grounded in any romantic, lyric way.[6] The language is often ironically at odds with Sweeny's madness and he traverses a mutable landscape, in which place names do not signal understanding or belonging, but alienation and loss. Although we relish its beauty, landscape is not presented as compensation for Sweeny's plight, as in Heaney; indeed, it intensifies it. The environment penetrates Sweeny, and he is taken over by, rather than undertaking, his exile, "lacerat[ed]", "lanc[ed]", becoming "a cave of pain" (22, 31). His plight resembles that of the passive lyric "I" of *Pentahedron*, which can neither express its selfhood nor map the object world adequately in language. However, the form of the translation, with its persona, destabilised and double narrative, and emphasis on emendation, distances the guilt attached to poetry's aestheticising aspect.[7] Moreover, the bicameral structure was one Joyce would use again to similar effect – in *Syzygy* (1998), 'Trem Neul' (1999) and elsewhere. In his note to the poem, he describes the relationship between his version and the original by applying to it James Mangan's description of his own inventive translations as "the antithesis of plagiarism" (236): in the "unoriginality" of translation lay the genuine originality of escape from the lyric ego, a potential "route out of the dilemmas of *Pentahedron*", as Nate Dorward puts it, "via a modernist poetics of translation" (3).

stone floods

Yet it would be more accurate to speak not of one, but two Poundian "models" of translation at work in *Sweeny*. Its back-cover blurb claims: "The model for this exciting and pioneering version is not Synge or Hyde but the Pound of *Cathay* and 'The Seafarer'".[8] This is the translation model Pound devised for trying to realise the past within the present by creating the impression of unmediated rapport with the dead, and both "The Seafarer", and *Cathay*, in which Pound merges his own voice with that of Li Po, are good examples. Revolutionary in its time, however, this model has now become the standard domesticating translation strategy for mainstream poets. But Pound also used a more radical, and in many ways antithetical, translation model. In Canto 1, the *Odyssey* is approached through the medium of Andreas Divus' translation of Homer – Pound translating a translation – signalling the fact that a translation is always already mediated by other texts, is always in some sense a betrayal of its original. It is an approach which, being unavoidably "foreignising", critiques the notion of direct "rapport" or presence.

Sweeny, Peregrine clearly resembles the *Cathay* model in its lyric second section, but its prose section is Poundian in the alternative sense. The dialectical tension between the two modes forestalls complete identification with Sweeny, and some of the problems Joyce had with the lyric "I" in *Pentahedron*. However, the potential of this "working" for his own poetry were not immediately apparent to him. Some intuition of it may be discerned in the way that, after 1976, Joyce pursued what can be described as a Poundian course of study in Japanese and Chinese poetry and philosophy, coming to an understanding of the cultural counterweight they represented to eurocentricity and Western binary modes of thinking.

Unlike Pound, however, Joyce never uses translation to pass ironic judgement on the present, nor does he succumb to linguistic idealism concerning the ideogram, or the belief that China offered a desirable social model.[9] *stone floods* offers a lyric mode which combines the presencing and distancing aspects of these two kinds of translation. The title indicates paradoxical states in which what is fixed and solid becomes fluid; it announces the book's themes of impermeability and porousness, closure and openness, fixity and movement, transgression and control, a concern with purity, dirt and waste, with boundaries and frames. The cover photograph displays a photograph of part of the famous buried terracotta army of Qin Shi Huang Di, the First Emperor of China. It shows, startlingly, the still half-excavated life-size figures apparently borne along in a river of rock, the effect of rock-as-fluid being to undermine the qualities usually associated with both stone and water.[10] The poems within probe the same paradoxical condition, with translation in the broadest sense playing a central role. Deserts and beaches figure heavily, because sand – a stony substance which flows – embodies the *stone floods* paradox. The themes of these poems stemmed from Joyce's own thinking through of his poetic dilemmas and some, such as 'The Opening' (a "threshold" poem), were written as early as 1983, to be followed by "sand" poems such as 'The Turlough' and 'Strands'. But the discovery of Beckett's poetry in 1991–1992, and especially his "je suis ce cours de sable qui glisse", which brings together several of these paradoxical conditions, or themes, acted as a confirmation and a validation for work in this vein.[11]

This was not simply a question of content: Beckett's work also makes striking structural use of the doubling and parallelism found in many of the *stone floods* poems. Sand, of course, is the principal ingredient of that ambiguous solid-liquid substance, glass, while its silicon is also used to capture another kind of flow, that of information, in the silicon chip. In this regard it should be noted that Joyce has been fascinated by information technology since taking a job in the computer section of a Dublin cigarette manufacturer in the mid-1970s; on moving to Cork in 1984, he worked for Apple. References to "circuits and gates" in 'The Turlough', or to software testing in 'Golden Master', flagged up the language of Joyce's daily grind as a Business Systems Analyst for them, but were also part of a Frankfurt School-informed critique of the way in which electronic media was increasingly shaping the contemporary world. Joyce's intention was to expunge or twist conventional narrative in many of these poems, placing the burden of conveying temporal change instead on repetition, either incremental or with calculated variation. "My models for this", he has noted, "were in the refrain structures of folk-song, often mediated through the likes of Yeats or Lorca, and in the interplay of stasis and movement in Chinese parallel verse".[12] Stylistically, *stone floods* "translates" the fixities of *Pentahedron* into forms which, while repetitive, can be made to embody change – stone floods – overcoming its aesthetic impasse. Thus, while these lyrics often seem intensely personal, they are at the same time non-confessional; they possess a quality of translationese which hovers somewhere between the verbal densities of, say, Pound or Basil Bunting, Chinese poetry, and folk lyrics. In many ways, Joyce writes in English as though it is Chinese, without connective particles, using a vocabulary, word-division and minimal punctuation which makes syntax ambiguous, as in 'Lines in Fall', which "take on the voice of the first two *Autumn Meditations* by Meng Jiao (751–814)" (*first dream* 237):

> Bag of bones cant lie down
> to night
> timbers settling
> crack them up right
> under Orrery Hill (103)

Here, for example, the "Bag of bones" can't "lie down / to night" (that is, can't get to sleep, or has nowhere to sleep) and/or, more existentially, refuses to succumb "to night", or "night / timbers" – the forest of the night – in the sense of accepting "night" (as oblivion), or wishes to avoid nightmares. There is a similar play between the antithetical pairs "settling / crack" and "up right / under", which multiplies meaning depending on how the reader understands the subjects and objects of the verbs, or what the verb is: "crack", for example, is intransitive with respect to "timbers" and, simultaneously, transitively with respect to "them". And who are "them"? The "timbers" or the "bones" of the first line? This kind of fruitful doubleness leads in 'The Turlough' towards a modified version of the Japanese *renga*, in which each verse takes its cue from the one preceding it, usually written by a collaborator, and reflects back on that verse, changing its meaning. Originally *renga* took its form from the movement of the seasons and the hours in the day; like the turlough itself, which is a limestone lake prone to flash-flooding, it is a body in a perpetual state of change, a poem defined by Octavio Paz as one "which effaces itself as it is written, a path which is wiped out and has no desire to lead anywhere. Nothing awaits us at its end; there is no end any more than there is a beginning: all is movement"

John Goodby

(Roy 27).[13] Such open-endedness and interconnection are particularly appropriate to Joyce's desire at this point to find a poetic strategy capable of sustaining the seemingly incommensurable complexities of word and world, of undermining linear narrative, and he developed it further in the poem 'Chimaera', which actually uses the multiple voices of *renga* proper.

'Trem Neul'

The poems of *stone floods* are recognisably in traditional free verse lyric forms, despite the radical disruption of narrative through parataxis, condensation and the limited collaging of texts found in 'Chimaera'. In its wake Joyce felt dissatisfaction that these forms did not sufficiently register the "flow" of information in the modern world. As he put it:

> I was forced to recognise... [with *stone floods*], that the "lyric" mode... I practised was quite as prone to exclude the incoherent world as was the mannered narrative I so distrusted. I had also encountered Cage for second time, and with more understanding of how the play of ambient noise across the receptivity of his spaces might circumvent those exclusions and admit what might otherwise not be acknowledged.[14]

In a series of poems written soon after *stone floods*, Joyce attempted, by the use of aleatory sampling and collage techniques, to break up the unitary "finish" of his lyric voice, devising forms in which impurity, in the sense of meanings which Joyce himself could not wholly control, could enter his poetry. Several intercut the texts of others – Tom Raworth, Randolph Healy, Michael Smith – with Joyce's own, and can be read in more than one way. Others use a variety of external structures, such as the shamanic 'Summons of the Soul' in the ancient Chinese *The Songs of the South*, in 'Data Shadows', or a palindromic medieval musical form, the cancrizan, in the more complex *Syzygy* (1998). In each case, Joyce tries to create a form in which unforeseen effects can occur within more or less rigorous imposed procedures.

'Trem Neul' (1999) is no exception to this trend. It is a longish, complex collage work in which Joyce finds new ways of using the concept of translation. The poem is bicameral, like Sweeny, but in two columns down each page: on the left-hand side a column of prose, on the right a column of free verse. J.C.C. Mays has claimed that the two narratives these present "can be read in two ways simultaneously, downward or upward" (62–63). In practice this is difficult, since both columns have their own punctuation schemes and do not encourage "reading across" the gap between them. However, his claim that while the left-hand column is "peopled with named characters who… inhabit a western part (of Ireland?) [and whose] sources are presented in their original form… undigested", the right-hand one presents people who "speak… in what seems to be an eastern (Chinese?) landscape", is suggestive (62). Is Joyce here obliquely aligning his two main translation sources?

Both narratives splice together snippets from a host of texts, many of them translations – by R. Luria, Magdalena Abakanowicz, Alain Prochiantz among others – as Joyce constructs what he has, perhaps with tongue in cheek, called "an extended autobiography in prose and verse from which everything personal has been excluded, and whose spaces instead are crowded with the memories and apprehensions of others".[15] Sections of the right-hand column read as if they were excerpted from a Teach Yourself language book, or were being addressed to someone who had just learnt the basics of a language ("What will be the issue / of this? / What will they do / in this matter? / Had we been early / we should have / arrived / by this time") (194). The narratives occasionally touch, glancingly, but shed no consistent light upon each other; they exist separately, although both concern memory and forgetting, loss, change, preservation and destruction. Joyce has argued that his work is,

> in part, an attempt to recoup part of the history of my world from what Beckett terms "the uniform memory of intelligence" – that is, to test the ways in which narratives construct plausibility, become discourses, and this because of "the dominance of contending master-narratives in the interpretation of the Irish past and… my present world".[16]

Yet one major source is familial: Patrick Weston Joyce (1827–1914), who is the nineteenth-century translator from Irish and author of *Irish Names of Places* and numerous works on Irish history, folklore and music, and a great-uncle of Trevor Joyce. A brief memoir by Joyce in the *Catholic Book Bulletin* supplies the work's primary left-hand column narrative, that involving the only named figure in the piece; this concerns a fiddler named Ned Goggin, who was caught in a snowstorm in the winter of 1838 and forced to seek shelter in P.W. Joyce's home. He heard Goggin play "The Tuning of the Colours" on that occasion, but forgot the tune until many years later when the memory passed through him, "trem neul, as the song-writers would say – 'through my dream'… and I woke up actually whistling the tune". The learning and forgetting of the air, and then its retrieval 'Trem Neul', are crucial to the concern with memory (and false memory, which it tries to create in the reader) and how the mind works displayed in 'Trem Neul'. Again, it seems to me, the poem is about translation, carrying across (from one culture or medium to another), in a metaphorical, broader than usual sense.

Courts of Air and Earth / What's in Store / Rome's Wreck

'Trem Neul' has as oblique and opaque a relation to Joyce's translation-derived poetics as anything he has written. In 2008, however, he published some direct translations, of Irish poetry. *Courts of Air and Earth* collects the previously published *Sweeny, Peregrine* and "Cry Help" (a working "from the Irish of Aogán Ó Rathaille" from *stone floods*), but also includes new work: 'Love Songs from a Dead Tongue', a sequence of eighteen Gormlaith poems "Worked from the Late Middle Irish"; the folk song 'Sean O'Duibhir of the Glen'; and two lyrics from the *Dánta Grádha* anthology (one, the famous "I will not die for you" translated twice). Like the second section of *Sweeny*, the Gormlaith "workings" are not translations in the usual sense; neither faithful renderings nor modern versions, they hover between tradition and modernity. Pungent, concrete, stark and spare in style, they also flag up the corruption of their originals, as in the first part of *Sweeny* (perhaps since "corruption is fertility", as 'Trem Neul' claims); thus, the third poem includes the interpolations "[This is doubtful]" and "[This translation is difficult]".[17] Overall, the additional translations indicate a wish to fill the gap between *Sweeny*, which possibly dates to as early as the eighth century, to Ó Rathaille in the eighteenth, when the Gaelic tradition was at its last gasp. If this was a more or less straightforward use of the mode perfected in *Sweeny*, however, work in Joyce's 2007 poetry collection *What's in Store* was anything but. In this case, the material is made more difficult to interpret because of the volume's complex arrangement and its mixture of original poetry and different types of translation. To complicate matters, all of the Irish poems in *Courts of Air and Earth* except *Sweeny* were included in *What's in Store*, differently arranged.

At the centre of *What's in Store* is a longish prose poem, 'STILLSMAN'. On either side are nineteen separate sections of different kinds of poem. The most important of these are 36-word poems, original lyrics clustered in nineteen groups of between three and twelve. Most of the other poems are translations, however; 'Outcry' (in two parts, on either side of 'STILLSMAN') is "a working of some of the surviving poems by Juan Chi (210–263), while 'Capital Accounts' is 'worked from' Ch'ang-an: Ku-i by Lu Chao-lin (635–684)".[18] There are also two groups of folksongs, 'Folk Songs from the Finno-Ugric and Turkic Languages' and 'Folksongs from the Hungarian'.[19] One of the first group of folksongs contains a version of the book's title and gives a good idea of the brevity and limpid beauty of these pieces:

> In the dark wood
> swifts don't fly.
> What's a blue dove
> doing there?
>
> With no mother,
> with no father,
> for you, what lies
> in store? (17)

Like the Hungarian folksongs which balance them in the second "half" of the collection, these apparently artless lyrics focus unsentimentally on the brevity of youth, the vulnerability of love and the inevitability of death. In this sense, they tell of what's "in store" for everyone. This is a quality they share with the material in *Courts of Air and Earth* too (there are also stylistic resemblances between the Central European and Irish translations). It is no surprise, therefore, that *What's in Store* opens with 'Folk Songs from the Finno-Ugric and Turkic Languages' and closes with 'Love Songs from a Dead Tongue' ('Folksongs from the Hungarian' and 'Anonymous Love Songs from the Irish' also occur at roughly the same points within their respective "halves" of the book). Apart from 'STILLSMAN', the exceedingly heterogeneous material in the book is not strictly demarcated – some sequences, indeed, have no title – and Joyce has claimed that "the whole book is constructed like one long poem, with the sort of checks and balances, diversions and obsessive foci one might expect from that".[20] A major impetus for *What's in Store*, and something of its structure, was, again, the work of P.W. Joyce, and also of his brother Robert Dwyer Joyce. R.D. Joyce was best known for *Ballads of Irish Chivalry* (1872) and it is possible to discern in his adaption of traditional Irish folksongs to produce Fenian propaganda a foreignising stance on translation, in contrast to his brother's "domesticating" contextualisation of his own translations, although one would not wish to push this too far.[21] What is clear is that Joyce is interested in the way that cultures "translate" their concerns by using analogues taken from previous historical periods: 1798 as a way of writing about a hoped-for Fenian rising, for example. As Joyce has explained of the book's Finno-Ugric and other material:

> Th[is] comes largely from the same interest as spurred 'Tocharian Music' [a poem in *stone floods*]: awareness of how the history of nomadic and "oral" cultures (or those strains within literate cultures) is written from the outside, by the settled, the lettered. Remember the Irish proverb at the start of *Rome's Wreck*, which is translated at the very end of the last sonnet. The Irish were seen as vagrant by the English.[22]

'Tocharian Music' deals with the fate of the Tocharians, a Central Asian people who were unique in being the only known Indo-European language speaking group to migrate eastwards, rather than westwards, from the Indo-European linguistic source. The poem tells of their rebellion against the Chinese in the sixth century CE:

> Eleven thousand
> died in the reprisal
> and the city laid waste
> the airs dispersed
> only the names survive (*first dream of fire* 108)

The Tocharians were dispersed; only fragments of their language now survive. Crucially for Joyce, however, the dispersal of their dancers and musicians, for which they were famed, meant that the Tocharians had a profound influence on the poetry and music of the Golden Age of Chinese T'ang Dynasty culture a century later. What the poem reflects on, in part, is the return of the repressed, the marginal, the impure. As in the traditions of the West, art may be seen both as complicit with power, and definitive of cultural difference from power. Opening and closing *What's in Store* as it does, this material exists at the margins of the book (but is given the first and last word in it) and frames the material emanating from "literate cultures", including imperial China. This oral culture is "within" the book and "literate cultures" too; it is the dirt, or leaven, depending upon point of view, in all human cultures. The dialectic between nomadic/"oral" and settled/literate, and the dilemmas involved in the latter representing the former, are therefore woven into the book.

As Joyce notes, the parallels between the Tocharian language and Irish, a language almost, but not quite, crushed by an imperial centre, are pertinent to these considerations. In his latest work, *Rome's Wreck*, another striking use of translation (and a redefinition of it), Joyce performs an act of what Roman Jakobson called an "intralingual translation" – that is, "an interpretation of verbal signs by means of other signs in the same language" – on Edmund Spenser's sonnet sequence *Ruines of Rome* (1591).[23] This work, consisting of thirty-two sonnets, plus an envoi, is itself a translation from the French of Joachim du Bellay and was a significant contribution to the golden age of the English sonnet. In his "translation" Joyce retains the form's fourteen lines and observes the volta, but changes Spenser's rhymed iambic pentameters into unrhymed hexameters and, more remarkably, irreverently reduces his rich Renaissance language to a series of single vocables. A comparison of the opening lines of the first sonnet gives the general idea:

Spenser:

Ye heauenly spirites, whose ashie cinders lie
Vnder deep ruines, with huge walls opprest,
But not your praise, the which shall neuer die
Through your faire verses, ne in ashes rest; (1: 509)

Joyce:

Hey, you great ghosts, you ash and deep
set dust that hefts the weight of walls,
your fame lives on in verse that won't
now leave you limp there in the dumps. (1)

Joyce's periphrastic ingenuity matches the many challenges he has set himself, particularly when polysyllabic proper nouns are involved: thus, "Such as the Berecynthian Goddesse bright / In her swift charret" becomes "Think a she god, quick in her cart / of war". The object of the exercise, however, is serious enough: to take the language of the imperialist planter Edmund Spenser, possessor of 30,000 confiscated acres at Kilcolman,

John Goodby

proponent of the brutal subjugation of the native Irish (and their poets), and strip it bare; to render it alien to itself, just as Ireland was made alien to its own inhabitants by the war and dispossession which accompanied the Plantations. The result is not so much pidgin mockery, however, as a form of Basic Poetic English that has its own gravity and humour. It also resembles, of course, the pared-back language of the "workings" of Irish poetry and the versions of Hungarian, Finno-Ugric and Turkic folksongs. Spenser the settler on the land of others, the first professional print poet in English, has himself been made dispossessed, made nomadic and "oral", through Joyce's translation.

Spenser's final sonnet, the thirty-third, is an 'Envoy' which is additional to du Bellay's sequence. In it, Spenser praises du Bellay and looks to a future in which Rome has been "revived" by du Bellay's work, as a result of which du Bellay himself enjoys immortality. Joyce, however, does not acknowledge his source, Spenser, in the same way. Instead, he translates the thirty-second sonnet, in which the poet looks to the future and his own possible fame, but alters its final lines. Spenser's sestet runs:

> Nath'les my Lute, whom *Phœbus* deignd to giue,
> Cease not to sound these olde antiquities:
> For if that time doo let thy glorie liue,
> Well maist thou boast, how euer base thou bee,
> That thou art first, which of thy Nation song
> Th'olde honour of the people gowned long. (32: 514)

Spenser anticipates a future in which, by praising Rome, his own efforts to raise the dignity of English poetry in the vernacular will be recognised too. This is a basic Protestant humanist aspiration. However, by an irony Spenser could not have foreseen, the empire has retrospectively written back; Joyce's "translation" of *Ruines of Rome* is the future to which Spenser looked, and the English poet's poem, like his language, has become part of the "Nation song" of Ireland. Joyce has therefore to write himself into the translation. He concludes it with a version of the Irish proverb which provides his work's epigraph: "Maireann lorg an phinn, ach ní mhaireann an béal a chan", which translates literally as "the mark of the pen lives, but the mouth that sang does not (live)":

> I use the tools I've got: hard words
> passed down, passed on, may speak on some

days when the live voice breaks.
Not all words bear the weight. I mean;
    but they may not. And these? Pen's mark
    lives on, but not the mouth that sang. (32)

The anti-imperialist point broadens to a general one concerning art's melancholy capacity to outlive the artist: Horace's *vitas brevis, ars longa*, Keats' Grecian urn. It may be that Joyce is also reminding us of another aspect of Spenser, namely his obsession with mutability. *The Faerie Queene* runs into sand in the Mutability Cantos, in which the Goddess Mutability is silenced, but wins the debate: and to admit to the ceaselessness of change is to acknowledge the ultimate futility of imperial permanence and grandeur. In this sense, *Rome's Wreck* is a brilliantly ingenious and yet literal reminder to Spenser of his most profound insights, even as it takes us back to Joyce's own fascination with translated states, a version of stone that floods, dreams to be travelled through, nomads who become emperors, in writing which translates the idea of translation itself in order to create one of the most remarkable bodies of poetry in contemporary Irish literature.

John Goodby

Notes

1   As the latest anthology of translations of poetry from the Irish edited by Gregory Schirmer shows, there is still widespread ignorance of, or resistance to, the translation strategy opposed to this one. This contains work by Mangan, but no twentieth-century translations that are the products of a foreignising aesthetic. See, Gregory Schirmer, *After the Irish: An Anthology of Poetic Translation*.

2   See David Lloyd, *Nationalism and Minor Literature: James Clarence Mangan and the Emergence of Irish Cultural Nationalism*.

3   In 1967 Joyce co-founded New Writers' Press (NWP) with Michael and Irene Smith; in the decade that followed, it published translations of Borges (the first in English), Machado, Quevedo, Vega, Vallejo, the *Dánta Grádha*, St John of the Cross and Huerga, and carried in its house journal *The Lace Curtain* (1969–78) a plethora of translated poetry by (among others) Bartusek, Andrade, Jiménez, Colinas, Bachmann, Desnos, Trakl, Neruda and Benn, as well as Irish poetry in translation by Mhac an tSaoi, Ó Direáin, and MacSíomóin. For an account of these activities see Trevor Joyce, 'New Writers' Press: The History of a Project', in Patricia Coughlan and Alex Davis (eds.), *Modernism and Ireland: The Poetry of the 1930s*.

4   This collection was published by Cusp Books in 2014.

5   Seamus Heaney, Introduction, *Sweeney Astray*, London: Faber, 1984, n. pag. This articulates Heaney's own concerns of the time of course, as reflected in *Station Island* (1984), especially its 'Sweeney Redivivus' sequence, and the criticism collected in *The Government of the Tongue* (1989).

6   As J.C.C. Mays claims, he is "the etiolated subject at a second or further remove [who] sings with the kind of lucid detachment achieved by the American Objectivists… Put another way, Joyce is not in control of the persona Sweeny – he identifies and resists identification, by turns – but he is in full control of the lines of poetry and this rescues him from excess" (57–58).

7   It's relevant here to note that Patrick Crotty's new Penguin anthology of Irish poetry includes only Sweeny's final lyric; stripped of context, its references to God and Christ read not as a distantiating palinode and possible pious corruption, as intended, but rather as representing an *echt* religious conversion. In this way, mainstream poetic discourse misreads and seeks to "domesticate" Joyce's estranging translation strategy.

8   The blurb is probably by Michael Smith, Joyce's editor, not by Joyce himself.

9   For Pound the deconstructive ambiguities inherent in the Chinese written character, and the lack of logical connectives in Chinese, allowed access to "a prolonged and rich heritage of intensity, precision, objectivity, visual clarity and complete harmony with nature – all key elements of Modernism itself" (Qian 3). Pound was fascinated by the fact that the Chinese written character eliminates the fixed concepts of agent and agency, its syntax allowing "agents to act as recipients as well, and vice versa", and this – so he believed – had the

potential to undo the binaries that hobbled Western thought and linguistic systems (104). Through immersion in a non-Western culture, particularly that of China, a measure of linguistic-cultural purity and social order could be accessed: in his words "China is solid", it is "a new Greece" (Pound 155).

10 For a fuller description of these aspects of the collection, see John Goodby and Marcella Edwards, "'glittering silt": the Poetry of Trevor Joyce and the Myth of Irishness'.

11 je suis ce cours de sable qui glisse
entre le galet et la dune
la pluie d'été pleut sur ma vie
sur moi ma vie qui me fuit me poursuit
et finira le jour de son commencement
cher instant je te vois
dans ce rideau de brume qui recule
où je n'aurai plus à fouler ces longs seuils mouvants
et vivrai le temps d'une porte
qui s'ouvre et se referme (Beckett 56–57)

12 Trevor Joyce, 'Why I Write Narrative', 1999, sent as a personal email to the author; posted on *The Narrative Site*, online Poetry Center San Francisco State University.

13 See also Edwards and Goodby, 2002, 190–193.

14 'Why I Write Narrative'. Cage's works are noted for their use of aleatory composition techniques and incorporation of ambient noise; in fact, for Cage there is no such thing as "noise" in the sense that any sound, depending on the context in which we listen to it, can give aesthetic pleasure. Trevor Joyce's later work resembles Cage's in the sense that it tries to marry extremes of formal constraint with procedures which allow for unforeseen irruptions of material from outside the structure figuring the struggle between the information-saturated lifeworld and the artist's attempt to create meaningful form.

15 Trevor Joyce, dustjacket of *with the first dream of fire they hunt the cold*.

16 Trevor Joyce, 'Why I Write Narrative'.

17 '*Love Songs from a Dead Tongue*, Worked from the Late Middle-Irish'; the Gormlaith poems, "probably composed around the year 1200, but manuscript copies continued to be made even as late as the nineteenth century". "They speak in the voice of the famous queen Gormlaith (d. AD 948), whose three husbands were all kings." Eleven of the originals were published in Osborn Bergin's *Irish Bardic Poetry* (1970) and another six come from a scholarly paper by Anne O'Sullivan, 'Triamhuin Ghormlaithe', published in *Ériu* in 1952. Joyce observes, "As far as I am aware this extended sequence of the Gormlaith poems had not previously been published together... prior to my gathering them into this set". Trevor Joyce, *Courts of Air and Earth*, Exeter: Shearsman, 2008, 95. Hereafter *Courts*.

18 Trevor Joyce, *What's in Store*, 311–312. Hereafter *Store*.

19 As Joyce explains in a note, his sources are the lyric sheets supplied with Hung-
    aroton LPs. The Finno-Ugric and Turkic languages in question are: Tatar,
    Voytak, Cheremis, Mordvinian, Chuvash and Bashkir.
20 From email correspondence with Trevor Joyce, 27/11/2009.
21 *What's in Store* also includes (Trevor) Joyce's version of 'Seán O'Duibhir a'
    Ghleanna' or 'John O'Dwyer of the Glen', another lineal ancestor, hence his
    translation of the ballad. R.D. Joyce used 1798 as an analogue for the hoped-
    for Fenian rising of his own day (in, for example, 'The Wind that Shakes the
    Barley'); this is echoed for Trevor Joyce in the use of Han Dynasty history to
    figure Tang Dynasty realities in the source he uses for 'Capital Accounts'; thus,
    part of his process of "translation" is to provide another layer of history (as
    Pound did in Canto I of *The Cantos*), applying that retrospective application to
    his own time, the working being done during the invasion of Iraq. From email
    correspondence with Trevor Joyce, 23/9/2010).
22 From email correspondence with Trevor Joyce, 23/9/2010.
23 Jeremy Munday, *op. cit.*, p. 5.

Works Cited

Beckett, Samuel. *Collected Poems in English and French*. London: Calder &
    Boyars, 1977. Print.
Dorward, Nate. 'On Trevor Joyce.' *Chicago Review* 48.4 (2002/2003): 82–96.
    Print.
Edwards, Marcella and John Goodby. '"glittering silt": The Poetry of Trevor
    Joyce and the Myth of Irishness.' *Hungarian Journal for English and American
    Studies* 8.1 (2002): 173–198. Print.
Joyce, Trevor. *Rome's Wreck: Translated from the English of Edmund Spenser's Ruines
    of Rome*. Los Angeles, CA: Cusp Books, 2014. Print.
——. *What's in Store: Poems 2000–2007*. Dublin: New Writers' Press;
    Willowdale, ON: The Gig, 2007. Print.
——. 'The Poems of Sweeny, Peregrine'. *with the first dream of fire they hunt the
    cold: A Body of Work 1966–2000*. 2nd ed. Dublin: New Writers' Press; Exeter:
    Shearsman Books, 2003. 9-44. Print.
——'Why I Write Narrative'. *Narrativity* 1. The Poetry Centre, San Francisco
    State University, Mar. 2000. Web. 3 Aug. 2013. <https://www.sfsu.
    edu/~poetry/narrativity/issue_one/joyce.html>
——. 'The Point of Innovation in Irish Poetry.' *For the Birds: Proceedings of
    the First Cork Conference on New and Experimental Irish Poetry*. Ed. Harry
    Gilonis. Sutton: Mainstream; Dublin: hardPressed Poetry, 1998. 18–24. Rpt
    in 'Six Poets: Views and Interviews.' Ed. Nate Dorward. Special issue of *The
    Gig* 2 (2001): 45–50. Print.

———. 'New Writers' Press: The History of a Project.' *Modernism and Ireland: The Poetry of the 1930s.* Eds. Patricia Coughlan and Alex Davis. Cork: Cork University Press, 1995. 276–306. Print.

Lloyd, David. *Nationalism and Minor Literature: James Clarence Mangan and the Emergence of Irish Cultural Nationalism,* Berkeley, CA: University of California Press, 1987. Print.

Mays, J.C.C. 'Scriptor ignotus, with the fire in him now.' *Dublin Review* 6 (2002): 42–65. Print.

Munday, Jeremy. *Introducing Translation Studies: Theories and Applications,* London: Routledge, 2007. Print.

Pound, Ezra. *The Selected Letters of Ezra Pound: 1907–1941.* Ed. D.D. Paige. New York, NY: New Directions, 1971. Print.

Qian, Zhaoming. *Orientalism and Modernism: The Legacy of China in Pound and Williams.* Durham, NC: Duke University Press, 1995. Print.

Roy, Claude. *Renga: A Chain of Poems by Octavio Paz, Jacques Roubaud, Edoardo Sanguineti and Charles Tomlinson.* New York, NY: Braziller, 1971. Print.

Schirmer, Gregory. *After the Irish: An Anthology of Poetic Translation.* Cork: Cork University Press, 2009. Print.

Spenser, Edmund. 'Ruines of Rome'. *The Poetical Works of Edmund Spenser, Vol. 2.* Eds. J.C. Smith and E. De Selincourt. London: Oxford University Press, 1912. Print.

John Goodby

Call Help

FANNY HOWE

At number 5 Church Street in Cork, you are safe from too much future. The webbed conservatory kitchen and a high wall outside provide time and chance to huddle among books and friends and translate, steal, verify and count.

> am
> out of
> harm's
> way
> here
>
> stone
> streaming
> glass
> opaque

Cork City holds the archetypal shape of an older Ireland, a Dublin of the fifties, with the river Lee reflecting bright Havana-like colors from the faces of buildings along the water. Neither idealised nor gentrified, Cork keeps its order intact. Stone naked in a surge of hills. Revolutionary graffiti and the bells of Shandon bang out the hours over the house where Trevor Joyce lived and wrote for years. In a sense, he is Cork. History marked, the dust of it rained on and modern life modest, orderly.

His poems, among other things, expose a supernatural nerve-connection between Early Chinese and Early Celtic poetry: I-empty poems at the point of being nature itself speaking: a mountain, a flower, a boat at sea, a tree, a latitudinal sympathy. What interests me is the ontological inversion that happens when things are turned around, and broken down, studied, then reclassified as poetry. This seems to me a prescient occupation. We may yet, soon, discover we have it all backwards. It isn't the desiring body that shapes the form, but an invisible coherence that creates the body which then tenses into sensation.

§

Once Trevor came down to Union Hall in West Cork to give a talk to some young Americans staying at a house that belongs to the Irish philosopher and novelist Richard Kearney.

We sat out in a glass room at a long table while Trevor talked about his poetry, then read some.

Geraniums were dried crisp against the hot glass, flies caught in webs and buzzing, but a bee was still free. He spoke about syllables, measures, history, corrupt texts, chance and deliberate appropriations like an expert on insects and biochemistry. I had never heard him talk like this before, not about his method of composition, and was bowled over when he read the resulting poetry, that was limpid, emotional.

This event and more since have made me know myself inadequate for the task of writing about his process. Nation and poetry are as intertwined as past and future and we each have our ways of thinking about them.

Luckily (for me) his thought turns hot in the process of preparing its appearance, and this way it acquires a deeply recognizable color.
With all the coded numbers and charts and beats, the little machine of a poem stands on its own two feet and bangs its drum.

§

A systems analyst for many years Trevor became a rare poet of the post-Cage matrix years: hyper-aware of what logical composition, grids, patterns, cubes, codes, and chance is engraved in lines of words. His translation of a painting by Botticelli doesn't seem to be seeking for a more perfect world as much as it is looking to see what figure might break out of the constraints As is so often the case, the figure is demented and deluded.

Above all, the figure is poor, naked, a body of failure, wrapped in social constraint and social contracts.

> court
> tombs
> constitute
> our earliest
> examples…

only the
largest
slabs
remain

fallen
displaced

smaller stones
purloined for
nearby walls
or roadworks

the ideal form
exists
in imagination
only

Corrupt texts and multi-revised ones, texts that are no longer available for us in their original English and other languages altogether (Chinese) are the sources of many "new" poems for him.

It was the "generation of complex formal dispositions of language which might correspond in some way to certain aspects of the world which interested me," he has written.

The poem that attracts him is loaded with gaps and errors but the desire that made it, keeps it: *amor fati*. Like Penelope's repetitive weave and unweave, the material is soaked in love and needs no more from anyone.

Translation work (for me) is an exercise in humility. The poem is not yours but each word is. The translator is the future, leaning over the given, which will never be his, because it is deceased, beyond ever finding except as a patch of DNA. Even in a resurrection, you do not see the same figure, the original, but a stranger.

No wonder we are fretful, prophetic even.

"Take charge

of the hoard
record

                    each unit
               of beauty
                    to calm
                         the storm."

                              §

Language holds secrets close to itself. Gershom Scholem said that irrational
insights "color" the results.

> "Just as the covenant is sown by 42 matings from a single seed, the
> engraved and holy name is sown by the 42 letters that describe the
> act of creation."

Out of his intense philological labors, Trevor happened on a wild figure,
farouche, sexually on fire, and ready to murder. Sweeny Peregrine.
(Frankenstein)

> Breaks the heart keening
> as the edge keen the king
> keen Niall Blackknee
> gracious as great.

                              §

Weapons and coins immured in the walls around him, are now visible;
straw and blood, the tools of composition for "the immediate future"—
because what he has been seeking is a world synonymous with our own,
locked into the casing of first texts, even into the walls of 5 Church Street
and the nearby cathedral and its strict tolling of the bells: are signals of an
evolving body, gracious as great.

Fanny Howe

Works Cited

Joyce, Trevor. 'The Phantom Quarry: Translating a Renaissance Painting into Modern Poetry'. *Enclave Review* 8 (2013): 5-8. Print.

——. 'torrential / penetrates / and rots'. *What's in Store: Poems 2000–2007*. Dublin: New Writers' Press; Willowdale, ON: The Gig, 2007. 218. Print.

——. 'court / tombs / constitute'. *What's in Store: Poems 2000–2007*. Dublin: New Writers' Press; Willowdale, ON: The Gig, 2007. 224. Print.

——. 'Causes of Affects: A Sentimental Retrospect.' *What's in Store: Poems 2000-2007*. Dublin: New Writers Press. Willowdale, ON: The Gig, 2007. 230. Print

——. 'Breaks the heart keening'. *What's in Store: Poems 2000–2007*. Dublin: New Writers' Press; Willowdale, ON: The Gig, 2007. 289. Print.

Joinery: Trevor Joyce's Lattice Poems

ERIC FALCI

A pair of lines from *Sole Glum Trek*, Trevor Joyce's 1967 debut volume
and the first publication by New Writers' Press, founded by Joyce with
Michael and Irene Smith that same year, offers a proleptic clue about the
kinds of poetic projects he would take up a quarter of a century later.
The final short section of 'Construction', which is dedicated primarily to
cataloguing the solidity and make-up of the substances – walls, pavements,
cobbles, "built stone", "each individual limestone cuboid" – that the
speaker encounters while walking in Dublin begins with these lines: "My
brain had built / A scheme of echoes" (20). 'Construction', unsurprisingly,
is densely constructed. Its topic is the materiality of the built environment
and the ways in which individuals come to know and relate to those spaces,
and its form mimics the divisions and subdivisions that would appear to,
inhibit, guide and coerce a city-walker. Its 36 lines are divided into three
main sections, each of which has one or two subsections; rather than a
smooth flow of lyric voicing, 'Construction' draws attention to its own
constructedness. This is not to say, however, that the poem radically
upends lyric conventions. As with the great majority of Joyce's early work,
"Construction" relies on a coherent lyric speaker whose tone draws in part
from earlier poets of urban alienation, with Baudelaire, Eliot and Kinsella
as key presiders. It is built out of irregular stanzas and features a number
of rhythmical patterns without submitting to a consistent metre. It is
primarily imagistic and, like many other poems from Joyce's three early
volumes – *Sole Glum Trek*, *Watches* (1969), and *Pentahedron* (1972) – it
remains within a fairly narrow scenic and atmospheric range.[1] In his early
poems, it is often raining or icy, usually grey or dark, and consistently
desolate, apart from the occasional appearance of a vagrant, an anonymous
worker or passer-by, a blackbird, various kinds of corpses, a set of gulls,
or rats – many rats inhabit these books. Instants of violence, brutality or
anomie surface frequently, and a sense of grim despair is pervasive.

So, in many ways, 'Construction' is a typical early Joyce poem, and
within their context the lines that I quote above function mainly as a
moment of self-reflexivity: the speaker, after having spent several stanzas
observing his surroundings, now turns inwards. This is a prototypical

lyric manoeuvre. While Joyce and Smith positioned the poets published by New Writers' Press and within its house journal, *The Lace Curtain*, as radical alternatives to what they saw as the debilitating conservatism and tired pieties of most Irish poetry, it is clear in retrospect that Joyce's early work is valuable not because it offers a full repudiation or reimagining of the basic modes of modern Irish lyric, but because it so fully displays its dissatisfaction with those modes while remaining unable to provide a viable formal alternative.[2] "A scheme of echoes" is a good description of the thematic concerns of Joyce's early work, but it also gets at its limitations: it remains caught in the echo chamber of modern Irish poetry's lyric topoi. It registers its discontent with the usual practices of Irish poetry, which he later describes as "a provincial literature, unambitious in its concerns, formally conservative, and rural in its outlook" ('New Writers' Press: The History of a Project' 276). However, it finds little room to manoeuvre outside of the conservative modes of modern Irish lyric.

If, however, we consider that phrase – "A scheme of echoes" – within the context of Joyce's more recent poetry, it provides a prescient primer to the formal innovations that this work undertakes. After three initial slim volumes and his version of the early Irish text *Buile Suibhne*, published in 1976 as *The Poems of Sweeny, Peregrine*, Joyce didn't publish any poetry for almost twenty years. During this period, Joyce turned his attention to reading Chinese and Japanese poetry and worked in the software industry. His reappearance on the poetry scene – with his 1995 volume, *stone floods* – initiated an extremely prolific period for Joyce, one remarkable for its range of formal experimentation. If one of the limitations of Joyce's early work was its tendency to stick to a small repertoire of motifs, techniques and shapes, then his later work is marked by a nearly obsessive desire not to repeat himself. The twenty-three poems in *stone floods* each seem to operate according to a different formal law, as though Joyce is deliberately working through a slew of lyric modes and rhetorical registers in order to understand the possibilities embedded within them. And several of his longer works largely abjure lyric form, whether the three prose pieces that comprise *Hopeful Monsters* (1998) – a bird parable and mythic bestiary, a cryptic forensic report and something that resembles an instruction manual putatively on governance, each featuring amalgamations reminiscent of the "New Sentence" writings by Language poets in the United States – or the double-entry form of 'Trem Neul' (1999), which is composed from an array of found materials and divides into information-rich prose passages on the left-hand side of the page and a series of simple questions, answers and statements that seem to come from a phrasebook on the right-hand side. The work collected in *What's in Store* (2007) continues this path of consistent reinvention, and it is filled with all manner of texts – translations, prose pieces, conceptual work and short lyrics. This hasty digest is meant to highlight one point: Joyce has worked diligently over the past fifteen or so years to forestall a characteristic style of, or approach to, poetic composition. The overdependence on a consistent style among Irish poets was one of the targets of early polemics by Smith and Joyce, and one can argue that Joyce's early work suffers from its reliance on one sort of stance – the alienated and belated *flâneur* picking over the remains and disgraces of modernity. His later work eschews such a consistent voicing, primarily by means of formal reinvention, but also by incorporating found texts that function in place of a unified lyric speaker.

The most intriguing set of poetic experiments that Joyce has so far attempted, and the set that is most illuminated by my touchstone phrase – "A scheme of echoes" – are his lattice poems of the late 1990s, and for the remainder of this essay I will work to illuminate their place within his larger body of work. After outlining the basic workings of these lattice poems, I will look in more detail at *Syzygy*, the most complex instance of this form. I will conclude by using these lattice poems to consider Joyce's place within the varieties of experimental poetry in Ireland. It seems significant that Joyce's return to poetry in the mid-1990s coincided with a moment of increased attention to linguistically innovative poetry across the United Kingdom and Ireland. It also seems significant that Joyce devoted a great deal of energy to his lattice poems at that time but has not gone back to them since. I will ultimately argue two related points: Joyce's lattice forms constitute a simultaneous reinvigoration and undermining of lyric form; and these poems in particular help to differentiate Joyce's poetry – as well as poetry by other innovative Irish poets such as Maurice Scully and Catherine Walsh – from many British and North American poetic experiments. They do not fully abandon the possibilities of lyric utterance, while simultaneously submitting the usual features of lyric to disruptive compositional strictures. The "scheme of echoes" that was a second-order observation in the early work becomes in the lattice poems a fully realised formal model, one that allows Joyce to render the actualities of late modernity's technocratic and brutal conditions (where schemes of all sorts abound), as well as to edge towards a critique of those conditions by way of a procedural deranging of lyric form.

There are eight lattice poems in total and all of them appear in Joyce's 2001 collected volume, *with the first dream of fire they hunt the cold*, hereafter *first dream of fire*. Seven appear in two groupings within a section of the volume titled "Shorter Poems (1995–1999)" and the eighth is *Syzygy*, which was initially published separately in 1998. Joyce's lattice poems take two forms, and I'll take each in turn before moving to a more extended reading of *Syzygy*. One type of lattice poem occurs when Joyce writes a poem "with" a previous text. There are three such poems in the volume: in two, Joyce embeds his own poem in between lines of poems by Michael Smith and Randolph Healy. In these poems, "Joinery" and "Let Happen", Joyce indents his own lines in order to differentiate them from the precursor poem. "Joinery" includes the entirety of a poem from Michael Smith's "Dedications", while in "Let Happen" Joyce takes ten discrete phrases from Healy's poem "The Rodin Sculpture Garden" and positions them as the first and last lines of each five-line stanza, with Joyce's own writing making up the interior lines.

'DARK SENSES PARALLEL STREETS' is the most ambitious of these "written-through" poems and differs from the other two. In this double-columned poem, Joyce places the entirety of Tom Raworth's "Dark Senses", sixteen quatrains in all, in the left-hand column of the page and joins it to a composition of his own on the right, which he titles "Parallel Streets" and which matches Raworth's poem line for line. As with the poems written through Smith's and Healy's texts, 'DARK SENSES PARALLEL STREETS' provides three different orders of reading. One can read only the left-hand column (Raworth's poem), only the right-hand column (Joyce's poem) or across the columns in order to produce the joint Raworth–Joyce text. "Dark Senses" cycles from topic to topic through a series of fiercely rendered images and scenes that explode into one another with Raworth's signature alacrity. Beginning with a description of an x-ray image, the poem moves quickly to recount a dream of walking "parallel streets / of tropical flames", then to a dinner scene and then to the various behaviours of the "unthinking insects" that come in and out of the "open window" where the "farewell meal" takes place. After considering the insect world and its "skeletons of organizations", the poem moves by way of "likenesses" back to the human world and its "gestures and rites" (180–181).

What seems to be an emerging commentary on the falsity and timidity of contemporary life soon turns into an almost hopeful – or entirely sarcastic – invocation of the power of tradition: "the experience of generations / proved far more effective // acts of representation respond / in order to survive desire / cheated by false hopes" (181). This, however, gives way to a series of images of mediatised reality (television weather forecasters) and environmental destruction, which shows the previous moment to be just another "false hope". Raworth's poem ends by questioning the ideology of the aesthetic and art's inability to effect actual change in the world:

> the nightmare atmosphere of ruin
> washes away in close-up
> striking spatial effects predicted
> if the mask is joyful
>
> produce a sublime gesture
> opposed to voice or action
> a system of reflections ordering
> the necessity of ornament (181)

The damaged world is obscured when ideology's "joyful" mask is brought back into the foreground (a "close-up / [of] striking spatial effects"). The "sublime gesture" produced does not actually work to improve the "atmosphere of ruin" but rather functions as a hall of mirrors, a "system of reflections" that, instead of encouraging "voice or action", merely details the necessary ordering of "ornament".

In addition to submitting to the constraint of writing within Raworth's original poem, Joyce adds a further limitation: each of the combined lines must contain eight words. Here we see Joyce's deep abiding interest in numerical patterns. The sixteen quatrains of 'Dark Senses' is doubled by Joyce's 'Parallel Streets', and the thirty-two quatrains that make up 'DARK SENSES PARALLEL STREETS' result in sixty-four lines of precisely eight words each. The poem squares itself. This formal perfection, perhaps problematic considering the critique of mere aesthetic fulfilment with which Raworth's poem concludes, is undercut by the multiple relationships that Joyce pursues between Raworth's original lines and his own graftings. At times the relationship is continuous, as in the first composite line of the poem:

> bones show through images   more opaque than tissue (180)

Here, Joyce's own line furthers the monologic voice that begins Raworth's poem, extending that voice's description of the x-ray image by explaining why it appears the way that it does. This is the most common stance that Joyce's lines take up in relation to Raworth's: they echo, annotate or amplify the phrase in the left column, and in this way Joyce aims to make his poem what he terms a "continuation" of 'Dark Senses' (240).

At other times, Joyce takes a slightly riskier approach. The beginning of the second stanza models a different relationship between the two sides of the text:

forgive me it's a dream	don't mention it
standing alone waving	it's easy to be fooled (180)

Joyce's poem is in conversation with Raworth's at this point, wryly putting the original poem "at ease" by responding to its anxieties. Instead of running parallel to 'Dark Senses', 'Parallel Streets' talks back to it, shifting into a colloquial register that has no precedent in Raworth's poem in order to subtly undercut the earlier poem's own "sublime gesture". Such interjections appear often enough to interrupt the overall sense of continuity between the two poems and, by the time we get to the final combined stanza, Joyce is conducting a much more complicated argument, both with Raworth's poem and with his own combinatory project:

the nightmare atmosphere of ruin	admitting sensory leakage
washes away in close-up	what could you expect
striking spatial effects predicted	to attract all comers
if the mask is joyful	after so much

produce a sublime gesture	when several significant figures
opposed to voice or action	question whether pleading
a system of reflections ordering	direct and material interest
the necessity of ornament	can openly be countenanced (181)

Several of Joyce's additions to Raworth's final stanzas clarify the terms of Raworth's critique – the "close-up / striking spatial effects" are merely a mode of advertisement, a way "to attract all comers" – but others, especially in the final stanza of the poem, seem to construct a different sort of argument out of Raworth's more elliptical conclusion. The "voice or action" foreclosed in Raworth's poem become actualised in Joyce's: they are attached to "several significant figures" who ask a fairly straightforward question: "whether pleading / direct and material interest / can openly be countenanced". Here, Joyce's joinery heightens the menace implied in Raworth's poem. The absence of "voice or action" in Raworth's poem becomes the wrong sort of "voice or action" in Joyce's. That is to say, the "several significant figures" who can speak and act are "opposed to voice or action" and the poem devolves into a cross-cut of bureaucratic discourse and a blank system of "reflections" and "ornament". In these final stanzas, the relationship between the two texts becomes more fully dialectical, with Joyce working to reshape the implications of Raworth's poem rather than to make local comments on or additions to it.

The written-through poems allow Joyce to experiment with stitching other texts – both found and chosen – into his own poetic structures. In this way, they serve – in part, and perhaps only within the retrospective context of his later work – as preparatory studies. One can suggest something similar in regards to the other four lattice poems that appear in the 'Shorter Poems (1995–1999)' section of *first dream of fire*. However, instead of providing Joyce with a space to work out strategies of intertextuality, 'Approach of Bodies Falling in Time of Plague', 'Proceeds of a Black Swap', 'Data Shadows' and 'behaviour self!' each give him a chance to tinker with methods of procedural rearrangement. He brings these two modes together in *Syzygy*, and it is tempting to see the seven lattice poems that occur later in the collected volume as studies for *Syzygy*. Joyce was clearly working on these poems at around the time he was working on *Syzygy*, but it isn't at all clear whether the seven lattice poems grouped in two sections within the collected volume can actually be construed as études for *Syzygy*. For one reason, Joyce places those poems later than *Syzygy* in *first dream of fire*, which is ordered, with some adjustments, chronologically. For another, I don't know whether in fact Joyce wrote *Syzygy* after the seven other lattice poems, even though it is certainly a much more complex example of the same type of procedural text. Nevertheless, the seven "preparatory" lattice poems do help to get a better handle on the structure of *Syzygy*, and so I'll begin with them before spending more time detailing *Syzygy*'s complexities. In two of the three written-through poems, the stable unit is the precursor poem itself. When writing with poems by Smith and Raworth, Joyce includes all of the lines of those poems in their original order. He takes more liberties with Healy's work in 'Let Happen': he doesn't use every part of Healy's poem and doesn't maintain the order of the lines he does use. He doesn't, however, alter the phrases and lines from Healy that he does incorporate into 'Let Happen'. In a similar way, the line is the fixed unit in the four "shorter" lattice poems. In each, Joyce offers a series of unpunctuated lines arranged into stanzas and then offers a second iteration of those lines, rearranged and divided into differently shaped stanzas. All four of the poems share a similar pattern of line rearrangement, which leads one to think that Joyce used the same spreadsheet program to compose each of them. They, even more than the "written-through" poems, have the feel of studies in a procedural method. 'Approach of Bodies Falling in Time of Plague' and 'Proceeds of a Black Swap' have the same number of lines, share the same stanzaic pattern and their lines are rearranged in precisely the same way. 'Data Shadows' and 'behaviour self!' are each longer than the other two, but Joyce uses a similar, though extended, procedure for determining the ordering of lines in the second iteration in each poem. To get a clearer sense of Joyce's project in these texts, I'll focus on 'Proceeds of a Black Swap', after which I'll turn to *Syzygy*.

'Proceeds of a Black Swap', like the other lattice poems, does not contain a clear narrative, and the individual lines only sometimes coordinate with each other. The opening couplet is, then, something of an anomaly:

> this morning we saw blood on the floor
> of all the major exchanges (161)

In his notes, Joyce includes the definition of a "black swap", as taken from P.W. Joyce's *English as We Speak It in Ireland*: "when two fellows have two wretched articles – such as two old penknives – each thinking his own to be the worst in the universe, they sometimes agree for the pure humour of the thing to make a *black swop*, i.e. to swop without first looking at the articles. When they are looked at after the swop, there is always great fun" (*first dream of fire* 239). Joyce posits a rather different outcome than the "great fun" the two fellows have when they see the proceeds of the swap. He translates the scene from an out-of-the-way place in Ireland to the world's major stock exchanges, but keeps the two fellows who exchange, as P.W. Joyce's example has it, "old penknives". Based on all of the "blood on the floor", the two fellows seem to have been less than pleased with the exchange – they each get back exactly what they were trying to get rid of – and so proceed to get into a knife-fight.

Such speculations about the poem's created world, as wild as they might be, are quickly made irrelevant, as it soon shifts away from the bloody scene:

> here fire displays its worst intensities
> we entered into certain of them found us embarrassed
> discovering some factor in the difficult atmosphere
> as deeds grow vague remembrance falls from vogue (161)

Gone is the blood on the floor and the world of finance, replaced by a lyric space – "here" – inhabited by lyric figures, a "we" / "us" grouping that is purely textual. Some kind of event – fire-based, intense, difficult – has wrecked the atmosphere in which the band of adventurers (the "we" who enter into the "worst intensities" of "fire" in order to discover "some factor in the difficult atmosphere") are placed. As the event fades, their "deeds grow vague", and the vocalic drop from "vague" to "vogue" mimics the dropping from memory of whatever event has occurred.

The next quatrain recategorises the obscure events of the previous two stanzas while reintroducing the poem's plural subject:

> redress turns myth and cruentation a lost hope
> made weep again the irregular
> when it came our turn for we too have had our losses
> where growing fields still answer to good names (161)

A series of "swaps" occur here: the attempt to redress the forgetting of events turns them into myth. The unattributed blood in the opening couplet has been connected to a body and to an act of murder ("cruentation" refers to the notion that blood seeping out of a corpse indicated the proximity of the murderer). The presence of the blood itself, which would – if we were operating according to some forms of medieval Germanic law – be "hopeful" in that it would provide evidence of the murderer, becomes here merely a "lost hope" and the irregular weeping in the second line refuses to provide anything like a locatable subject. The second half of this quatrain brings back the poem's protagonists, who now are facing losses – another black swap perhaps – and who are relocated back into an environment, though one now suggestive of the pastoral spaces ("growing fields") of the aristocracy ("good names" to which the fields are still answerable). Another sort of economic system is put into play, one that is quite far from the mutual poverty of the black swap.

The third quatrain begins by indexing the effects of the system of ownership implied in the previous line and then works through a series of images of economic hardship or dispossession:

> to fix obliterate possess and cleanse
> often been broke then perforce broke odd eggs to feed ourselves
> dark maps that underfoot have grown familiar
> the least upset is not to recollect their dole (161)

The same system of ownership and power that calls fields to "answer to good names" is the one that will "fix obliterate possess and cleanse". Compacted within this line are many of the crimes and horrors committed in the name of progress and rationality. The voicing shifts in the second line of the quatrain and we move from a position of near-infinite power (the verbs in the first line remain unconjugated, infinitive forms unswayed by questions of duration or person) to one of brokenness and disadvantage. After a line in which possession of, or at least knowledge of, the land is derived from experience rather than inheritance or ownership, the final line of the stanza is almost entirely untethered from normative grammar. The reference to the dole places the poem within the context of the welfare state, although there is little else in the line to further such a context. This line refuses to conform to the rules of grammatical exchange, with the first half of the line disjointed from the second. If we take "the least upset" as a singular subject (so that it agrees with "is not") then it fails to "swap" with the plural object at the end of the line ("their dole"). There are other failures of sense and reference: What does it mean to not "recollect" one's dole? That someone has forgotten to remember to collect it? Is there an extremely sidewise allusion to that famous phrase from Wordsworth's preface to *Lyrical Ballads*? And if so, in what way does this allusion "work" within the context of the rest of the poem? Perhaps one way to momentarily settle things is to conceive of this final line as another kind of bloodletting, as a moment of grammatical violence that has brought all manner of exchange to a halt.

If we entertain this possibility, then the final line of the poem, set off by itself, becomes an almost too apposite return to the context of the beginning:

they mopped up quick could our strong agents err? (161)

The blood that has been on the floor since the beginning of the poem is finally cleaned up and the collective speaker – now morphed into something like the security services or a dark outfit assigned to protect the sanctity of the exchanges – asks the reader sardonically whether there was ever any doubt that the mess would be cleared away: "could our strong agents err?" This act of obliteration is one that is both irrevocable (the poem is over) and potentially redemptively ambiguous: once we remind ourselves of Paul de Man's reading of the final lines of Yeats' 'Among School Children', then any rhetorical question is not an instance of certainty or authorial assurance, but of the text's uneasy fissuring. Considering that the crucial aspect of this poem is that it is repeated, reconfigured, on the following page, then the reassertion of systemic power that occurs at the end of this poem is not, in fact, conclusively total.

And this seems to be the burden of Joyce's lattice poems. They are ceaselessly interested in tracking the various modes of coercion and brutality by which the globe is run, and this, coupled with their tendency to front the public languages of commerce, bureaucracy and instrumentalised abstraction, makes for texts seemingly enthralled by power. The undoing of such enthralment, if it is to occur, has to occur at the moment when the poem is shuffled and replayed. Like the other "minor" lattice poems (with *Syzygy* as the major lattice poem), 'Proceeds of a Black Swap' cannot entirely reconfigure its materials, bound as it is to maintaining the integrity of each line within the process of rearrangement. But what the second poem of 'Proceeds of a Black Swap' can do is to cancel, or at least partially invalidate, the progression of the first poem. As I've mentioned, the first poem consists of stanzas of two, four, four, four and one lines, respectively. The second poem consists of stanzas of four, five, five, and four lines, respectively, with each stanza separated by a black dot. In addition, the second poem restarts itself twice, beginning the first two stanzas with the first line of the first part of the poem, and the second two with the first poem's second line. The other minor lattice poems proceed in the same way and this has the effect of factoring out the poem into interrelated, but non-progressive, bundles. The composition of each of these bundles is presumably predetermined by whatever procedural constraint Joyce has put into place. But procedurally rearranging the lines of the poem, while keeping each individual line intact, makes for a reading experience that is oddly freeing.

Because each stanza in the second poem stands apart as its own unit, and because the first two poems and the last two poems begin with the same lines, the kinds of micro-narratives that emerged in the first stanza are no longer fully plausible, even as we are unable to fully forget them. Both of the first two stanzas begin with the same moment of unexplained violence that we originally encountered:

> this morning we saw blood on the floor
> as deeds grow vague remembrance falls from vogue
> redress turns myth and cruentation a lost hope
> the least upset is not to recollect their dole

Eric Falci

•

this morning we saw blood on the floor
discovering some factor in the difficult atmosphere
made weep again the irregular
dark maps that underfoot have grown familiar
they mopped up quick could our strong agents err? (162)

In the first stanza, this moment of violence is compacted with its forgetting
and potential remembering (the "redress" through myth), but the final line
remains stubbornly untethered to those around it. This could be partially
explained by pulling "dole" out of its immediate economic context and
thinking of it as more generally indicating a part of something or a division.
This, then, becomes a way to conceive of the poem as a structure, and we
start to get a clearer sense of it as a set of semi-articulating parts that don't
cohere into a totality. The second stanza restarts the poem, and the new
lines that now follow the repeated line initially begin to give an explanation
of the bloody scene, but this is quickly derailed as the third and fourth lines
gravitate towards each other, but away from the lines surrounding them.
The factor in the "difficult atmosphere" disagrees with the weeping of the
"dark maps" (both syntactically and sensically) and the vague narrative
about possession and ownership that arises in the first poem is disabled by
the second. The return of the final line of the first poem ("they mopped up
quick could our strong agents err?"), which in that earlier context indicated
a reassertion of a system of power, now seems less the nefarious statement of
an insider than the empty repetition of a structure locked into its patterns.
Although each of the four stanzas are kept apart on the page, the first two
and the last two constitute pairs, since they begin with the same line. In
the same way, the middle two stanzas are linked by the fact that they share
the same last line. The third stanza spins together two motifs from the first
poem: some band of adventurers in the process of discovery and images
of economic hardship. The fourth removes the scrim of socio-economic
activity (and human activity more generally) and operates in the elemental
register often favoured by Joyce:

of all the major exchanges
we entered into certain of them found us embarrassed
when it came our turn for we too have had our losses
often been broke then perforce broke odd eggs to feed ourselves
they mopped up quick could our strong agents err?

of all the major exchanges
here fire displays its worst intensities
where growing fields still answer to good names
to fix obliterate possess and cleanse (162)

The "exchange" in the third stanza initially is a kind of marketplace the "we" enters in order to better their economic position, with the double grammar in the second line – in which the "exchanges" ("them") moves from an object to a subject position – signalling a reversal that ends with the original "we" in a state of embarrassment, unable to escape their poverty and hunger. The mopping up that occurs at the end clears all human presence from the poem and the "strong agents" seem transformed into impersonal forces. This swap is fully realised in the final stanza, in which the exchange has lost its social connotations and becomes something nearer to a natural process, the fire that begins to overrun the still "growing fields" and which will lead to a quite different process of obliteration, possession and cleansing. The kind of totality darkly hinted at in the first poem has been reformulated to refer to the earth's own cycles of creation and destruction. The poem's final swap keeps the poem's basic processes but switches frames: we've moved from the realm of economic and social exchanges to the non-human exchanges of the earth – its elements, its atmosphere, its cycles of obliteration and repair. Even as the basic units of the poem stay the same, their exchange from one poem to the next makes for a reading experience that remains, like many of the poem's soldered phrases, decidedly unmoored but oddly fascinating.

This really shouldn't be the case. 'Proceeds of a Black Swap' does not offer its readers much in the way of aggregative pleasure. There are phrases of compelling strangeness, but these phrases are often repulsed by those around them. As I have been doing here, a reading can work through the two iterations of the poem in order to find points of contact and divergence. And a reading of the poem can be concretised at certain moments when a formal effect converges with a semantic possibility in the line, or when several lines in a row seem to build upon one another. But the simple fact that the poem is built out of discrete, reshuffle-able lines thwarts the desire to make them signify together. Individual lines may make more or less sense, but trying to make the abstract structure of the poem – its procedural lattice – work in tandem with its line-by-

Eric Falci

line unfolding proves to be frustrating. This frustration has, I think, value, much of which emerges as an incommensurably dual experience: the reader can take pleasure from comprehending the poem's procedure and can take pleasure from individual moments of the poem. But these two sorts of pleasure work against each other, which makes for frustration at a higher level. This frustration, however, is part of the design, and the value of Joyce's lattice poems is that they offer both kinds of pleasure without fully allowing either to stabilise or to hypostasise. A closer look at *Syzygy* will give a better sense of the kind of double reception that these poems provide.

Syzygy is certainly the most complex of the lattice poems and it has received the most attention from critics. It is also the poem for which Joyce has provided the most detailed compositional history. In the notes to *first dream of fire*, Joyce explains that the poem is based on a palindromic structure drawn from Guillaume de Machaut's medieval cancrizans *Ma fin est dans ma commencement*. In such a form, Joyce writes, "one or more parts proceed normally, while the imitating voice or voices give out the melody backwards", to which Machaut adds a third voice that is palindromic within itself (237). The first part of *Syzygy*, entitled 'The Drift', is made up of twelve stanzas of somewhere between ten and thirteen lines, each of which can stand alone as a discrete lyric, but which together comprise a digest of Joyce's favourite themes and strategies. He plays disparate scales against each other (geological time vs. human time, the galactic vs. the bodily), overlaps various systems of order and symmetry and watches them undo each other, presents moments of creation and traces their disintegration, sketches and critiques systems of control, juxtaposes stark images from the natural world with the human destruction of that same world and catalogues various instances and modes of violence.

Each of the twelve poems that make up 'The Drift' has its own internal logic, and several of the poems have quite straightforward topics. The first outlines a multi-scalar instance of creation and destruction, beginning with a sonic birth within an amalgam of minerals ("and then there is this sound / that starts with a scarcely audible / rustling inside gold the whisper / echoing within the diamond") and ending with a moment of human catastrophe ("eventually / you attend to the infinities / of numbers shattering / the shriek that is the change / of several millions") (136). The second sketches a scene of natural cyclicity – salmon "leaping from the mouth / up the cold fresh stream" in order to spawn – that has been captured and instrumentalised within systems of human industry: "until the fixed mesh abstracts / unerringly each hour / with all its clamouring brood / jerking routinely to the tune" (136). The fourth begins with a quasi-Beckettian roadside tableau and transforms into a disquisition on the construction of the vocal apparatus, the economy of speaking and listening and the voice's sounding of the "history / of all the ordinary / aches we suffer" (137). The fifth offers an instance of imperial power and of the urge to standardise and regularise that characterises regimes of political control. The eighth details a scene of environmental damage caused by a set of jugs that, supposedly "standing sealed and safe", "exhale", "intoxicating" their surroundings (139). The eleventh presents a seemingly tranquil nocturne that on second glance becomes a scene of frozen death, an "exposure to the extreme" (141). Others lack such a (somewhat) stable diegetic space and instead juxtapose disparate discourses and logics, allowing Joyce to combine more freely his favoured motifs. In each poem there are lines and phrases of stunning power and even of crystalline beauty, and part of the readerly interest in the poem is in watching such moments of penetrating lucidity get rearranged or deranged by the lines around them. We are made to experience moments of seeming lyric interiority being unrigged by alternate, and incommensurate, registers.

The relationship between 'The Drift' and the second text that comprises *Syzygy*, 'The Net', is both lucid and complex. Joyce has provided an extensive description of the composition of the two poems. He emphasises their cellular nature: 'The Drift' is made up of three groups of four poems, with, as he notes, "each lyric originally composed as a chain of twenty four phrases" ('The Construction of *Syzygy*'). Joyce constructed 'The Net' by procedurally rearranging the phrases that make up 'The Drift', using a spreadsheet to realise their combination and ordering. 'The Net' is composed of twenty-four tercets, with the first line of each tercet being composed of phrases from the first four lyrics in 'The Drift', the second line of each tercet composed of phrases from the middle four lyrics and the third line composed of phrases from the final four lyrics. So, for example, the first line of 'The Net', "and then there is this sound the red noise of bones", is constructed out of phrase cells from the first lines of the first four lyrics in 'The Drift'. The final line of each tercet reverses the order of the initial set of permutations, and so the final line of the poem repeats the first line of the poem. The first and third lines are analogous to the initial melodic voice and its inversion in Machaut's crab-canon, and the interior line of each tercet corresponds roughly to the interior melodic line, itself a palindrome. Joyce hit upon the structure of the poem first and then decided upon the words that would populate this structure. He settles on three found texts, one from a poem by Pablo Neruda (the line quoted above), one from a story within the Irish oral tradition that Joyce learns from Sean Ó Boyle's discussion of *The Irish Song Tradition* and one from "the financial pages of some paper I've long forgotten" (238–239). He adds to this trio a line of his own composition and then breaks the text down into cellular units and uses these to fill out the basic substance of the poem. Even without delving into every aspect of Joyce's compositional scheme, I think that this sketch of *Syzygy*'s genesis gives a sense of the complex constructivism at work in Joyce's lattice poetry. At one level, Joyce employs compositional constraints in the spirit of OuLiPo poetry and certain forms of conceptual writing, and so we can consider *Syzygy* as a machinic text in the sense that Joyce decided ahead of time on the kind of procedural machine that would govern the production of the text.[3] However, Joyce complicates such an approach, mainly because he decouples the structural mechanism for generating the poem from the process of choosing the words of the poem. He came up with the spreadsheet procedure ahead of time and so, as he says, had "already decided the mapping between each phrase of 'The Drift' and the corresponding composite lines of 'The Net'" before choosing the words and phrases of the poem ("The Construction of *Syzygy*"). So, while 'The Drift' provides the phrasal materials that get caught up in the procedural mechanism of 'The Net', some of the composite phrases that appear in 'The Net' actually "predate" 'The Drift', lines that were found or free-composed ahead of time. A systemic reciprocity is at work, and so it becomes impossible to definitively claim that one poem precedes the other. Of course, in the published volume 'The Drift' comes before 'The Net', but any reading experience would be likely to toggle incessantly between one text and the other, searching for their exact mode of relation. To put it somewhat too simply, 'The Drift' and 'The Net' comprise a syzygy.

What interests me most about *Syzygy* is that even as it is a procedural text, one whose complex constructivism would seem to banish all traces of lyric – expressivity, voicing, subjectivity, interiority – it is impossible to think about this poem entirely outside of the category of lyric, if we take *lyric* to designate a mode of concentrated writing (i.e. writing that is attuned in some way to its own processes and that manifests this attuning via formal concentration – rhythmic, metric, sonic, imagistic, rhetorical, morphological) whose primary function isn't narrative, dramatic, informational or propositional. Even a thorough awareness of the poem's construction doesn't exhaust an interest in the poem. One still feels compelled to *read* it, even after one has accounted for how it came to be and has determined its guiding procedure. This is, of course, not a structure of readerly feeling unique to Joyce's work. It seems as though much of the most powerful procedural or conceptual writing provides interest well beyond the knowledge of its construction or the understanding of its concept. Such works demand to be read through, to be experienced as processes and not merely as outcomes. *Syzygy* demands this kind of attention.

There are several reasons for this. Perhaps the simplest is that, on the evidence of the poem, Joyce is still heavily invested in producing moments of lyric density – moments generated by the triple impulse to describe the world, to reflect on and conceptualise such descriptions and to remake such moments in language. And so, the poem includes a number of passages that provide a great deal of readerly pleasure. Such moments – "the sun leans down / and lifts the sea", "the flickering of the fields whispering" or "the dream on the grass / hearing each hour" (139, 142, 144) – are strewn throughout both parts of the poem. However, because of the demands of the poem's composite structure, and because a reader knows that there is a predetermined structure at work that produces and orders such moments, it remains impossible to consider them purely within the category of interiority or expression even as one can't help but to keep such notions in play. Once a reader knows the construction of the poem – and Joyce has aimed to assure that any reader could easily attain this knowledge, either within the discursive notes to the poem or in ancillary texts, such as his brief essay 'The Construction of *Syzygy*', which is freely available online – passages of lyric intensity cannot remain simply that. They are neither the free and autonomous instantiations of writerly power, nor are they the determinate effects of structure. As readerly experiences, Joyce's lattice poems provide something like a cyborg lyric. They are co-composed by the machine that Joyce has established in order to write them and by a writerly agent who provides materials for the machine to work through and who adapts those workings-through according to a set of logics not determined by the writing machine.

'The Net' does not make for a coherent reading experience, and because – presumably – a reader will come to 'The Net' just after finishing 'The Drift', the way in which 'The Net' constructs a "scheme of echoes" from the previous text will probably be the most prominent aspect of the poem. All the words and phrases in 'The Net' have appeared before, often in more coherent configurations somewhere within the dozen lyrics of 'The

Eric Falci

Drift', and so uncanny and estranging frustration is likely to be a reader's initial affect. All is familiar – echoic – but of an exceeding strangeness. Neither 'The Drift' nor 'The Net' includes any punctuation, and the tendency for individual phrases and words in both poems to atomise makes it difficult to build up syntactic structures into hierarchical relationships. The micronarratives that are at least partially apparent in certain sections of 'The Drift' have been pulverised, and so one is often constructing one's own readerly net in order to catch what bits of sense remain. At other times, one simply catches the alienated shreds of sound and the unstrung words within the "echoing apparatus" (142) transfer of 'The Net'.

There is not space to provide a commentary on all of the poem's 24 tercets, but I would like to isolate a single tercet in order to concretise my sense of the kind of readerly attention that *Syzygy* demands. Taking a tercet out of context seems, of course, a wilful violation of the poem's crystalline structure, but it also seems to honour something of the poem's concept. One drifts through the net and brings to light a find. Here is the fifth stanza of the poem:

> the cold rustling on the road will get out
> surface of your voice exhale presence
> the flickering of the fields whispering (142)

In quite a number of ways, this tercet is not at all indicative of the poem as a whole. This is perhaps why I have chosen it: its clarity is deeply unexpected. Many of the other stanzas feature a-grammatical phrases and unmoored words. Considering the procedure that generates the poem – a spreadsheet divvying up phrases according to Joyce's pre-set rules – such non-normative word strings are exactly what we would expect. Here, though, in the fifth stanza, something truly strange happens. The procedure has thrown up an almost perfectly intact and utterly limpid moment of lyric intensity. There is a unified environmental space from which the poem emerges. It is cold, probably winter, or at least late autumn, since one can see one's breath: the exhalations have "presence". There is a road. A field. An icy wind that causes rustling on the one and the other to flicker (perhaps barren stems ruffled by wind, flickering into and out of the light). The "flickering" perhaps indicates an evening scene: the field flickers as though toggling between light and dark. Apart from the noise the wind causes as it passes along and through the earth's objects and scapes, the tercet is nearly silent. There is a voice mentioned – "your voice" – but it is a mechanism for breath ("exhale presence") rather than for speech. The tercet is referential, expressive, deeply felt. It makes a bid for sublime stillness. It attempts to animate the earth.

And yet, we know that this tercet is the outcome of Joyce's machine. And we can reverse engineer the tercet in order to source its materials. The first line must be drawn from the first four poems of 'The Drift' and its four cells (the cold / rustling / on the road / will get out) are taken from, respectively, the second line of the second poem, the third line of the first poem, the third line of the fourth poem and the second line of the third poem. The second line of the tercet must be taken from the middle quartet in 'The Drift', and its four cells (surface / of your voice / exhale / presence) are drawn from, again respectively, the third line of the sixth poem of 'The Drift', the third line of the seventh poem, the first line of the eighth poem and the third line of the fifth poem. The tercet's third line would be constructed from the final four poems in 'The Drift' and its four cells (the flickering / of / the fields / whispering) are taken from the third line of the eleventh poem, the third line of the twelfth poem, the second line of the ninth poem and the third line of the tenth poem. This all would have been what the spreadsheet demanded. As Joyce says in 'The Composition of *Syzygy*', the precise structural correspondences between 'The Drift' and 'The Net' were mapped before the words were in place. The wonderful winter lyric that appears as the fifth stanza of 'The Net' was predetermined. It depended on nothing like the impulses out of which we usually imagine poems happening. There is no recollection of a spontaneous overflow of powerful feelings. There is a grid, and a formula for filling out that grid. And there are words chosen later. Which are then given over to the grid. The winter nocturne created by this procedure is, simply, an outcome of that procedure. It is serendipitous.

And yet, one wonders, did Joyce rig the game? Was this a privileged, a lynchpin moment for the poem, when Joyce, instead of simply applying the procedure to the words freely and objectively chosen, chose the words to fit the procedure? Did he ensure that the spreadsheet found winter in the fifth tercet? This, I think, doesn't matter. Part of the pleasure of procedural works occurs when a presumably objective and non-feeling writing machine produces a moment of uncanny familiarity, of human feeling. And, in any case, one's reading of this tercet cannot rest upon either a fierce adherence to simply what is there in the three lines or upon an abyssal recourse to compositional design. These are merely three lines within a "scheme of echoes", and none of the echoes have been accounted for. Accounting for

Eric Falci

echoes dismantles the tercet's isolate wonder. The tercet's most mellifluous and exorbitantly poetical line, "the flickering of the fields whispering", is built from phrase cells that appear in quite different contexts in 'The Drift'. "The flickering" occurs in another wintry moment in the eleventh poem of 'The Drift', but it is a moment not of tranquil, but of deadly, stillness: though never mentioned directly, a corpse seems to inhabit the eleventh poem, a death caused by "exposure to the extreme". In a similar fashion, the alliterative partner of "the flickering" – "the fields" – is also drawn from a deathly moment in 'The Drift'. The ninth poem begins:

> millions are too vast
> cruelly they hunt the fields
> and bring down awkwardly
> the quickening in its course
> behind their staggering weakness
> leaves devastation and impersonal rage (140)

The tercet's calm winter fields are, in their earlier context, killing fields, where millions are hunted, massacred and left for dead by a total system of violence ("impersonal rage"). The fields' "whispering" is drawn from a less extreme moment of 'The Drift', although even here the earlier context troubles the tercet's winter scene:

> the tune of several mysteries
> what brought this on
> the sand whispering
> in your veins
> what wind of knives could
> buzz the nodding headbone blind (140)

The winter scene of the tercet is made partially from a desert scene in 'The Drift' and, as with "flickering" earlier, there is another corpse. Instead of a death from exposure to the cold, this tenth poem from 'The Drift' includes a death from exposure to heat. Or perhaps from violence: the "wind of knives" may refer not to the sting of sandy winds but to an attack by blades. In either case, the skull is left to nod in the wind and the peaceful winds across the wintry fields in the tercet are inverted grotesquely. Even the second cell of the tercet, the bare "of" that links "the flickering" and "the fields", is drawn from a sinister moment in the final poem of 'The Drift':

we suffer an old vertigo
that strikes with the first dream
of irresistible winds
across these settlements (141)

A scene of pastoral order in the tercet is partially constituted from a
scene of radical disorder in 'The Drift'. "Of" keeps its basic prepositional
function as it is shifted from one text to the other, but it drags along with
it turmoil, suffering and a sort of dream violence that takes place in an
ambiguous sort of human community. The passage of lyric simplicity that
I pulled from 'The Net' is built from moments of death, violence and
disorder. Because of the way in which individual words and phrases are
exchanged between 'The Drift' and 'The Net', it is crucial to account for
the implications of these exchanges. The construction of *Syzygy* enforces
a reciprocal reading that ultimately affords a readerly experience in which
neither of the two poems' parts is stiffened into an artifactual lyric. Both
remain in process. The unlikely and serendipitous tercet in 'The Net' is
prohibited from standing as a poetic moment that simply captures the
calm of a winter's night. Rather, the materials that make up that tercet
hold on to their earlier connotations and contexts, and so it can't be read
without keeping in mind the violence and disorder embedded within the
"scheme of echoes" underlying it.

In the lattice poems, and most powerfully in *Syzygy*, Joyce manages
to splice together lyric form and procedural practice, which ultimately
intervenes in and disrupts the radical/conservative split that has long
shaped our understanding of the range of poetry in Britain and Ireland
since the 1950s. He maintains the densities that we associate with lyric
form – indeed, what the lattice poems provide, perhaps above all else, is a
chance to watch highly charged and compacted bits of language interact
with other highly charged bits of language. At the same time, their
procedures and arbitrary operations foreclose on another aspect central
to lyric writing: its supposed basis in expressivity. By constructing a text
that necessarily requires multiple readings and that doesn't fully privilege
one progression over another, Joyce finds a way to preserve the critical
capacities of lyric. And by fashioning a poem that has to talk to itself, Joyce
has provided a way to dialectise lyric form.

This is, of course, not the only way to do this. Other Irish experimental
poets have taken different paths in order to find a way out of what they
perceive as the confines of lyric form. Like many innovative British poets
since the 1960s, both Catherine Walsh and Maurice Scully have drawn on

open field poetics – as formulated by Charles Olson and others who were following up on the modernist long forms of Ezra Pound and William Carlos Williams – in their attempt to move away from Irish poetry's dependence on traditional lyric structures and modes. They both employ different sorts of lattices, and a brief look at their work will serve as the conclusion to this essay, and will help me to better contextualise Joyce's project.

Just as *lattice* is my favoured term for describing the Joyce poems that I've discussed so far, *reticle* becomes the primary term in an account of Maurice Scully's long project, *Things that Happen*, a series of eight volumes covering about 600 pages and composed over twenty-five years. Three poems are entitled "Reticle", "reticulated" appears twice and "reticula" and "reticulate" each appear once. The words *reticular* or *reticulated* describe net-like structures, ranging from a net, trellis or lattice (another favourite Scully word) to a more abstract or virtual network. As a term to name poems, and, at a second remove, to describe them, it seems most important to note that a reticle can be both a material object and a non-material, abstract configuration. Imagining a poem as a net provides a new way to conceive of it as both a closed and open form. A net hold things and lets things go, and what "belongs" in a net is partly a function of what happens to have made it into its openings. As a way to describe individual poems and longer aggregations, it suggests both arrangement and porosity and indicates both structure and structure's hollows.

Scully's reticles are quite different than Joyce's procedural nets. Attempting to apprehend the immediacies of the actual world while fronting its own mediations of this engagement, *Things that Happen* undertakes an expansive epistemological project. Catching the immediacies of experience within the non-immediacies of the poetic page requires a commitment to detail acts of perceiving and modes of knowing, but also a relinquishment to the varieties of flux that aren't catchable. The "inner reticulate world" not only refers to the overlapping networks that make up our inner lives, but also to the limen between inner and outer worlds (*Humming* 93). For Scully, "our understanding's reticulated" because our means of ordering the world involves the maintaining of many, often incompatible, nets, and because our understanding gets "reticulated" each time it comes up against the world (*Five Freedoms of Movement* 70). This act of extensive "netting" is our means of experience:

> I mean, sifting the word *if* for many years brings clarity,
>   maybe. Flecks & spherules… (*Livelihood* 107)

Scully's work reticulates because it uses lyric's possible methods of netting (genres, figures, modes, stances) while abstracting, undoing or transforming those nets so that they are open to what eludes them.

Scully's poetry is reticular both in terms of theme and scope. Calling a very long set of poems *Things that Happen* is deeply cagey. It can signal that the poet-figure will be the organiser of all the things and their mode of happening, but it can also signal that the poems will include many things that happen outside of the poet's control but within his range, and this is the impulse that dominates Scully's work. Different voices, scenarios and contexts intervene and interfere. And considering that Scully's project extends over multiple volumes and many years, is threaded together primarily by way of motifs and repeated images and is both a single extended work and a collection of discrete poems (often with lyric titles like "Sonnet" or "Song", although without ever resembling sonnets or any other fixed forms), the net-like quality of *Things that Happen* is perhaps most powerfully apparent in Scully's general approach rather than in any overt theme or programme. The poem is a reticle because it will catch some things and not others:

> full of. everything differently
> precisely in each different net.
> full of the tiny bright word*k*s of
> discarded invention. our lives,
> glittering, reticulated. (29)

This passage, from *The Basic Colours*, the second volume in *Things that Happen*, is a distillation of Scully's larger project. "Each different net" is full of "discarded invention", which is at once "our lives" and "tiny bright word*k*s". This nearly unsayable neologism is the key to the passage. The "word" that is also an off-kilter "work" is a rescoring of "our lives", which are both glittering (Scully's lighting effects are systemic) and reticulated. "Word*k*s" itself is a reticulation. Two words are caught up in each other's nets. A funky bit of soldering, this bit of newness is an emblem of Scully's interpolation of activity and writing. Each poem is shot through with material unassimilable to it, distorting and morphing in every direction depending on the kind of material involved, and enacting all sorts of captures and counter-captures between the poem and the poem's recalcitrant materials. And as individual poems and passages are strung together into longer strands, both losing their status as autonomous lyrics and becoming caught up in and changed by proximate poems, Scully's reticulations become clearer. If Joyce's work is actively reticulated or latticed, then Scully's work is ambiently so: the sheer length and scope of the project requires a flexible, "net-like" arrangement of motifs and lyric modes, a poetics of extension and aggregation that subdues the reified power of the freestanding lyric while simultaneously refusing the kinds of epic stances characteristic of modernist long poems.

Catherine Walsh's books work by way of a different kind of reticulation, one that depends upon the page as a lyric net. Often appearing as a crash of fragments, isolated words and shards of public and private speech, the pages of Walsh's books atomise language and experience so as to fissure the presumption of continuity between the two, "delineating what takes / up space" (*City West* 44).[4] Deeply invested in the particularity of experience – her texts are "particularising to the point jot" (39) – they undertake an epistemological project as well as an ontological one whose most significant influence may be Beckett. Towards the end of her 2005 volume, *City West*, this remarkable page appears:

that   time
   strain   great
                                              exhaustion
love
                           vibrating
                           expanse
                                        indeed inhabiting
      same space   air
                                  breathing light
      as sound   vice versa
                              (viscera I
      opaque
                     chrysalis
sallies
            clarifying]   nothing

[yes

      sigh   light   displacement of what
      air   humidity   infinitesimal
      minutes   particles   mites (71)

There are of course a number of things that we can say about this passage, from noticing the gradual move from the general to the microscopically particular, the toggle between the elemental and the human, the swing from Beckettian negation ("nothing") to Joycean affirmation ("[yes"), or the bare catalogue of crucial lyric themes (love, time). But I want to notice just one thing: that odd near-anagram in the middle of the page, "vice versa / (viscera I." "Vice versa" provides readerly instructions in that it offers an improvisational mode of taking in the poem. One always finds oneself reading such pages not left to right and top to bottom, but lattice-wise, moving in a series of spirals and rotating the words and phrases around each other. It is reticular as well in that it provides a poetic superposition as much as a poem itself, as though we are meant not only to reconfigure the words on the page, but to use them as coordinates while evoking an additional set of words in the page's white hollows. When "vice versa" submits to itself and becomes "(viscera I" this surfaces not only the lyric subject that is reinvented in Walsh's poems, but also the actual writing and reading bodies, the precise network realised by the poem. But in doing so it undoes the lyric self by exposing it as merely entrails. This moment of stark reversibility (showing "I" to be "you", the subject to be simply guts) is indicative of the great power of Walsh's poetry and is also suggestive of the manifold ways that recent Irish poetry reconfigures our notions of lyric. For what is a better reticle than deixis itself, that lattice of subjects and objects, insides and outsides, which crucially underwrites the forms of lyric writing?

Each of these poets remains deeply interested in retaining certain formal and discursive characteristics of what we traditionally associate with lyric poetry. Joyce's lattice poems continue to privilege concentration, density and brevity; they rely on stanzaic regularity; and they are catalysed by brief packets of language that are charged on multiple levels. *Things that Happen*, as well as Scully's subsequent work, is based primarily on a prototypical lyric act: observing the particularities of the outside world and framing those observations within the complexities of the poet's inner life, even as the usual sense of lyric authority concomitant with this act is muted and redistributed in Scully's practice. By so thoroughly fragmenting language in a book such as *City West*, Walsh disrupts even more forcefully the connection between the observing writing subject and that subject's environment. Even as Walsh's work undoes this link, however, it maintains another central feature of lyric poetry: deictic play and transformation. These variegated commitments to lyric are, simultaneously, undoings

Eric Falci

of lyric. The full abandonment of lyric poetry is, particularly in Ireland, unlikely, and these poets seem to have registered this fact. Their echoic schemes, whether Joyce's procedural reiterations, Scully's hyperextensions or Walsh's atomisations, are lyrically minded critiques of lyric, and they constitute a unique intervention within the wide range of innovative practices that have shaped the field of poetry in Britain and Ireland in the late twentieth and early twenty-first centuries.

Notes

1   A selection of poems from these early books comprise the 'Pentahedron and others (1966–1976)' section of *with the first dream of fire they hunt the cold*.
2   Six issues of *The Lace Curtain* appeared between 1969 and 1978. For a checklist of New Writers' Press publications, see Trevor Joyce, 'New Writers' Press: The History of a Project'. The key polemical articulations of the press are essays by Smith. The fullest account of this line of Irish modernist poetry is Davis. For a briefer introduction to Joyce's work, see Dorward.
3   For a preliminary gesture towards a typology of machine writing, see McHale. For a useful English-language anthology of writings on OuLiPo, see Motte.
4   Such atomisation is much more apparent in the books up to *City West* (2005) than in her subsequent volumes, *Optic Verve: A Commentary* (2009) and *Astonished Birds Cara, Jane, Bob, and James* (2012).

Works Cited

Davis, Alex. *A Broken Line: Denis Devlin and Irish Poetic Modernism*. Dublin: University College Dublin Press, 2000. Print.

Dorward, Nate. 'On Trevor Joyce.' *Chicago Review* 48.4 (2002/2003): 82–96. Print.

Joyce, Trevor. 'The Construction of *Syzygy*.' *The Drunken Boat*. 2006. Web. 6 Nov. 2012. <http://www.drunkenboat.com/db8/oulipo/feature-oulipo/toward/joyce/construct.html>

———. 'New Writers' Press: The History of a Project.' *Modernism and Ireland: The Poetry of the 1930s*. Eds. Patricia Coughlan and Alex Davis. Cork: Cork University Press, 1995. 276–306. Print.

———. *Sole Glum Trek*. Dublin: New Writers' Press, 1967. Print.

———. *with the first dream of fire they hunt the cold: A Body of Work 1966–2000*. 2nd ed. Dublin: New Writers' Press; Exeter: Shearsman Books, 2003. Print.

McHale, Brian. 'Poetry as Prosthesis.' *Poetics Today* 21.1 (2000): 1–32. Print.

Motte, Warren F. Jr. *Oulipo: A Primer of Potential Literature*, 1986. Normal, IL: Dalkey Archive, 1998. Print.

Scully, Maurice. *Five Freedoms of Movement*. (1987) Buckfastleigh: etruscan
     books, 2001. Print.
——. *Humming*. Exeter: Shearsman Books, 2009. Print.
——. *Livelihood*. Bray, Co. Wicklow: Wild Honey Press, 2004. Print.
Smith, Michael. 'Irish Poetry Since Yeats: Notes Towards a Corrected History.'
     The Denver Quarterly 5.4 (1971): 1–26. Print.
——. 'The Contemporary Situation in Irish Poetry.' *Two Decades of Irish Writing*.
     Ed. Douglas Dunn. Manchester: Carcanet Press, 1975. 154–165. Print.
Walsh, Catherine. *City West*. Exeter: Shearsman Books, 2005. Print.

Trevor Joyce's *Pentahedron*:
Forms Hatched in Darkness

LUCY COLLINS

Pentahedron, published in 1972 by New Writers' Press, marks the culmination of the first phase of Trevor Joyce's poetic career. From 1976 there would be a long period of silence before the rich creative period heralded in 1995 by the volume *stone floods*. Though the early work represents an aesthetic still concerned with formal testing and innovation, we can see the seeds of ongoing concern with the relationship between movement and stasis that was to acquire more radical form in the experimentation of *Syzygy* (1998) and 'Trem Neul' (1999). Here I will argue that Joyce's early struggle to represent this important dynamic is significant for its contextual engagement with Irish poetic cultures of the 1960s and early 1970s.

Ireland in the 1960s was emerging from a long period of artistic constraint brought on by the isolation of its political and artistic life. The economic revival, led by Seán Lemass who succeeded de Valera in 1959, emphasised significant state investment in productive industry and incentives for foreign investors (Brown 242). These developments would pave the way for Ireland's entry into the European Economic Community in 1972, but almost a decade before that Lemass envisaged the larger harmonies of Europe addressing the difficulties of partition in Ireland.[1] Among Lemass's key achievements, Brown argues, was his capacity to distinguish modernisation from anglicisation, thereby removing ideological impediments that linked the nation state with traditional values and practices (247). Throughout the sixties Ireland experienced rapid social change shaped, at least in part, by a growth in consumer culture and by the introduction of television across the nation in early 1962. Within five years 80 percent of urban households owned television sets, and though the figures in some rural areas could be as low as 25 per cent at this time, the centrality of the broadcast media to Ireland's cultural life was already becoming apparent. Much of the material shown was of British and American origin, and though the programming was often far from current, British advertising drew the Irish consumer into the British commercial realm. This expanding materialism would affect cultural development in both direct and indirect ways, offering new opportunities for publishing and broadcasting while increasing the consumption of popular and imported cultural productions.

The drive towards modernisation that shaped Ireland in the 1960s also changed the infrastructure of Dublin in lasting ways, altering the relationship between the people and their capital city. As the state celebrated the fiftieth anniversary of the 1916 Rising, the building of the Ballymun flats was well underway. The aim of this scheme was to provide cheap and accessible public housing; together with building projects in Finglas and Tallaght it would irrevocably change the inner city communities that had shaped the architecture and character of Dublin for centuries. Andrew Kincaid draws a distinction between the pluralist, even playful, architectural modernisation of the twenties and thirties and the "monotonous repetition" of the corporate developments of the 1960s: a decade which saw

> the deliberate depopulation of inner-city neighbourhoods, the destruction of historic buildings, and the completion of dozens of high-rise blocks in an international style that had metamorphosed, by way of volume and function, into the overreaching blandness now commonly associated with the style (131).

Joyce picks up on the ensuing turbulence within Dublin communities in subtle ways in his early work. The dynamics of movement and stasis that inform these poems suggest that at the heart of social change lay increased entrapment for many – pessimism could not be entirely dispelled, in spite of Ireland's increased prosperity.

In keeping with this change in the country's fortunes, and especially its newfound confidence on the international stage, it was a time of increased publishing opportunities for Irish writers, as well as a broadening of thematic and formal range. Yet these changes, significant in retrospect, did not yield an immediate sense of freedom and optimism; instead these were years of moral and aesthetic disquiet, and a degree of tension over the shaping of Ireland's cultural identity for the future.

The foundation of Dolmen Press by Liam Miller in 1951 had a lasting effect on the reading of Irish poetry in the second half of the twentieth century. By the 1960s Dolmen Press had moved to new premises in Upper Mount Street, and Miller was embarking on a more ambitious programme of poetry publishing, broadly conceived as 'Poetry Ireland'.[2] Tentative early printing practices had grown into a respected publishing enterprise that offered an important outlet for Irish poets. From the mid-sixties to the

Lucy Collins

early seventies, when Trevor Joyce's earliest poems were written, Dolmen had published many significant poetry volumes, including collections by Austin Clarke, Denis Devlin, Thomas Kinsella, John Montague and Pearse Hutchinson. In publishing Clarke's late work, Miller created a fruitful continuity between generations but this decision is also suggestive of the ongoing tensions between tradition and experimentation in Irish poetry – Clarke, who began his poetic career as a late Revivalist, appears in the Dolmen catalogue alongside Thomas Kinsella, a poet influenced by modernist aesthetics and by British and American poetic developments. In spite of this apparent anomaly, many critics have pointed out the extent to which the modernist influences of the 1930s were largely excluded from the work of the next generation of poets. Alex Davis records "the gradually diminishing importance of Anglo-American and European modernism to Irish poetry from the closing decades of the nineteenth century to the middle of the twentieth", suggesting that the legacy of modernist techniques would be a limited one for Irish poets of the mid-century and beyond (81). Certainly, for this generation, the fragmented forms and dissonant voices of high modernism offered challenges to poetic identity that could not readily be assimilated in post-revolutionary Ireland.

The poetic world into which Trevor Joyce entered in the late 1960s was therefore one suspicious of challenge and experimentation. Though both the quantity and range of work being published was far greater than it had been a decade before, there was still a strong emphasis on Irish contexts, rather than on the processes of writing itself, as the chief concern for poets. These aesthetic limitations led Joyce, together with Michael and Irene Smith, to set up the New Writers' Press in 1967; Joyce explains the decision thus:

> We felt that the mainstream of contemporary poetry was passing us by. Only the Dolmen Press, under Liam Miller, was publishing substantial collections in Ireland at that time but the Dolmen was reliant on the small stable of writers it had helped to establish, it still leaned heavily on the legacy of Yeats, and it favoured the book as art-object, rather than as a cheap, fast, and effective means of getting new poetry before its prospective public ('New Writers' Press' 276).

The perception that certain poets had a special association with Dolmen Press was not misplaced, though Miller was still publishing work by new poets as well as established Dolmen figures. The importance of the book as art-object, however, was a greater impediment to producing poetry quickly and inexpensively, and this remained the key to Dolmen's aesthetic identity.[3]

Joyce's direct involvement in this publishing venture had an important effect on his early work, not only in facilitating its publication, but also in linking creative process with theories of artistic production and consumption. Through this project, Joyce and Smith expressed their individual poetic purposes, but they also articulated a shared desire to change the way poetry would be read in Ireland through the printing of work by new poets working in non-traditional forms. The first four publications from the New Writers' Press showed the important intersection between these interests. The first volume to appear was Joyce's own *Sole Glum Trek* in 1967, a 30-page gathering that was listed as the first of the "New Irish Poets" series; *Endsville* – a joint publication by Brian Lynch and Paul Durcan – emerged two months later. 1968 saw the publication of two volumes of Michael Smith's own work – *With the Woodnymphs* and *Dedications* – but it was the volumes that immediately followed these that indicated the press' vision and the range of its commitment to avant-garde poetries: in 1969 it published *Billy the Kid*, by American poet Jack Spicer and Jorge Luis Borges' *Poems*, in a translation by Anthony Kerrigan. Work by César Vallejo, and Antonio Machado would follow within the first ten years of the press's existence.

Another significant editorial achievement for Joyce was the foundation, in 1969, of *The Lace Curtain: A Magazine of Poetry and Criticism*, which again he co-edited with Michael Smith. This magazine became an important venue for the publication of new poetry, as well as a forum for critical debate. Other journals flourished during this period, including James Liddy's *Arena* and Hayden Murphy's *Broadsheet*, but *The Lace Curtain* was the most clearly committed to innovation in both poetry and criticism. It printed the work of poets who would later appear in book form from the New Writers' Press, but it also included material from those already in the Dolmen stable, or who would soon be published there, such as Thomas Kinsella, James Liddy and John Montague. As the journal became established, its links to the poets of the thirties became more pronounced: work by Brian Coffey and Denis Devlin appeared in Issues 3 and 4. In the latter publication poems by Samuel Beckett – together with his provocative 1934 essay, 'Recent Irish Poetry' – brought the conflict between experimentation and tradition under the spotlight. Joyce's own attitude, which can be gauged in his critical essay on James Liddy, placed emphasis on the pliancy of the creative process, on the value of emotions still in formation, rather than on those "the force [of which] is spent and the experience tidied up" ('Ideologist' 46).

The desire to render states of being with force and immediacy can be seen clearly in Joyce's earliest poems. In *Pentahedron* (1972), work from Joyce's first two publications – *Sole Glum Trek* (1967) and *Watches* (1969) – are gathered, together with some previously unpublished poems.[4] In these texts spatial representation plays a key role in linking the location of human experience and the enquiry into larger questions of poetic creation. Often a relationship between the dynamic and the static informs both the making of the text and its described settings: Joyce reaches beyond both natural and built environments to contemplate the realms of light and darkness, of air and atmosphere. This exploration brings the abstract into significant relationship with material form, and in doing so extends poetry's potential to address philosophical issues in a way that is meaningful to the human dwelling in a contextualised world.

The depopulated landscapes of these poems reflect both the condition of Dublin and a state of mind troubled by the dissonant realities of a nation state embracing late forms of industrialisation. Nate Dorward describes these early poems as representing "a series of objects, part-objects, and living creatures at once oppressively plentiful and yet failing to add up to anything like a full and living world" (84). By contrast, it is the 'de-organic quality' of the poems yet, conversely, their preoccupation with death and dying that strike Andrew Duncan (n.pag.). This impression calls attention to Joyce's capacity for detachment from the visceral world that he creates; a perspective that is vital to the conceptual developments of his later work. In spite of the important presence of the capital city in these poems, Marcella Edwards and John Goodby argue that they are most concerned with the representational power of language itself (174). This preoccupation with art evokes the troubled urban vista of an earlier modernism, where existential conditions are explored in spatial forms, and streetscapes permit the divergent realities of self and community to be explored.

Reaching further back into literary history, the gothic dimensions of Joyce's work hints at Irish precursors, especially James Clarence Mangan, but also speak to the fragility of forms of cultural identity that had been unchallenged a decade before.[5] In 'Surd Blab' – a noteworthy early sequence – the opening scene is one of gothic decay: there is a "violet halflight / between walls and hoardings / / where plaster, paint and torn advertisements / creep from their places" (*Pentahedron* 22). Here the difficulty in reconciling "memorials and neon signs" is rendered in the fragmented form and contexts of the poem, and in its sense of the divergence of singular and shared perspectives. An earlier draft of the poem begins not with this disintegrating environment, however, but in the originating mind itself: "Somewhere, / / somewhere at the back of my brain / there is a question" (*Records*). Rather than construing meaning – however ironically – as formed by the power of thought, the finished poem emphasises the need to seek it in the material world. This turning outwards acknowledges the opacity of the natural and created world and its resistance to poetic representation.

The structures that shape both aesthetic perceptions and ethical positions are important to Joyce even at this early stage in his career. He has an instinctive sense that the patterns that shape our vision of the world are indicative too of its systems of power and governance. In some poems this is confronted directly, such as in 'Gulls on the River Liffey' where poverty shadows the natural scene. The poem presents a fixed and partial view, made all the more striking by the choice of a fluid, mobile subject matter: "All is superstructure here, no gaps between forms / Through which to glimpse the basic groundplan of the scheme" (21). The presence of the superstructure indicates the power of modernity to obscure, rather than to reveal, the essence of things. This inability to see the "groundplan" also indicates the absence of a necessary connection between form and meaning. It is an observation that has both political and aesthetic ramifications, as the values on which the state is built have become obscured by ambitious modernisation.

John Goodby has commented on the claustrophobia generated in Joyce's early work by the depiction of Dublin's "bridges, monuments, vaults, churches and walls"; certainly the built environment exerts a shaping force on the poet's choice of imaginative landscape in these poems (615). The scientific form of 'Construction' offers perhaps the most immediate sense of the building as a creative device. Each section of the poem surveys a structured environment: first the "massive grey stone wall" suddenly encountered by the walking speaker; then the cobbles of enamelled rock (19). The contemplation of surface and substance that ensues appears in other poems too; often we encounter stone, sometimes concrete – limestone, coal, quartz, fulgurite testify to the poet's near-obsession with mineral states as well as other formations, such as glass, metal and steel. Many are indicative of the solidity of the built environment, yet obliquely also the slow process of change that underpins it. Sometimes these substances are indicative of the collective urban space, so that in 'Surd Blab' the town is described as "Cold and opaque / as a chunk of river quartz" (III 24). The rock, apparently impervious and lasting, is set within the "river's blab" – the endlessly changing soundscape of human voices and experiences. Yet this reworking of Yeats's "stone in the midst of all"[6] does not construe language as lasting commemoration, instead it is ephemeral – "blown / in the storm like old saurian / down" (24).

As well as the juxtaposition of stone and word, the architectural dimension of Joyce's work must be seen in tandem with the representations of nature that also shape the volume – images of rivers and trees approximating fixed forms; birds and animals struggling, and often failing, to survive. Indeed the enduring trope of the volume is this relationship between organic life and the built environment, and its potential to address the entrapment of the life force itself. Decades before such environments became important for critics examining the complex relationship between the individual and nature, Joyce was reflecting on this dynamic in ways that demonstrated its importance for the formation of self and poet. 'River Tolka and Botanical Gardens' interweaves different natural elements, though the poem's stanzaic structure separates the description into moments of observation, creating a tension in the work between form and idea. The deathly image of the rat's carcase is not fleeting though, but rather refuses to be dispelled from the imagination:

Below, a carcase in the snow,
smirched snow, rat's blood upon it,
crushed rat's bone upon it,
splintered on the bone-pale snow,
rat's marrow. (11)

Here alliterative effects, together with modulations of rhythm, make this an insistent scene. The cold preserves the rat's body, both in actuality and in the text, holding the reader in a condition without productive energy yet without degeneration. This state of suspension is an important dimension of Joyce's early creative life, as he embarked upon the important business of writing and publishing poems, while still searching for the form such poems might take.

The experience of cold, and the state of petrification with which it is associated, informs *Pentahedron* as a whole. The speaker in 'Death is Conventional' notes the "click of thawed ice" on the window pane, as well as the casualties of these freezing temperatures – the neighbour dying "in the first cold spell" and the vanity of Narcissus frozen above the pool (36-9). Here the combined effects of real cold and the ambiance of myth and story are starkly realised. 'The Fall' records "Stone cracked in the jaws of ice, / splintered, grinding" (41); paths of snow and icy streets chart the journey of 'Elegy of the Shut Mirror' (52-3). In the latter poem, states of estrangement and of paralysis emerge as specificities of place meet the landscape of the mind. In spite of the sun, "frost thickens on the gates" and the ice loosening on the streets does not mark a renewal but merely postponement.

This sense of postponement is an important dimension of the sequences from this volume, and none is more important in drawing together the impulses of the collection as a whole, and of Joyce's early achievement, than the title sequence –'Pentahedron'. The first and most important tension as the poem opens is that of rain and sleeping man. It reveals the vulnerability of the human in a late-twentieth century world and the fragility of sense experience in an industrial age. Marshall Berman understands the destruction of the city as a situation requiring human remaking: "It was as if people had to learn to see and to speak all over again" (129). For this a new language and a new way of seeing the world are needed. Similarly, in Joyce's poem, the disintegration of the body is mirrored in the cosmos:

Stars have grown up in the sky like fruit,
the moon corrodes, the moon
falls like ash and smoulders;
sourness of acid rain.

When your lips are falling through the ruined jaw
they will remember autumn
and the painful fruit. (47)

This apocalyptic landscape forms the texture of the volume as a whole – here it is explicitly connected to a nuclear winter, the falling of ash signalling a corruption of the earth so fundamental that it results in the disintegration of the human body as "lips [fall] from the ruined jaw" and later "melt from the bone" (47). This disintegration, visually reminiscent of Salvador Dalí's pliant skulls, is specifically one that links the sensory world with the world of language, so that the loss of direct engagement with the world is also the loss of the speech act through which such an engagement can be shared with others. The landscape in which this degeneration takes place is one of monumental proportions, its "central squares" and vast statuary suggestive of the cities of Eastern Europe suffering the ravages of war. The statues are as trees, yet their gestures are fixed, rather than at the whim of wind and weather. This juxtaposition of the static representations of the past, and the changing conditions of contemporary life recur at significant moments in this volume.

In many of the poems in this book the presence of children is subtly indicated, forming a counterpoint to faltering adult perceptions. Part II of 'Pentahedron' opens by situating a school close to the environment of stone and water that shapes Joyce's realisation of the urban here. The sleeping man lies on a plinth – seemingly a raised gravestone – from which his deathly form obscures inscription; language in this instance could take one of several forms, either the memorial carving that contributes to the narrative of past lives, or the graffiti that asserts the value of contemporary feeling. Fears of such eradication of language are everywhere in Joyce's early work, where the gothic mode creates a spectral city, silenced by past and present cultural loss. The persistence of nature does little to assuage these fears, however. Though "summer decorates the railway track", language demands reciprocal response:

Torture of the word and understanding
pain of the flesh in song:
the mouth, unanswered, falls away,
sorrow,
  and the beat of rain. (II, 48)

The need for understanding – and for the sympathy it makes possible – becomes clearer here, yet the gap between human states is not reduced by this realisation. Instead, the juxtaposition of youth and age confirms that division, suggesting a sundering of past and future that has ramifications for Ireland's sense of identity. Joyce hints here that the experience of childhood is intense and in 'Pentahedron' it exists in the mind of the sleeping vagrant, who imagines the dread of children "stoning a sheep's head at the lock".

The third part of the sequence places the process of disintegration under close scrutiny by linking natural patterns with the destruction of created objects. It begins by depicting "grey cones" dropping from the tree, in a direct mirroring of the rain-drenched oak boles of 'Surd Blab'. In that scene too greyness is omnipresent, though brightness emerges as the raindrops are shown not just to magnify the surface on which they fall, but also to reflect the entire cosmos. In this, the central poem of the 'Pentahedron' sequence, the tree is not part of a larger network of natural processes as it is in 'Surd Blab' however. Here, the orange bed of wood suggests the sawdust created by large-scale destruction of forest. Likewise the river's energies – its modulation of sound, its foam and fish – are buried "under a barren wall of stone". This process has already been rendered in 'Gulls on the River Liffey', where "The river, between bridges, lies rectangular, / A sheet of filthy linen, green on grey cement" (21). The perspective offered in this poem, which sees the river arrested into a static view, reveals lasting anxieties concerning the relationship between meaning and form in art. Here the gulls, at once individual creatures and a living group, are both subject to the stasis of the scene and able to float above it, refusing their place in the fixed pattern of urban life. Yet, in spite of this refusal, they can only be properly apprehended in relation to the surrounding structures, and in this sense they resemble the figure of the artist himself – part of the cultural context from which he writes, yet possessing the potential to move freely around this environment.

The third part of 'Pentahedron' has a still darker view of the dynamics of creative life, however. The rotting stone of the fountain speaks of the fragility of all man's creations, even those that rely on materials as lasting as stone. There is no rejuvenating water here, no promise of renewed speech; instead, even the sleeping human body turns to dust but without the promise of resurrection made by the language of ritual. This vision of the atomised self is reinforced by the fact that no form of redemptive sacrifice can be envisaged – neither the crucified man nor the body tested by fire are to be found, only humanity stripped of meaning:

> Never the nail through the shattered wrist,
> never the body mad with fire,
> only the mouth clogged with soft ash
> breathing the reek of pain.
>
> The moon's corrosion hunts your face
> and your flesh grows sweet in the wasted air.
> when your lips are falling through the calcined wreck
> they will remember autumn;
> > time of fruit. (III 49)

Lucy Collins

At this point in the sequence a more complex relationship emerges between the projected subject positions here. The figure of "you" appears, an unwitting agent of destruction that will in turn be destroyed, existing only in the minds of "they" for whom the season of mellow fruitfulness becomes a bitter end to the dark contest of life.[7]

The poem continues with its indirect evocation of literary precursors – its fourth part summoning T. S. Eliot's *Waste Land* directly, though this text has shadowed the volume from the start. The poem begins with singing, yet these sounds go unheard, and the fact this is so changes their interpretative impact for the reader. Again entwined with Joyce's other work, the girls in the cathedral garden sharing "knowledge and silence" (IV 50) can be linked to the solitary girl on the bridge in 'Elegy of the Shut Mirror' (52); in that poem too the ringing footfall of the child through the streets draws attention to a blend of visual and auditory effects. Yet these characters are barely present in the texture of the poem – they are glimpsed or faintly heard, and their futures cannot be fulfilled because of the disjunctions of memory and imagination evident here. Likewise the auditory quality of the opening line of 'River Tolka and Botanical Gardens' – "Eggshells of white hoar crackled underfoot" (11) – demonstrates the evocative and (literally) destabilizing power of the soundscape of these poems. In that poem too the calls of blackbirds punctuate a chilled environment and their black marks "jotted across the snow" suggest the printed page and the complex relationship of visual and auditory elements. In Part IV of 'Pentahedron' children reappear, this time playing in "ruined plots" where tramps and lovers find space away from the gaze of others. Here the fact that "decay has forestalled demolition" suggests passive neglect as the hallmark of modern Ireland, rather than the visionary decision-making projected by the decade's ambitious politicians.[8] It is here that the poverty of emotion first emerges in the poem, and it is more explicitly dealt with than in the other texts. The sounds of lovemaking bring only despair in the listener, and the need for "bread to live" makes love scarcely more than a transaction.

Moons through the night sky fall,
futility. in a deserted lane
the moan of lovers from an upstairs room.
poor sour despair. this guilt
of needing bread to live.

The thoroughfares and pubs are full,
where all things move in their circle
and all emotion has its root
in misunderstanding. (IV 50)

The increased punctuation adds to the poem's fragmentation: full stops without capital letters break the natural flow of syntax and reduce language's sense of purpose here. This is a poem that doubles back on itself; by both opening and concluding with the lilac and the unheard birdsong Joyce makes these images his own, reclaiming them from the larger modernist store. The "cripple's dream" (IV 50) echoes the "cripple's song" (48) of Part II, adding to the sense of this landscape as one peopled by those made immobile by circumstance.

Peter Sirr has remarked of Joyce's poems that "Even at their most abstract [they] retain the texture of a speaking voice" (150), a feature thrown into particular relief when a singular voice emerges – as occurs at the opening of the fifth and final part of 'Pentahedron':

I know these streets,
as crammed with dream as a clock with time;
yellow groundsel through the broken flags
grows into the mouths of children:
even the stone ages. (51)

By shaping this poem through experience, Joyce offers a way of grounding the multiple facets of the poem. While the opening line here is resonant with factual assertion, the phrase continues with a significant irony: just as the clock does not contain time but only marks its passing, so this flawed urban world cannot realise dreams but only trace their fleeting existence. Even children adopt a deathly posture at this stage in the poem, as stone and body meet in a form of abjection. The extent to which even what is thought to be permanent is in fact subject to decay changes the relationship between the cyclical life of plants and the seeming endurance of the rock beneath. The poem now locates itself in the Jewish quarter, in the Portobello area of the city – a place where communities are clearly delineated but marked by struggle. It is in this place, apparently, that "curious dreams / of histories and of old men's deaths" (51) can be experienced, and the weight of the past can be made meaningful. From the darkness of such dreams a form of awakening at last seems possible, but this awakening brings only

Lucy Collins

consciousness of the depth and endurance of human suffering: vagrants are roused by the early light and the laughter of the mad persists from night to morning. This is not an entirely existential plight, however, but one shaped by specific circumstances. The allusion to merchants returns us to T. S. Eliot, but evokes Shakespeare too, and a world shaped by the rise and fall of wealth and status.[9] The singular speaker here can bear witness to the inchoate suffering of the city but is powerless to render it less.

The volume *Pentahedron* ends with 'Elegy of the Shut Mirror' so that the closing of light marks the closure of the book itself. The mirror world of the poem reverses the normal expectations of space and time in ways that will become more radical in Joyce's later work: the text shuts down from imagined materiality to the fine abstraction of ideas in formation and also reflects – in its own figurative incarnation – the anxiety of the creative self that has played itself out over the course of the earlier poems. The ambiguous relationship between presence and absence here indicates the importance of this volume as a first step for this young poet, and one that will shape Joyce's later radicalisation of poetic form. For this reason *Pentahedron* does not only serve to illuminate the shifts in poetic production of the late sixties and early seventies in Ireland, it also confirms the importance of aesthetic risk-taking to the larger progress of cultural innovation in Ireland.

Notes

[1] Seán Lemass outlined these ideas in an article in *The Spectator* published in 1962. See Brown 241-266.

[2] The concept 'Poetry Ireland' followed from the earlier 'Dolmen Poets' designation, and was intended by Miller to embrace poetic activity in Ireland at the time. See Redshaw 147-8.

[3] It is an interesting irony that the same year that Joyce published *Pentahedron*, Thomas Kinsella would move away from the book as art-object with his publication of *Butcher's Dozen* in a cheap, throwaway format. See Tubridy.

[4] *Sole Glum Trek* (1967) contains 37 poems, ten of which are reprinted in *Pentahedron* (1972). The earlier volume was a cheaply produced pamphlet in black and white throughout, in contrast to *Watches* (1969), which showed more attention to design and layout; all but one of the poems in *Watches* would re-appear in *Pentahedron*. In preparing the latter volume, Joyce made some revisions to these early poems but the changes were generally minor, most involving the removal of capitals at the beginning of lines. A selection from *Pentahedron* was included in *with the first dream of fire they hunt the cold* (2001) under the head-

ing 'Pentahedron and Others'. Here 20 poems from the 1972 volume were reprinted, together with one from *Watches* and four additional poems.

5 Mangan's practice of translation also influenced Joyce as he began work on the medieval Irish text *Buile Suibhne*.

6 "Hearts with one purpose alone / Through summer and winter seem / Enchanted to a stone / To trouble the living stream". W. B. Yeats, 'Easter, 1916'. *Collected Poems* 202.

7 Keats's 'To Autumn' is obliquely suggested in these lines – the "season of mists and mellow fruitfulness" is invoked a number of times by Joyce in this collection, indicating the potential for creative production in the darkening days towards the end of the year.

8 David Andrews, Charles Haughey and Brian Lenihan were major figures to emerge onto the Irish political scene in the late 1950s and early 1960s.

9 T. S. Eliot's merchant from Smyrna is a possible reference here, though Shakespeare's merchant of Venice is more powerfully suggested by the proximity of Jewish identity and the important theme of trade.

Works Cited

Berman, Marshall. 'Falling.' *Restless Cities*. Eds Matthew Beaumont and Gregory Dart. London: Verso, 2010. 123-37. Print.

Brown, Terence. *Ireland: A Social and Cultural History 1922-1985*. London: Fontana, 1981. Print.

Davis, Alex. '"Deferred Action": Irish Neo-Avant-Garde Poetry.' *Angelaki* 5.1 (2000): 81-93. Print.

Dorward, Nate. 'On Trevor Joyce.' *Chicago Review* 48.4 (2002/2003): 82-96. Print.

Duncan, Andrew. 'Pale angel exuvial who can mix it with the chicken: Rev. of *with the first dream of fire they hunt the cold: A Body of Work 1966–2000* by Trevor Joyce.' *Jacket* 20. Dec. 2002. Web. 12 Aug. 2014. <http://jacketmagazine.com/20/dunc-r-joyc.html>

Edwards, Marcella. '"A scheme of echoes": Trevor Joyce, Poetry and Publishing in Ireland in the 1960s.' *Critical Survey* 15.1 (2003): 3-17. Print.

——— and John Goodby. '"glittering silt": The Poetry of Trevor Joyce and the Myth of Irishness.' *Hungarian Journal of English and American Studies* 8.1 (2003): 173-98. Print.

Goodby, John. '"Repeat the changes change the repeats": Alternative Irish Poetry.' *The Oxford Handbook of Modern Irish Poetry*. Eds Fran Brearton and Alan Gillis. Oxford: Oxford University Press, 2012. 607-28. Print.

Joyce, Trevor. 'Ideologist of Love: The Poetry of James Liddy.' *The Lace Curtain* 1 (1969): 43-46. Print.

——. 'New Writers' Press: The History of a Project.' *Modernism and Ireland: The Poetry of the 1930s*. Eds Patricia Coughlan and Alex Davis. Cork: Cork University Press, 1995. 276-306. Print.

——. *Pentahedron*. Dublin: New Writers' Press, 1972. Print.

——. *Sole Glum Trek*. Dublin: New Writers' Press, 1967. Print.

——. *Watches*. Dublin: New Writers' Press, 1969. Print.

——. *with the first dream of fire they hunt the cold: A Body of Work 1966-2000*. 2nd ed. Dublin: New Writers' Press; Exeter: Shearsman Books, 2003. Print.

Keats, John. *The Complete Poems*. London: Penguin, 2003. Print.

Kincaid, Andrew. *Postcolonial Dublin: Imperial Legacies and the Built Environment*. Minneapolis MN: University of Minnesota Press, 2006. Print.

Records of New Writers' Press. MS 40, 128/2, National Library of Ireland.

Redshaw, Thomas Dillon. 'Liam Miller and Poetry Publishing in Ireland, 1951-1961.' *Irish University Review* (Special Issue on Irish Poetry Cultures, 1930-1970) 42.1 (2012): 141-54. Print.

Sirr, Peter. 'Ways of Making: Rev. of *Collected Poems* by Pearse Hutchinson and *with the first dream of fire they hunt the cold* by Trevor Joyce.' *Poetry Ireland Review* 73 (2002): 145-51. Print.

Tubridy, Derval. *Thomas Kinsella: The Peppercanister Poems*. Dublin: University College Dublin Press, 2001. Print.

Yeats, W. B. *Collected Poems*. London: Macmillan, 1982. Print.

Rome's Wreck : Joyce's Baroque

David Lloyd

Some dozen years ago, in an *Irish Times* review of Trevor Joyce's first collected poems, *with the first dream of fire they hunt the cold* (hereafter *first dream of fire*), I suggested that the poems collected in *Pentahedron* could be seen as "mannerism in the best sense that designates an art tired of the habits of a style that has become commonplace in its very common sensicality and that forces the limits of style at the risk of excess and artificiality. Mannerism as one recognises it in Baudelaire, Kafka, Mangan, the early Beckett, all of whom used conventions to burst conventions" (10). The limits of a newspaper review did not give me space to elaborate that comment, one that might all too easily be misread as implying a negative judgement of the achievement of the poems, given the still-prevalent critical assumptions that associate "mannerism" with stylistic artificiality and poetry itself with sincere subjective expression. In the present essay, I want to explore further this association of Joyce's early work with mannerism and to devote some sustained attention to the singular and important achievement of that early work in its moment, an achievement that has frequently been too easily undervalued in light of the subsequent direction of his work as a whole. I also hope to add to that still inadequately developed judgement some further reflections on what I continue to consider the "baroque" elements of Joyce's work that are as striking now as they were in his early poems. Once again, the colloquial association of that term with over-elaboration or excessive ornamentalism demands a richer specification of the term as I intend it here.

In the first instance, both mannerism and the baroque most commonly refer to the stylistic unities of art historical periods and characterise the common traits of various arts in those periods. Mannerism designates the period of the sixteenth century that emerged between the classicism of the Renaissance and the seventeenth-century baroque. Strongly associated with Michelangelo's late work, as with his imitators, it is characterised by stylistic self-consciousness and by the extreme awareness of the conventions within which its formal elaborations take place. In a certain sense, one might say that mannerism involves the deliberate exaggeration of the traits of a received style, in this case those of Renaissance classicism, even to the point of being a criticism of them. It is on account of this stylistic self-consciousness that, on the one hand, mannerism is often regarded as demanding a very high degree of intellectuality and, on the other, is associated so strongly with being "mannered"; that is, as betraying insincerity or inauthenticity. A more sophisticated but still pejorative usage of "mannerism" would be the acute remark of Samuel Beckett's friend, the painter Avigdor Arikha, that, by the late 1950s, abstract painting had become a form of mannerism, in the sense that it was "painting from painting" (Tuchman 44).

A quite different understanding of mannerism, however, is that of Arnold Hauser, who, drawing on pioneering work by Ernst Curtius, argued that mannerism should be seen not so much as a single stylistic epoch but as a recurrent, critical moment in the dialectical oscillations of Western art forms. Whereas, for Curtius, mannerism became a generalisable set of stylistic traits, for Hauser it names formal attributes that emerge quite specifically at certain moments of social transition in which accepted conventions lose their legitimacy. He reads mannerism in its strict art historical sense as symptomatic of the cultural impact of the rise of capitalism in the sixteenth and seventeenth centuries and then understands its recurrence as bound to similar moments of crisis in later centuries. If, as Hauser argues, mannerism, with its exacerbated tension between subjection to convention and its exaggeration into excess, is correlated to a destabilisation of the relation between the individual and traditional institutions, then any consistent projection of mannerism as a term applicable to other historical moments would have to be grounded in both an apprehension of the moment of transition itself and of the stylistic or aesthetic institutions that are, for any given moment, in dominance. That is precisely the kind of context I will want to give for what I understand as the mannerism of Joyce's *Pentahedron*.[1]

Art-historically, the baroque follows mannerism and is usually understood as a stylistic period marked by the intellectual moment of the Counter-Reformation and bounded by the eighteenth-century resurgence of neo-classicism. Accordingly, it is marked by the tension between the new, propagandistic requirement of the Catholic Church to produce work legible to the illiterate, which demanded dramatic and often sensational depictions, and the tendency to a visual grandiosity, especially in architecture, that emphasised the power and opulence of Church and State. One could say that its extreme tendencies would be represented by Caravaggio, on the one hand, with his emphasis on the worldliness of his religious subjects, and Bernini, on the other, whose grandiose architectural projects and exuberant sculptural forms synthesised the baroque emphasis on the passions with its orchestration of masses and perspectival effects. There are, however, other and less official modalities of the baroque, a baroque of the margins, one might say, such as the colonial baroque forms that characterise the religious architecture and sculpture of Latin America or the Philippines, with an intense emphasis on human suffering and on ornate, almost labyrinthine, forms. Here the baroque lends itself to the articulation of what may be quite different, more subversive affects, often associated with melancholy and resistance, and with a far less bounded periodisation.[2] Like mannerism, the baroque suggests (as its colloquial usage implies) not so much a bounded period as the recurrence of formal and affective motifs whose elaboration – in the sense of their rigorous working-out rather than their excessive ornamentation – undercuts the institutional functions in which they may have originated.

So much is already implicit in even the most conventional characterisations of the baroque:

> Classical compositions are simple and clear, each constituent part retaining its independence; they have a static quality and are enclosed within boundaries. The Baroque artist, in contrast, longs to enter into the multiplicity of phenomena, into the flux of things in their perpetual becoming – his compositions are dynamic and open and tend to expand outside their boundaries: the forms that go to make them are associated in single organic action and cannot be isolated from each other. The Baroque artist's instinct for escape drives him to prefer "forms that take flight" to those that are static and dense; his liking for pathos leads him to depict sufferings and feelings, life and death at their extremes of violence, while the Classical artist aspires to show the human figure in the full possession of his powers. (Bazin 6–7)

In a somewhat more sober account of the baroque, which derives its aesthetic principles less from Counter-Reformation religious requirements and more from philosophical and mathematical foundations that cut against a later, post-Kantian aesthetic, Gilles Deleuze characterises the baroque in terms of a certain "operative function" rather than a historical period:

> The Baroque refers not to an essence but rather to an operative function, to a trait. It endlessly produces folds. It does not invent

things: there are all kinds of folds coming from the East, Greek, Roman, Romanesque, Gothic, Classical folds… Yet the Baroque trait twists and turns its folds, pushing them to infinity, fold over fold, one upon the other. The Baroque fold unfurls all the way to infinity. (3)

Formally, Deleuze associates the enfolded traits of the Baroque both with the labyrinthine, composed of multiple folds, and with a peculiar characteristic of its disposition of material, where "matter tends to spill over in space, to be reconciled with fluidity at the same time fluids themselves are divided into masses" (4). "Stone floods", one might say. These formal traits of the baroque, independent of its periodisation, permit Deleuze to think of the baroque as a concept that "can be stretched beyond its precise historical limits" and which, indeed, by its very definition as "enfolding", must always exceed the limits prescribed to it by a concept (33). Hence, for Deleuze, it includes not only Tintoretto or El Greco, but also Mallarmé, or the Boulez who composed the song-cycle 'Pli Selon Pli' ("Fold upon Fold") after the former's poems, or the contemporary Hungarian-French artist Simon Hantaï, with his techniques of folding, or even Paul Klee (30–38).

This emphasis on the definition of the baroque through a specific trait or "operative function" could run the double risk, as Deleuze well knows, of seeming at once overly reductive and too all-enfolding. While Deleuze does continue to specify at some length the particular differentiating elements of the baroque through which it recurs at various moments (34–38), here I want to follow him rather in his emphasis on what he calls the baroque's "division into two levels", the high and the low, its "two stages or floors: the pleats of matter, and the folds in the soul" (35, 3). This principle of severance, "between the lower floor, pierced with windows, and the upper floor, blind and closed, but on the other hand resonating as if it were a musical salon translating the visible movements below into sounds above", furnishes an architectural "allegory" (as well as an actual architectural paradigm) that grounds the opposition between the baroque and the classical (4). In place of a stable harmony and proportion between the world and its sense, the elaborated fold of the baroque "moves between the two levels" in a potentially infinite process (35). If, for Deleuze, this division produces, not a direct conciliation, but a *process* of harmonisation, "a perfect accord of severing", it is not hard to see how so rigorous a principle of division could equally produce, in another key, so to speak, an apprehension of a world utterly sundered between sense and matter, the redeemed and the fallen, the historical and the absolute.

It is at this joint that Deleuze's reflections converge, if only tangentially, with those of that other great theorist of the baroque, Walter Benjamin. As is well known, Benjamin's work focuses not on architecture or the visual arts, but on that "minor" dramatic form, the *Trauerspiel*, or "mourning-play", which flourished not amidst the material and religious triumphs of Counter-Reformation Rome but in the wake of the crises of sovereignty effected by the Thirty Years War in Northern Europe. Accordingly, the baroque in Benjamin's work takes on a quite different and darker tonality, even as he equally envisages it as a stylistic or formal tendency that exceeds its historical moment and furnishes an analogy for the expressionist work of his moment (*Origin* 54). Though Benjamin does not stress this, and cites critical work from an earlier decade, the conjunction he perceives between the *Trauerspiel* and expressionism may well be driven by the analogy between the effects of the Thirty Years War and those of the First World War, which likewise threw into question the sovereignty of empires and nations in the wake of catastrophic violence.[3] This emphasis on the recurrence of formal traits in analogical moments, on the concept of the baroque as one that exceeds its temporal boundaries, clearly connects Benjamin to both Hauser and Deleuze.

At all events, it is on the baroque sense of the catastrophic rather than the harmonic that Benjamin focuses:

> The religious man of the baroque era clings so tightly to the world because of the feeling that he is being drawn along to a cataract with it. The baroque knows no eschatology; and for that very reason it possesses no mechanism by which all earthly things are gathered in together and exalted before being consigned to their end. The hereafter is emptied of everything which contains the slightest breath of this world, and from it the baroque extracts a profusion of things which customarily escaped the grasp of artistic formulation and, at its high point, brings them violently into the light of day, in order to clear an ultimate heaven, enabling it, as a vacuum, one day to destroy the world with catastrophic violence. (66)

We may recognise here the negative version of Deleuze's "perfect accord of severing" with its Leibnizian optimism: Benjamin's baroque severance is between an unredeemed thingly or creaturely finite world and an abstract and perhaps absconded absolute. This irrevocably fallen world is "haunted by the idea of catastrophe" (66); it is the temporal world of

David Lloyd

"natural history" – that is, of a creaturely history subject to nature rather than to a redemptive eschatology; its predominant affect is the perpetual mourning of melancholy, "the state of mind in which feeling revives the empty world in the form of a mask" and which "emerges from the depths of the creaturely realm" (139, 146). Its privileged material figures are stone and ash, or the ruin that is the sign and remnant left by the process of "irresistible decay" that is natural history (177-78).

"Allegories are in the realm of thoughts what ruins are in the world of things" (178): for Benjamin's baroque theatre and its ruined, fallen world, allegory is the dominant tropological mode. In part, this preference for the allegorical explains the modern disquiet in the face of the baroque and its typically pejorative usage as a term. As Benjamin may have been the first to articulate critically, it is with romanticism that allegory was subordinated and marginalised by the discourse of the symbol. The symbol, "as it were categorically, insists on the indivisible unity of form and content", thus distorting "the unity of the material and the transcendental object" in the theological symbol (the transubstantiation of bread and wine in the Eucharist) into a secularised "relationship between appearance and essence" (160). Benjamin cites Goethe's antagonism to allegory:

> There is a great difference between a poet's seeking the particular from the general and his seeing the general in the particular. The former gives rise to allegory, where the particular serves only as an instance or example of the general; the latter, however, is the true nature of poetry: the expression of the particular without any thought of, or reference to, the general. Whoever grasps the particular in all its vitality also grasps the general, without being aware of it, or only becoming aware of it at a late stage. (161)

As anyone who has ever been subjected to the study of poetry in college will recognise, Goethe's pronouncement stands even now as an unassailable orthodoxy. It is not only an aesthetic, but also a categorically moral orthodoxy that organises both the relation of the particular to the general in post-romantic theories of representation and the idea of the individual's development from partial fragment to participation in the whole with which it is one: "What is typically romantic is the placing of this perfect individual within a progression of events which is, it is true, infinite but is nevertheless redemptive, even sacred" (160). The symbol, the part which represents the whole in a "momentary totality" (165) that anticipates an infinitely deferred reconciliation or redemption, lies at the core of a whole pedagogical theory, aesthetic, moral and ultimately political, of the modern human under whose sway we continue to live.

Allegory, on the other hand, describes a dialectical "movement between extremes" (160), a movement that partakes of the violence of an unredeemed world:

> Whereas in the symbol destruction is idealised and the transfigured face of nature is fleetingly redeemed in the light of redemption, in allegory the observer is confronted with the *facies hippocratica* of history as a petrified, primordial landscape. Everything about history that, from the very beginning, has been untimely, sorrowful, unsuccessful is expressed in a face – or rather in a death's head. And although such a thing lacks all "symbolic" freedom of expression, all classical proportion, all humanity – nevertheless, this is the form in which man's subjection to nature is most obvious and it significantly gives rise not only to the enigmatic question of human existence as such, but also of the biographical historicity of the individual. (166)

Allegory resides in the severance of extremes, both in its formal antinomy "between the cold, facile technique and the eruptive expression of allegorical interpretation" and in the gulf it registers between the worldly and the transcendent (175). Both that formal technique, which may arbitrarily lay hold of any thing and force it violently into the sign of another (allegory is the domain par excellence of substitution), and in the division of spheres it signifies, allegory consigns things to a realm of indifference utterly divorced from the domain in which they attain significance or redemption:

> Any person, any object, any relationship can mean absolutely anything else. With this possibility a destructive, but just verdict is passed on the profane world: it is characterised as a world in which the detail is of no great importance. But it will be unmistakably apparent, especially to anyone who is familiar with allegorical textual exegesis, that all of the things which are used to signify derive, from the very fact of their pointing to something else, a power which makes them appear no longer commensurable with profane things, which raises them onto a higher plane, and which can, indeed, sanctify them. Considered in allegorical terms, the profane world is both elevated and devalued. (175)

David Lloyd

Of this allegorical domain where the indifference or devaluation of the object is the condition of its signifying, the skull or death's head is the apt figure, as a fragment of the dismembered body consigned to a contemplation for which the individuality or particularity of the human no longer matters.

This relation between allegory and the fragment is constitutive and profoundly opposed to the symbol, the part fully integrated or translucent with the whole:

> It is not possible to conceive of a starker opposite to the artistic symbol, the plastic symbol, the image of organic totality, than this amorphous fragment which is seen in the form of allegorical script. (176)

Fragmentation, the reduction of the body to its severed parts, is the very condition of allegory, for "the human body could be no exception to the commandment that ordered the destruction of the organic so that the true meaning, as it was written and ordained, might be picked up from its fragments. Where, indeed, could this law be more triumphantly displayed than in the man who abandons his conventional, conscious physis in order to scatter it to the manifold regions of meaning?" (216). If Isis is the allegory of the allegorical interpreter, it is Osiris who figures allegory itself. Only when broken and scattered into its constituent parts, like language itself after Babel, can the material enter into the domain of meaning and value: "the image is a fragment, a rune", and "the false appearance of totality is extinguished" (176). It is this state of dissolution, of a radical separation of the elements, rather than through particularity and individuality, that things can come to point to or substitute for one another.

Any reader of Marx might recognise in this description of allegory's tropological system an allegory of capitalism as a system of exchange. Transposed from the theological terms, which, not yet secularised, formed the interpretive matrix for the crises of sovereignty and political power, into those of the critique of political economy, the movement of the fragment from fallen, natural history to the elevated domain of signification where substitution is the rule replicates that of the commodity from a thing in use to the domain of exchange value. In the realm of exchange, any thing's operative function is to substitute or be substituted for another, as its being as a particular thing succumbs to indifference in the face of its circulation as a sign of value. In that domain it becomes, as Marx put it, "changed into something transcendent", into "a social hieroglyphic", an allegory for the social process (76, 79). Allegory as an aesthetic mode recurs as the correlative of reification, where the very arbitrary violence of its appropriation of the thing as figure is the mark of a totality that is instituted through coercion rather than through the organic integration that the symbolic falsely promised. The melancholy of the baroque, as it appears in Benjamin's critical construction, is the melancholy of a persisting attachment to things that have become devalued as the means to their abstraction as signs of value, in a world where "the frenzy of destruction, in which all earthly things collapse into a heap of ruins", furnishes both the limit and the necessity of allegory (232).

It is within this double construction of the baroque, as a formal elaboration or folding–unfolding of the severance of matter and meaning, and as the recurrence of an allegorical mode that registers the effects of a contemporary intensification of reification, that I wish to situate Joyce's poetry and its critical practice. It was not, however, in the first instance in its formal or rhetorical procedures that I first apprehended the baroque or mannerist dimensions of the earlier work, especially *Pentahedron*. It was, rather, in the insistence of certain elemental figures that underlay the bleak urban lyrics of that volume, figures that recur throughout Joyce's work no matter what procedures he employs in its production. Throughout *Pentahedron*, stone, water or river, ash, moonlight furnish the underlying ground of lyrics that otherwise foreground the histrionic images of a derelict humanity – drunks, beggars, mad men and women, and children whose uncanny, shrieking laughter furnishes a kind of inarticulate chorus seaming the poems. The volume's central preoccupation is the severance of an indifferent, cosmic or geological time from the "natural history" of human or biological decay:

> Cold and opaque
> as a chunk of river quartz,
> the town that inroads these eyes.

> The effort to impress
> rock results
> in the quick fixed,

> or a fossil mote
> sprouting in our late
> damp climate.

David Lloyd

> The hazel leaves,
> the hazel wands
> scream in storm winds.
>
> Words are blown
> in the storm like old saurian
> down. ('Surd Blab' III 57)

The city itself in its architectural decay becomes a kind of parody of such geomorphic forces, a petrification of human design and labour that has become an alien rather than a lived landscape:

> Each individual limestone cuboid
> Chisel-squared and weathered
> Rough and grimy, holding on its face
> All its past history and the threat
> Of its future. Streams
> Of rust-brown rain had stained
> The entire wall; each
> Block realized its presence
> In this pattern and the wider
> Patterns of sunlight, shadows, tone
> And the complete distributed
> Weight of rock
> Combined for the present. ('Construction' 52–53)

Against the backdrop of this stone geometry, where cobblestones resemble skulls and seem to undergo a slow, vegetal decay, the volume's personae appear as little more than types, allegorical *faciei hyppocraticae* that render the sheer disposability of mortal flesh:

> All forms are savaged as they come:
>   maimed men who limp on club-leg,
>   garrotted men with meths-blue faces,
>   women whose secretive survival
>   shuns the predatory light,
>   and all the ashen faces of the dead. ('Dynamic' 71)

The title of this poem is surely ironic: such savaged forms of the human are not parts in a dynamic whole, but fragments, any one of which could substitute for another – madman for maimed man, beggar for drunken woman – in the hostile city whose emblem may be the "countless wheels" that "revolve / on distant rails" (*first dream of fire* 71).

The icon of the volume as a whole is the skull, through whose "ruined jaw" the lips fall and whose "cage of bone" forms the cell or crypt of the monadic subject's anxious circulations (77). The skull, a *memento mori* that represents the human reduced to its inorganic substrate, is not a symbol, offering no prospect of reassembly into a living whole of which each part is the representative. By the same token, *Pentahedron* as a book is rather "a ruined web / bent with death's freight" than the progressive cycle of poems its recurrent, desiccated figures might suggest. The finest single poem in the volume, the unrhymed sonnet 'Christchurch. Helix. 9th Month', seems to thematise the impasse of the volume:

> Passages of labyrinth repeat;
> the crypt gives vellum thighs to the dead,
> mark our return in this way;
> again we hollow dust-caves, ankle deep.
>
> Paths are furrowed by rats' feet,
> scribbled as cryptic schemes, motifs
> of death and propagation;
> here the fruit of death dilates.
>
> Arid courses interplay, rivers of dust,
> graphs wrought in frost, dust-falls interpret sunlight.
> A cat plays knucklebones with something grey
> and we move into daylight: (68)

The poem plays knowingly with the relation between the crypt as site of burial and the cryptic scripts or graphs it may secrete, but what it elicits, in this space where both human flesh and the rivers of life revert to dust, is a subjectless reading of allegories that encrypt only their evacuation. And the return from this cave to the light in turn yields no Platonic truth, only the dazzle of light on surfaces: "for mornings the roads are chrome / and the sun is a citron stain on a limed wall" (68).

There is a relation between this labyrinthine repetition of familiar passages and the evacuation or desiccation of the form. 'Christchurch' mimes perfectly the characteristics of the fully achieved lyric poem, with its steady conversion of the elements of the real place into laden metaphors, prepared for by felicitous adjectives like "vellum", its movement from dark to light that apparently parallels a movement from sensuous immersion to sense. Its formal qualities are no less striking: the turn to the sonnet form (the "narrow room" or "cell" of Wordsworth's metaphor), the internal rhymes and half-rhymes that echo the repetitions and turns of its thematic statement (dead-deep, feet-motifs), the double anapaests of the twelfth line that might imitate the upward movement that the line describes. As does any high parody, the poem repeats the lyric mode in a way that emphatically betrays its exhaustion as a form. And what it repeats, with precise knowledge of the conventions, was certainly the dominant manner of Irish lyric of the moment – one has only to evoke a poem like Seamus Heaney's 'The Forge', another sonnet, from his 1969 collection *Door into the Dark*, to instantiate perfectly the ideal type of that mode.

Joyce has since expressed often enough his dissatisfaction with that mode of poetic writing, the "well-made", subjective and expressive lyric, what he has recently called "the standard Irish bag of tricks: lyrics of description and expression dressed in the most transparent of formal attire; the emphasis being almost entirely on the language as carrier of information, with little heed to other possibilities" ('Phantom Quarry' 6). That "bag of tricks" we might consider an etiolated offshoot of the romantic symbolist tradition as Benjamin describes it: the descriptive element corresponds to the moment of the particular through which the subjective experience is elevated to a generalisable, transferable meaning whose continuity with the experience is guaranteed by the function of metaphor (etymologically the trope that performs transfer). In its late usage, however, what had in romanticism represented the revolutionary value of the emancipated individual whose unique particularity was an embodiment of universality betrays its secret tendency: rather than conveying the universality of the particular, the expressive lyric obeys the laws of general equivalence that were always the occult condition of the individual's emancipation. The exhaustion of that mode of which Joyce had grown tired was also its declension into untruth, the falsity of putatively spontaneous or free lyric expression or the fallacy of the analogy of poet with craftsman (as in 'The Forge') in an era of intensified commodification. The "originality" of the subject that finds expression in the symbolist lyric succumbs to the automatism of repetition as the particularity of the experience described becomes merely the alibi for the momentary reproduction of a totality that is over and again the same. Joyce's achievement in *Pentahedron*, which certainly exceeds the mere reproduction of this "standard bag of tricks", is that of a very specific mode of mannerism. And, in keeping with Hauser's understanding of mannerism's recurrences, it emerged at a moment of transition, when the Irish state's commitment to economic modernisation seemed to have produced more devastation than progress and had consigned to redundancy, along with much of the nationalist tradition, the conventional forms of lyric subjectivity and the ideological assumptions they embedded. Thus, in place of the conventions of Renaissance classicism that art historical mannerism extended and challenged through exaggeration, Joyce exaggerates the tendencies of the Irish lyric in such a manner that symbol and metaphor pass over into allegory, bearing with them the spectres of ruination and petrification for which the skull is the just emblem. The disjointures of the poems, between their fleeting and derelict human figures and the chill simulacra of geological permanence against which they appear, between the decay of natural history and the cycles of cosmic time, mark a severance of spheres that no symbol could bridge. Nor do they affect a "natural" or ordinary language use. Benjamin remarks on what links the language of baroque *Trauerspiel* and that of German expressionism – with whose rhetorical traits Joyce's early style has much in common – that "Exaggeration is characteristic of both".[4] That quality of exaggeration in Joyce is manifest both in the somewhat hyperbolic emphasis on figures of death, deformity and decay that endow the poems with a certain grotesque quality and in the pushing of metaphor into deliberately tasteless terrain:

> Acts are expectorated,
> and when the spittle hardens
> into facts, our lives
> are emerald threads of mucus. ('The Importance of the Bells' 48)

The tastelessness of such hyperbolic metaphor nonetheless remains true to the logic of metaphorisation: it merely projects comparison beyond the bounds that convention usually sets. In that process of projection, the poems of *Pentahedron* perform a kind of anatomy of the contemporary Irish lyric, one that exposes its structure like a skeleton it then reduces to fragments.

Projection, in the mathematical sense, is itself a metaphor entirely in keeping with similar figures that punctuate the poems: construction, geometric planes, gnomon, surd, spiral, diagram, circle, graphs, parallax and, of course, in the title poem itself, pentahedron. Such terms, in most cases separated from the body of the poems to function as titles, work to suggest an abstract, formal dimension of the poems that is the correlative of its thematic emphases on abstraction and reification. But they remain metaphors, signalling a tendency that the poems are unable to realise formally, working as they do still in a lyric mode of expression that has yet to be fully subordinated to the kind of algorithmic constraint that would exhaustively determine the disposition of the poem's linguistic materials. The pursuit of such forms of constraint, it is well known, would preoccupy Joyce through the next decades, including those of his virtual silence as a writer between the publication of *Pentahedron* in 1972 and that of *stone floods* in 1995. What is less often observed is that Joyce's turn to successive modes of procedural production, restlessly experimented with in various versions and combinations, is intimately linked to his perception of the socio-political bankruptcy of the expressive lyric and the subjective spontaneity it assumes. As he would put it, reflecting recently on his three-decade-long elaboration of the "hyper-sestina":

> My approach was to try to set up certain constants of texture or structure, and then to set loose within those constraints an apparently free subjective voice, the intent being to simulate in various ways the common experience of seeming to act freely and spontaneously, while even a minimal self-awareness reveals that this freedom is to a great extent generated and governed by forces and concerns in which one has no hand, act, or part. Without some reframing of this sort, I fear that the language of description, expression, aspiration, is constantly being sucked down the sink of calculated, monetized use. Moreover, even our means to refresh it have been appropriated. (6)[5]

Assumed in the relation between "description" and "expression" is the movement from outer to inner that is at once the movement from material to value, matter to sense, establishing the subject as a kind of processing plant for its raw experience. Constraint and procedure do not abandon the idea of a material that is subjected to labour; on the contrary, the working of a variety of materials, from found language like legal phrasing or astronomical terminology to others' poems, is crucial to their concept, for which the autonomy of the poem derives from its formal operations rather than from original subjective utterance. What they do contest is the naturalisation of that work as either craft or as spontaneous expression:

constraint is the foregrounding of the mediation of the material in a fully intentional formal structure. It requires what Benjamin described, in relation to the kinship of the baroque and expressionism, as an "unremitting artistic will" (55). What Benjamin ascribes to specific periods of artistic production may in fact be the formal condition of modern art in general. As Adorno put it of the new music:

> Competence is no longer what it was once supposed to be, but in reality never was, namely a treasure trove of acquired methods that could be exploited by talent. Instead, every element of the structure, from the smallest up to the totality, has to spring from the sustaining intuition of the specific musical insight, without regard to traditional skills. And conversely, every musical intuition, every involuntary, subjective impulse, must be transmuted into the rule-bound procedure that retroactively takes over what had started out as an irrational origin. (150)

One might correspondingly understand Joyce's poetic career after *Pentahedron* as involving an unremitting pursuit of procedures that would allow the material to be mediated through the form with ever-increasing thoroughness, from the mostly binary "axes" around which, as he explained to Michael Smith, *stone floods* was structured, to the assemblages of found language from which 'Trem Neul' is constructed, with the aim of producing "an extended autobiographical essay . . . from which everything personal has been excluded" ("On *stone floods*" 3).[6]

At least one phase of this pursuit culminates in *Syzygy*, with its thoroughly musical elaboration of its elements in the medieval form, the *cancrizans*. Any reader of *Pentahedron* would recognise in the later poem the continuities of tone or theme, the recurrence of certain elemental figures and of the severance between cosmic time and natural history:

> exposure to the extreme
> stillness of fire
> the flickering rock
> disturbs
> all night across an empty sky
> the high frosts creak
> and strike the clumsy sun
> leaves on the grass
> the shadow of the vaulting white

> beyond the bounds
> no silence no noise (*first dream of fire* 141)

The "voiceprint" of these almost obsessive figural motifs remains, as if deeply inscribed in the DNA of the work: it is their formal disposition that has changed and transformed them. In *Syzygy* and other procedural poems, the figural elements cease to be the mannered remnants of referential signs and are certainly no longer representations of "particulars" elevated to generality. Its very deliberate detachment from any directly representative function, its increasingly thorough mediation, produces the characteristic austerity of Joyce's mature language, as if it echoed with the sound of high cosmic winds and "grows to take in snatches / from high stars from elsewhere", as the opening stanza of *Syzygy* puts it.

As the fugal form of the *cancrizans* suggests, the procedural forms that Joyce invents are – like the baroque compositions of which Bazin writes – "forms that take flight", from *Syzygy* to the 36-worders that spin off from the extended hypersestina project of the last decades. The non-referential language generated by these algorithmic forms is no less a language in flight, determined not by its anchorage in the real and the particular, but by a series of departures that take place as words take off in a "cascade of splayed ambiguities" from their signifying function into an autonomous realm through which their relation to the world is thoroughly mediated ('Phantom Quarry' 7). This is not at all to say that the works bear no relation to the world and are merely "language games". The apt figure for this detached and mediated relation of the formal work of the poem to its world is another cube than that of the four-dimensional hyperstina, that of the closed room into which light filters indirectly. Joyce uses this figure at least twice. One is in connection with the poem 'Approach of Bodies Falling in Time of Plague', of which he explains that the poem takes off from Isaac Newton, who, during the London plague of 1663, "locked himself up and excluded the world" in a room that became a kind of camera obscura, illuminated by a small slit that admitted a ray of light which he then split with a prism ('Approach of Bodies' 17). Newton's experimental practice resembles the use of the camera obscura by baroque painters to which Joyce alludes in the beautiful, transitional poem, 'Mirror: of Glazier Velazquez':

> Where shutter, wall, and lock
> exclude the casual sun
> a new light illuminates
> long darkened and abandoned rooms.

Light that is natural has failed;
an angular course delivers this
through systems of reflections,
enfilading in its route
chambers where pose manifold
still dwarf and her princess
introvolute and incessantly,
or where, upon a bed, a graceful girl
approves herself in slender contemplation. (88)[7]

This "closed arcanian space" forms a kind of passage between the failed natural light that still fitfully illuminated the poems of *Pentahedron* and the cryptic later work whose autonomy from the real is established by the absolutely systematic determination of its materials (Marin 160). For Deleuze, the baroque camera obscura is the closed space of the monad, "a cell" or rooms "with neither doors nor windows, where all activity takes place on the inside" and yet where "a crushing light comes from openings invisible to their very inhabitants" (28). Composed of grids and "linear and numerical tables", this Leibnizian monad resumes a variety of interior spaces of display or performance – "a cell, a sacristy, a crypt, a church, a theatre, a study, or a print room" – to destroy the traditional model of representation as a window opening on the outside: "The painting-window is replaced by tabulation, the grid on which lines, numbers and changing characters are inscribed" (27). Emancipated from capture by the external "model", in which the Platonic ideal is always secretly at work, these monadic forms are enabled to take flight, "introvolute and incessantly".

Resumption of these closed spaces, the monad is, however, also their ruination. We might say that the sealed interior of the hermetic room bears the same relation to the ruined building as Giovanni Battista Piranesi's series of etchings, *I Carceri* (The Prisons), do to his other series, *Vedute di Roma* (Views of Rome), which depicts the ruins of ancient Rome. If the one dwells almost claustrophobically on the unfolding of obliquely illuminated spaces, in flight on flight of perspectival elaboration, the other exposes through the ruin the inner structure of repetitions, passages, apertures, that underlies the facade of the intact structure. "In the ruins of great buildings", as Benjamin puts it, "the idea of the plan speaks more impressively than in lesser buildings" (235). Both are anatomies, analytical procedures that reveal a structure through fragmenting and reassembling it, "articulated with a precision characteristic of the analysis of a skeleton"

(Stafford 69).[8] The features of the ruin are predicted by the structure itself, and the principle of ruination, the condition of always being a fragment as opposed to a part representative of a whole, is contained in the very idea of the procedural in poetry, even as it operates through the closed monadic chamber of the work. The constraint, like the *stretto* of the fugue, intensifies the flight of signification beyond its function of containment. Accordingly, the structural capacity of the procedure to generate exceeds the actual realisation of work that can never exhaust its productive potential, such that the work is always a fragment, the ruin of a never completed plan. Always, the work that results "remembers the calculation and ruin which generated it (Joyce 'Phantom Quarry' 8).

One of the modes of constraint that Joyce has favoured from his earliest work is translation. Like "writing through" or the lattice works constructed in relation to poems by other poets that appear at the end of *first dream of fire*, translation in the first place obeys the non-expressive constraint of inhabiting another's language, perhaps the most rigorous prescription possible. Furthermore, as Joyce has put it, "any translation now must take its place within a recursive series of previous versionings, each with its own significant subtractions and additions ('Phantom Quarry' 5). Here the crypt or chamber becomes a box within other boxes, or a series of enfoldings. As Benjamin strikingly put it, "While content and language form a certain unity in the original, like fruit and its skin, the language of the translation envelops its content like a royal robe with ample folds" ('The Task' 75). In a Deleuzean sense, translation is baroque, a matter of folds. It is also a process of ruination: not only is every translation a shadow of the original, at its best laying bare the latter's inner structure or isolating its context, it works moreover in the shadow of Babel. Its recursive force is not only to be a fragment in itself, but to reveal the original as such also: "a translation, instead of resembling the meaning of the original, must lovingly and in detail, incorporate the original's mode of signification, thus making both the original and the translation recognisable as fragments of a greater language, just as fragments are part of a vessel" (Benjamin "The Task" 78). Translation is thus not as bound to the original as its initial condition of constraint might suggest: its departure from the original is an intrinsic quality of translation, rather than the index of inept execution of the task. That, in translation, language takes flight from its original was signalled in the resonant pun that Joyce embedded in the title of his version of the *Buile Suibhne*: *Sweeny, Peregrine*: Sweeny who wanders, peregrinates, and Sweeny who, in his becoming-bird, takes flight. And flight itself, the

David Lloyd

poem reminds us, is double: a horizontal movement of displacement and a vertical movement of elevation or metamorphosis.

Sweeny, Peregrine, Joyce's first published work of translation, was already a version of a ruin or fragment subject to "significant subtractions and additions": its original is a distressed text, "somewhat the worse for *lacunae* and the pious interpolations of monks" (*first dream of fire* 236). His most recent work of translation, on the other hand, operates by distressing an existent and complete text, which is itself already a translation. In *Rome's Wreck,* Joyce "translates" Edmund Spenser's English translation of Joachim du Bellay's *Les Antiquités de Rome* (1558) as *The Ruines of Rome* (1591). Rather than an interlingual translation, then, Joyce's is a translation from one English into another, subject to a singular constraint: that it be completely done over into monosyllables. My reference earlier to Piranesi's *Vedute di Roma,* usually referred to as *The Ruins* (rather than *Views*) *of Rome,* was not arbitrary: like Piranesi's etchings, *Rome's Wreck* is a kind of anatomy of an anatomy, of both Du Bellay's and Spenser's descriptions of Roman ruins and of their moral meditations on fame and mortal decay.[9] In a fashion familiar from Renaissance *aere perennis* poetic convention, Spenser follows Du Bellay in invoking the possibility that his own written language might outlive in fame that of Rome itself:

> If vnder heauen anie endurance were,
> These moniments, which not in paper writ,
> But in Porphyre and Marble doo appeare,
> Might well haue hop'd to haue obtained it.
>   Nath' les my Lute, whom *Phœbus* deignd to giue,
> Cease not to sound these olde antiquities:
> For if that time doo let thy glorie liue,
> Well maist thou boast, how euer base thou bee,
>   That thou art first, which of thy Nation song
>   Th' olde honor of the people gowned long. (32: 514)

Joyce's austere rendering – to use that term in its industrial or culinary as well as poetic sense – of the poems into octosyllabic verse almost automatically ironises that desire for elevation, reducing Spenser's tentative triumph and steady pentametric beat to faltering rhythms and emphasising both the secondariness of his language and the rift between spoken and written words:

David Lloyd

> The skies grow dark. No fame stands fast
> or these stones spread round, clean cut, cold
> and hard, dressed by sharp steel, so far
> less frail than script, should have it made.
>   I use the tools I've got: hard words
> passed down, passed on, may speak on some
> days when the live voice breaks.
> Not all words bear the weight. I mean;
>   but they may not. And these? Pen's mark
>   lives on, but not the mouth that sang. (32)[10]

Joyce's ear for ambiguity in colloquial phrasing is here fully at work, as in "should have it made" or in the reader's momentary hesitation as to the possible and expected predicate of "I mean", which surely brings to mind Browning's 'Fra Lippo Lippi': "The world's no blot for us, / Nor blank; it means intensely, and means good: / To find its meaning is my meat and drink" (576). Just as surely, "I use the tools I've got" resonates both with Clov's "I use the words you taught me" in Beckett's *Endgame*, that ultimate drama of ruination (51), and with Caliban's "You taught me your language", to which Beckett alludes (Shakespeare 1.2). In turn, the complicated plays in "Hard words / passed on, passed down, speak on" run the gamut of meanings, from transmission through tradition, with its connotations of descent and then decline, to death ("passed on") as opposed to the continuity of voice ("speak on") – a meaning suspended and completed in turn by one of the more aggressively interruptive enjambements in the poem: "speak on some / days when the live voice breaks", an odd six-syllable line that exactly breaks off.

Joyce's rendering of Spenser thus performs a double operation: on the one hand, it radically simplifies the diction of the poem by confining its linguistic options so radically; on the other, with half an eye on Borges' Pierre Menard, it subjects the poem to a recursive cascade of accreted possible meanings along a line of flight that splays and frays, unravelling the texture of the original. That Joyce's rigorously monosyllabic rendition is so analytical in its effect may seem paradoxical. It is, after all, a deeply held prejudice that the monosyllabic element represents the most fundamental layer of English, its roots in Anglo-Saxon, as opposed to the later Latinate vocabulary that enters with Norman-French and with the learned speech of the educated or professional classes. The putative "earthiness" of Anglo-Saxon is, by way of a metaphor that becomes an assumption, associated with its status as the most primitive and therefore most authentic, if less developed, part of the language. Spenser himself may have had no small part in the shaping of such assumptions, given his own studious incorporation of older English words, like "wight" or "shreik", into the verse pattern of this and other poems. This practice gives rise to some of the odder energies of *The Ruines of Rome*:

> If so be shrilling voyce of wight aliue
> May reach from hence to depth of darkest hell,
> Then let those deep Abysses open riue,
> That ye may vnderstand my shreiking yell. (1: 509)

> Behold what wreake, what ruine, and what wast (3: 509)

It was also a practice which, much like Du Bellay's ambitions for French poetry, was at once nationalist and imperialist, aimed at producing a distinctively English vernacular literary language that might accord with the rising nation-state's visions of empire. The language, unifying the various historical strands that composed the national culture and furnishing a fully adequate medium for poetry, might rival Latin even as the nation's expanding territory and geopolitical power seemed set to rival Rome's imperial expansion.

Joyce's monosyllabic text works peculiarly in an opposite direction, its effect being not only analytical, but abstract, rarefied even. Compare Spenser's lines to Joyce's:

> Triumphant Arcks, spyres neighbours to the skie,
> That you to see doth th' heauen it selfe appall,
> Alas, by little ye to nothing flie,
> The peoples fable, and the spoyle of all… (7: 510)

> arch that's pure win, spires shot up so
> they scare the sky, tick tick, too bad
> that bit by bit you end in ash,
> scarce worth a laugh, your spoil our source. (7)

The spare economy of Joyce's diction succeeds simultaneously in appearing to impoverish the language and in exhausting all its resources. Spenser's "spoyle" becomes at once an allusion to Joyce's travesty of his source,

The Ruines of Rome, and the analogous process of despoiling that led to Rome's ruin, the cannibalising of the ruined buildings as materials for new structures. Thus it is that the passage of time – condensed here ironically to a Baudelairean "tick, tick" – that "bit by bit" Rome "ends in ash", and thus it is that Joyce's appropriation of Spenser's text not only "spoils its source" but furnishes the materials for a renewed text. That text in turn seems to obey Goethe's dictum that the ideal translation does not domesticate its original but draws the translator's language into the orbit of the original's, thus estranging the former from itself. This, Goethe claims, is achieved by going back "to the primal elements of language itself" (Benjamin 'The Task', 80-81). Joyce's reduction of the resources of English to its monosyllabic "roots" performs a parodic version of such estrangement on Spenser's translation and on the English language. In a certain respect, *Rome's Wreck* performs on Spenser a work analogous to that which Joyce performed on his own *Pentahedron*: where Spenser creates a kind of triumphal progress while invoking ruin, naming ruination as a figure but still standing off from it, Joyce reworks Spenser's poem by drawing ruination into the very process and language of the poem. The elements that resonated as figures throughout *Pentahedron*, constituting its affective palette – ash, stone, dust, flood, ruin, the whole natural history of decay – recur in *Rome's Wreck*. In the latter, however, they are integrated into the very process of the poem, as the rationale of its desiccated language.

Joyce's procedures in *Rome's Wreck* remain thoroughly baroque, both in the persistence of certain fundamental affective registers and in the procedures that renovate the allegorical and reaffirm the validity of a poetics of fragmentation and of "forms that take flight". But that it should be a reworking, and quite a violent reworking, of a poem by Spenser may remind us that this is a baroque of the margins, rather than one of the expanding, imperial Europe of the seventeenth century. Spenser was, after all, a colonial servant, dispatched to County Cork in order, as Joyce himself puts it, "to wreck the lineage (Aogán) O'Rahilly praises" ('On *stone floods*' 8). Counterpart to those other forms of colonial baroque of Latin America and elsewhere, and sharing in their sense of ruination and in their melancholic refusal to abandon the fragments that history has stranded, Joyce's Irish baroque constitutes a counter-poetic with its own broken and dispersed lines of transmission. This is a baroque in which Benjamin's crisis of sovereignty, of the subject no less than of the state, remains in play because it has never ended. If this poetic "remembers the calculation and ruin which generated it", we should perhaps recall that the ruination that afflicts it is not only an effect of its procedural destruction of all naturalised models of reference and representation, but also an echo of unrelenting historical catastrophe. The wager of this counter-poetic is that it may be the black box of the crypt, the monad only obliquely penetrated by the real it refracts, that furnishes the most adequate echo chamber for the reverberations of a disaster that remains unfinished.

Notes

[1] See Arnold Hauser, *Mannerism: The Crisis of the Renaissance and the Origin of Modern Art*. For an extended discussion of Arnold Hauser's approach to mannerism, see David Lloyd, *Nationalism and Minor Literature: James Clarence Mangan and the Emergence of Irish Cultural Nationalism* 197–200.

[2] Germain Bazin points out that, in Latin America, the baroque persists well into the nineteenth century, and one might argue that, in popular forms, baroque elements persist, at the risk of kitsch, down to the present in many regions where the effects of colonialism persist (7).

[3] For a discussion of Benjamin's concern with the question of sovereignty in this and other contemporaneous works, and in particular his debate with the political theorist Carl Schmitt, see Giorgio Agamben, *State of Exception* 52–64.

[4] Benjamin, *Origin of German Tragic Drama* 54. In an interview with Marthine Satris, Joyce remarked on his intense interest in the German expressionist poet Georg Trakl at this time, when "it was sort of a little bit rarefied as a taste" (Satris 23).

[5] Joyce, 'The Phantom Quarry' 6. It would require another essay to elaborate the ways in which Joyce's developing poetic is embedded within the history of the Republic of Ireland's efforts and failures at capitalist modernisation during the 1960s, '70s and '80s, projects within which his own career as a computer systems analyst was intimately bound up. There is certainly a close relation between the branding of Ireland as simultaneously a space of surviving traditionalism and one of readiness for development and the lyric forms that continued to dominate in the face of the monetisation and capitalisation of the Irish economy. On the relation of tradition to modernisation, see Luke Gibbons, 'Coming Out of Hibernation? The Myth of Modernization in Irish Culture', in *Transformations in Irish Culture*. For an account of Ireland's economic modernisation and its cyclical failures, see Peadar Kirby, *Celtic Tiger in Collapse: Explaining the Weaknesses of the Irish Model* 13–68.

[6] Anonymous jacket note to *with the first dream of fire they hunt the cold*.

[7] This poem was initially not included in *Pentahedron* and was first published separately in *The Lace Curtain* (1978). It may be the last poem Joyce wrote prior to his return to the poetic work that became *stone floods*, hence its transitional status.

8   On the relation of Piranesi's *Vedute* to actual anatomical drawing in the eighteenth century, see the brilliant pages of Barbara Stafford's *Body Criticism* 58–72. I am grateful to Trevor Joyce for introducing me to this work.

9   As we worked on the visual design of *Rome's Wreck* for Cusp Books, Joyce and I discussed at length the appropriateness of working over fragments of some of Piranesi's *Vedute* in combination with anatomical drawings reproduced in Stafford's *Body Criticism*. Our thanks to Susan Guntner, the graphic designer, for the execution of this working over.

10 That effect of halting or uncertain rhythm may derive straightforwardly from the monosyllabic texture of the verse. As Joyce comments to Marthine Satris, "How do you fix the rhythm of something that's monosyllabic?" (Satris 25).

Works Cited

Adorno, Theodor W. 'Criteria of New Music.' *Sound Figures*. Trans. Rodney Livingstone. Redwood City, CA: Stanford University Press, 1999. 145-196. Print.

Agamben, Giorgio. *State of Exception*. Trans. Kevin Attell. Chicago, IL: Chicago University Press, 2005. Print.

Bazin, Germain. *Baroque and Rococo Art*. Trans. Jonathan Griffin. New York, NY: Praeger, 1964. Print.

Beckett, Samuel. 'Endgame.' *Endgame and Act without Words*. New York, NY: Grove, 1957. Print.

Benjamin, Walter. *The Origin of German Tragic Drama*. Intro. George Steiner. Trans. John Osborne. London: Verso, 1985. Print.

——. 'The Task of the Translator.' *Illuminations: Essays and Reflections*. Ed. Hannah Arendt. Trans. Harry Zohn. New York, NY: Schocken, 1969. 69-82. Print.

Browning, Robert. 'Fra Lippo Lippi.' *Men and Women*. 1855. *Poetical Works 1833–1864*. Ed. Ian Jack. Oxford: Oxford University Press, 1975. 568-578. Print.

Deleuze, Gilles. *The Fold: Leibniz and the Baroque*. Trans. Tom Conley. Minneapolis, MN: University of Minnesota Press, 1993. Print.

Gibbons, Luke. 'Coming Out of Hibernation? The Myth of Modernization in Irish Culture.' *Transformations in Irish Culture*. Cork: Cork University Press, 1996. 82–93. Print.

Hauser, Arnold. *Mannerism: The Crisis of the Renaissance and the Origin of Modern Art*. 2 vols. London: Routledge, 1965. Print.

Heaney, Seamus. *Door into the Dark*. London: Faber, 1972. Print.

Joyce, Trevor. *Rome's Wreck: Translated from the English of Edmund Spenser's Ruines of Rome*. Los Angeles, CA: Cusp Books, 2014. Print.

——. 'The Phantom Quarry: Translating a Renaissance Painting into Modern Poetry.' *Enclave Review* 8 (2013): 5–8. Print.

—. *What's in Store: Poems 2000–2007.* Dublin: New Writers' Press; Willowdale, ON: The Gig, 2007. Print.

—. 'On *stone floods*: A Commentary from a Letter to Michael Smith'. 'The Fly on the Page'. Special issue, *The Gig* 3 (2004): 3–15. Print.

—. '"Approach of Bodies Falling in Time of Plague" and "Proceeds of a Black Swap": Some Explanatory Notes'. 'The Fly on the Page'. Special issue of *The Gig* 3 (November 2004): 3–15. Print.

—. *with the first dream of fire they hunt the cold: A Body of Work 1966–2000.* 2nd ed. Dublin: New Writers' Press; Exeter: Shearsman Books, 2003. Print.

—. 'Surd Blab' III. *with the first dream of fire they hunt the cold.* 2nd ed. Dublin: New Writers' Press; Exeter: Shearsman Books, 2003. 57. Print.

Kirby, Peadar. *Celtic Tiger in Collapse: Explaining the Weaknesses of the Irish Model.* 2nd ed. Basingstoke: Palgrave, 2010. Print.

Lloyd, David. 'An Impressive Collection'. Review of *with the first dream of fire they hunt the cold*, by Trevor Joyce. *Irish Times* 8 Sept. 2001: 10. Print.

—. *Nationalism and Minor Literature: James Clarence Mangan and the Emergence of Irish Cultural Nationalism.* Berkeley, CA: University of California Press, 1987. Print.

Marin, Louis. *To Destroy Painting.* Trans. Marjorie Hjort. Chicago, IL: University of Chicago Press, 1995. Print.

Marx, Karl. *Capital: A Critique of Political Economy.* Vol. 1. Trans. Samuel Moore and Edward Aveling. London: Lawrence, 1954. Print.

Satris, Marthine. 'Interview with Trevor Joyce'. Spec. issue of *Journal of British and Irish Innovative Poetry* 5.1 (2013): 13–35. Ed. James Cummins and Rachel Warriner. *Gylphi.* Web. 14 Feb. 2014.

Shakespeare, William. *The Tempest.* Eds. Virginia Mason Vaughan and Alden T. Vaughan. 3rd ed. London: Arden, 1999.

Spenser, Edmund. 'Ruines of Rome'. *The Poetical Works of Edmund Spenser.* Vol 2. Eds. J.C. Smith and E. De Selincourt. London: Oxford University Press, 1912. Print.

Stafford, Barbara Maria. *Body Criticism: Imaging the Unseen in Enlightenment Art and Medicine.* Cambridge, MA: MIT Press 1991. Print.

Tuchman, Maurice. 'A Talk with Avigdor Arikha'. *Arikha.* Ed. Richard Channin. Paris: Hermann, 1985. Print.

Twanging the Zither: Trevor Joyce and Chinese Poetry

JEFFREY TWITCHELL-WAAS

On the cover of *What's in Store* is a photograph by the poet of a stone wall that displays its history: the remnants of an ancient-looking rubble wall of red sandstone mesh with rough-cut blocks of silver limestone interspersed with red bricks, including the arch over a door or window now sealed up. An image of recycling and reassembling, the photo is an apt entrance into a volume that so vigorously multiplies voices through various improvisational, collaging and procedural methods. One sense of Joyce's typically punning title signifies the storehouse necessarily latent in any text, "the awful vastness of the *not-I*, densely populated with individual experiences" ("Interrogate" 157). Letting in the not-I means writing is always self-consciously rewriting. What is of interest lies not behind that sealed door because if we are attentive everything is on the surface of the wall-text, the play of relations and antitheses. We are situated within this play or we are played by the text as an enlarged sense of these latent stores, rather than witnessing or commenting on some reality over there. If Joyce's particular politico-poetic circumstances determine that his meta-poetic statements, whether inside or outside his poems, tend to align themselves with the forces of dissolution against those of limit and control, his poetry as a whole offers no such choice. There is an unsentimental focus on order and mortality, form and disintegration as inextricable, and therefore no question of choosing where any choice necessarily evokes its antithesis.

During his nearly two decades' sabbatical from poetry, Joyce developed a serious interest in Chinese and Japanese literature and thought, which provided suggestive models when he returned to writing. There is no reason to argue that these models alone were decisive in his thinking during this time, but *stone floods* clearly enough registers the impact of such reading: from the front cover with its photo of half-excavated terracotta warriors, to the epigraph from Dōgen, to the handful of poems in this slim volume that quote, rework or otherwise use materials especially from classical Chinese. Here I will examine a range of poems in which Joyce has explicitly drawn on classical Chinese materials in a variety of ways. Particular attention will be given to Joyce's renditions from Lu Zhaolin (Lu Chao-lin) and Ruan Ji (Juan Chi) in *What's in Store*, which I will treat as translations while trying to indicate just what that means. Joyce himself consistently prefers to speak of his various translations as "'worked' from the original languages in order to dispel any temptation to read them as 'translations' in the generally accepted sense" (*Take Over* 4). When he published a number of his Chinese and Irish translations as a chapbook, he aptly gave it the punning title *Take Over*, pointing on the one hand to translation in the etymological sense of to carry over, while on the other to a strong, even aggressive, over-writing of the original – although it remains an open question who has the upper hand in this take over.[1] Joyce's translations are firmly within the Poundian tradition, while benefiting from a century of sinological scholarship in English, so that the signs of translation's intrinsic doubleness remain explicitly in play. Actually Joyce's versions of Lu Zhaolin and Ruan Ji remain quite close to the structure and semantic sense of the original Chinese poems and, particularly in the case of the former, they are by some distance the best translations we have, if what one wants is a readable poem rather than simply a crib.

Translations from classical Chinese into English are necessarily exercises in illusionism. This is not merely due to the obvious differences between the languages, but because classical Chinese was a literary language no one spoke and which developed over a couple of millennia within a group nurtured on a well-established canon of texts. Consequently, the poetry is usually heavily allusive and the imagery thoroughly coded. Furthermore, the sophisticated and complex formal principles of classical poetry pose insurmountable difficulties, not simply because there are no plausible analogous forms in the tradition of English poetry, but also because these formal principles generate so much of what is quintessentially poetic in Chinese poetry. It is a wonderful irony that the most influential translations into English were an extremely successful event in the campaign for free verse. Most subsequent literary translations have found it necessary to make the same fundamental choices as did Pound, for whom these "choices" were more in the nature of inspired ignorance, to jettison the allusive coding and ignore the forms of the originals. We end up, as T.S. Eliot famously discerned, with an "invention", which then became a remarkably pervasive style and sub-genre inhabiting modern English poetry and poetic translation. But then illusionism is what all literary translation is about, and illusionism is not necessarily, although it might encourage, delusion. In the case of poetry such as classical Chinese, this illusionism will always be more mirror than window. There is simply no such thing as a translation from classical Chinese that is a near equivalent to the original, whatever that is.[2]

An important factor in whether or not translations tend to encourage delusion is their contextualisation. In this regard *What's in Store*'s presentation is exemplary in limiting the identification of poems as translations to the detailed tables of contents in the back and suppressing clear demarcations between all the poems other than the unpunctuated rock of 'STILLSMAN' set off at its centre. Framed by sets of translations with others distributed throughout, we could just as well call this is a volume of translations with poems "by" Joyce scattered in-between as the other way around, given the egalitarian presentation. Particularly with the weaving throughout of groups of Joyce's 36-word poems and the overall predominance of short line poems, the presentation encourages a seamless reading between groups of poems, which ingeniously enhances the echo chamber effect that clearly interests the poet. Poems and voices run from one to the next with relentless variation but equally with a tendency to counter and bounce off each other, which seems to invite us to read in a different order each time. So, in this sense the translations from the Chinese are folded into the cacophony of the larger volume, contributing their distinct landscapes and tonal variations. Set alongside other groups of poems designated as translations, mostly representing various folk song and ballad traditions from the fringes of Europe, the Chinese poems offer – as so often to the Western imaginary – what might be characterised as a hyper-civilised and decadent culture. One cannot imagine Queen Gormlaith describing herself as "too highstrung" as does Ruan Ji in the first of Joyce's renditions (118). Usually Joyce maintains the basic historical illusionism of his translations, so that even when he freely interpolates modernisms he nevertheless retains a sense of distance in time and place – Ruan Ji still plays his zither and has not yet taken up a guitar.[3] However, within the context of the volume this only raises more acutely the question of where translation begins and ends. There is a pervasive translation effect throughout Joyce's work in the sense that he is self-consciously transmuting found or pre-given materials. If one is to enjoy Joyce's work, one has to get used to never being sure who one is reading.

Before turning to the translations from Lu Zhaolin and Ruan Ji, however, it will be useful to consider a very different work from *What's in Store*. In a detailed explanation of the formal method of 'The Peacock's Tale', Joyce gives some prominence to the model of Chinese parallelism ('The Structure'). The structural brick of most classical Chinese poetry is the couplet, within which evolved complicated principles of parallelism and antithesis. This can be grammatical, in which the syntactical sequence of the grammatical categories of characters – nouns, verbs, adjectives, participles – mirror each other in the two lines. This can be tonal, in which a set tonal pattern (roughly analogous to the metre) of the first line is antithetically mirrored in the second. This can be semantic, in which the second line repeats the sense of the first, or more often gives an antithetical sense or image. So, to give a crude example, we might have: sun falls one bird roosts / moon rises many spirits wander. From here the parallelism/ antithesis principle expands out to relationships between couplets which can dialectically develop larger themes. Not all couplets in classical Chinese poetry use parallelism, and obviously too mechanical an adherence to this pattern would quickly become monotonous, so there are innumerable variations. Nevertheless, the logic of parallelism and antithesis is pervasive. This is typically explained as deriving from the philosophical and cosmological background of the *Yi Jing* and the principles of yin and yang; that is, the general assumption of the natural process as an endless interplay of interdependent opposites.

In the lyrical half of 'The Peacock's Tale', Joyce uses this principle of parallelism – that is, semantic and aural rhymes – as a procedural method: strings of related vocabulary are input into a predetermined form or matrix using a spreadsheet.[4] He then freely massages the results into grammatical constructions with an eye and ear to further rhymes while attending to his initial thematic prompt, which is two lines from a poem by Fanny Howe, "The human is a thing / Who walks around disintegrating" (242). The result has little enough relation to a classical Chinese poem, and in fact many of the original rhymes become buried in the compositional process in which new rhymes are discovered. What is of note is Joyce's interest in the structural principle of parallelism and antithesis, what he has elsewhere described as the "interplay of stasis and movement in Chinese parallel verse", and how one might imaginatively redeploy it in a quite different manner ('Why I Write Narrative'). 'The Peacock's Tale' is also one of Joyce's many bicameral works, in which two halves are set in antithetical relation, affecting and complicating each other. Here the prose first half, substantially adapted from a nineteenth-century encyclopaedia entry on Ireland, describes in ethnographic detail the shabby clothing and personal hygiene of the Irish poor. This grim description contrasts sharply with the lyrical second part, full of high-society imagery and light talk, in which references to clothing are also notably prominent. Yet the instigating lines from Howe with which this lyric ends, as well as the longest and most central vocabulary string worked into it, are all about disintegration.

Disintegration, of course, appears everywhere in Joyce's work, and clothing imagery frequently recurs with its suggestion of the poetic body and its textures.

Joyce's deployment of this principle of structural parallelism is never merely formal, since it is inextricable from his persistent thematic concerns with time, transience and mortality. Allowing the outside in means accepting temporality and change, which forever threatens any sense of the singular integrity of the poem. Parallelism implies and enacts antithesis, the rhymes of form resonate their dissolution; therefore, "with the first dream of fire they hunt the cold". Thus Joyce's self-conscious interest in forms, often very complicated and symmetrical, function to allow in rather than keep out all the forces of their undoing and result in the characteristically unpredictable diversity of his body of writing.

'Capital Accounts' from Lu Zhaolin

In terms of thematic development, Lu Zhaolin's poem divides into 6-6-2 sections. The first six describe the decadent bustle of the city, then zooms in on one of the denizens of the prostitute quarters as she prepares herself for a night's work. The next segment complements the first but focuses on corrupt officials who prefer to dally with the courtesans rather than fulfil their civic responsibilities. The final two sections, then, make clear the satiric intent by first abruptly switching to an image of the city as abandoned and reclaimed by nature, and then sketching a portrait of a lone Confucian scholar. Most of the sections within each of the two larger thematic segments are linked by the convention of repeating the final phrase or image in the first line of the following stanza, and in most cases Joyce has retained this feature. Each of Joyce's stanzas renders a single line of the original, which typically are end-stopped and represent a complete semantic unit. Each section, which Joyce has marked off by large dots, is a stanza in the original, where they are distinguished from each other by changes in end rhyme. These stanzas are predominately four lines (two couplets) each, although three are of eight lines. Overall Joyce respects the formal structure of the original, rendering each line and each section as an integral unit, except in a few sections where a line is added or subtracted. As is common practice in literary translations of Chinese poetry, Joyce largely ignores the many allusions in this poem, although as we shall see in many cases he freely substitutes his own interpretive inventions. The elimination of proper names also has the effect of toning down the exotic colour, but given the poem's decorative descriptive manner there remains more than enough chinoiserie. By using a short line that breaks each seven character Chinese line into four units, Joyce highlights the phrasal subdivisions into which the Chinese line naturally divides. I do not mean to suggest that each of Joyce's lines equates to a phrase in the original but simply that the Chinese lines have one and often two caesuras, which allows for a complex play of phrasal units. Highlighting the sub-units draws more attention to the subject and image rhymes within and across the stanzas. Equally important the short line enhances the conciseness of the translation. Of course concision is precisely what Western readers particularly associate with East Asian poetry, and a key reason why Chinese translation into English was 'invented' with the onset of modernism. Nevertheless, even literary translations are usually heavily padded out in order to maintain a natural English syntax. Literary Chinese is, relative to Western languages, undergrammaticalised and often highly elliptical or ambiguous – generally speaking there are no tenses, plurals, conjugations or articles, and pronouns are usually suppressed (those ubiquitous "I"s in translations are mostly added in). Strictly speaking Joyce's version is no less wordy than most other translations and maintains a natural syntax. However, the short lines give the effect of concision and tend to draw attention away from the continuity of syntax to the juxtaposition of lines and phrases. This also suits Joyce's lyrical gifts (the short line dominates *What's in Store* overall), and at times he manages wonderful effects, such as the word string threaded through stanzas four to seven in the first section: glitz, golden, glinting, glittering, gossamer. If Joyce perhaps sacrifices some of the sobriety of the Chinese, this is preferable to the ponderousness of most translations of the long seven character line, and in this case he effectively captures the gaudy commotion of the cityscape.

The first section shows clearly the antithetical principle previously mentioned: main boulevards / narrow lanes, black / white, beasts of burden / sedan chairs, cross re-cross / circulate, celebrity / old money, dragons / phoenix, gnaw / vomit, early sun / evening clouds, one / assemblies, encompasses / unify (from within). The philosophical and cosmological significance is most obviously signalled by the appearance of the dragons and phoenix, traditional symbols of the Emperor and Empress respectively and thus of male / female, yang / yin principles, which for all the glamour and power of the depicted capital assure that this is only a momentary manifestation of the cosmic process. This transience comes out clearly in the third section where the poem turns to the portrait of an aging courtesan. This section is initiated by the link with the preceding: the

Jeffrey Twitchell-Waas

antithetical idea that everyone is a stranger and alone amid the multitude of the city. The subsequent portrait of the courtesan is organised around this sense of aloneness and therefore of incompleteness and mortality. She is representative of the moral state of the capital, which for all its glory and size consists of isolate particles lacking any principle of cohesion or harmony and is therefore ephemeral. As the courtesan sits down at her mirror to make herself up – a conventional poetic setting which might remind the English reader of *The Rape of the Lock* – there is an ironic allusion to the purple mist into which Laozi disappeared and generally signifying the Taoist realm of the immortals. In this case Joyce retains rather than interprets the allusion so that it remains an exotic detail that nonetheless is suggestive enough of the unreality of the courtesan's desires. Her sense of aloneness and her hope for a husband is expressed in the latter half as akin to being one-eyed or one-armed, which in the Chinese are readily recognisable allusions to legendary or symbolic animals: a fish with two bodies that share one eye and mandarin ducks, a conventional symbol of conjugal harmony.[5] Joyce has turned these allusions inside out to stress the sense of mortal decay and sickness – the courtesan's sense of incomplete singleness evokes the image of disintegrating into bits. This play on one and two continues into the following section, whose two halves antithetically mirror each other: first the courtesan is "sick" at the sight of healthy couples since they remind her of her aloneness and mortality, and then similarly the single phoenix depresses her so she is cheered by the image of lovebirds together (presumably all these images are decorative motifs in her boudoir, like the earlier dragons and phoenix decorating the sedan chairs). The point here is to indicate how Lu Zhaolin's poem and Joyce's handling of it to a large extent generates itself out of the principles of parallelism and antithesis on more than merely a formal level. Within the individual sections or in the poem as a whole there is little sense of narrative, but instead through repetition and antithesis there is a constant thickening of the thematic texture.

An obvious feature of Joyce's rendition is the use of anachronistically modern interpolations, in the manner of Pound's 'Homage to Sextus Propertius', with the similar aim of drawing a contemporary target for the poem's satire. Joyce's punning title immediately clues us into this doubled reading of the poem. The Chinese title is simply 'Changan, Ancient Thoughts', identifying the city described as what is today Xian, which served as the imperial capital for many early dynasties from the Qin (221-207 BC) through the Tang (618-907). Just outside Changan, the terracotta warriors guard the as-yet unexcavated tomb of the so-called First Emperor of Qin, that grandiose image of the denial of mortality in Joyce's 'Cold Course'. Joyce translates the literal meaning of Changan, "long peace", in the first line, and it is perhaps not altogether irrelevant that Changan also designates the main boulevard of Beijing, running east-west through the centre of the city with the Forbidden City on the north side facing Tiananmen Square and Mao's mausoleum on the south side. Changan, like Beijing, is carefully laid out according to cosmological principles, an elaborate symbol of the centre of imperial power and indeed of the universe. In Lu's poem, however, we are immediately waylaid from this symbolic grid into the small irregular back alleys, into the shadows of the city.

Although Changan was still the capital during Lu Zhaolin's day, Chinese readers would recognise that his description is set during the Han dynasty half a millennium previous. This was a standard convention, in large part because subsequent dynasties looked back on the Han as establishing the template of the Chinese Empire both geographically and administratively, including the institutionalisation of Confucianism, but also because of the dangers of commenting directly on contemporary society. This of course fooled no one, but Chinese intellectuals have been and continue to be addicted to the elaborate and often risky game of seeing how far they can get away with the social obligation to criticise bad government. After all, Qu Yuan, the earliest poet for whom we have a name and one of China's greatest, is the prototype of the faithful minister who paid the consequences for giving good advice to his prince, and in theory the Confucian ethos mandated a similar forthrightness. The biographies of Chinese poets often do not make for happy reading. However, this convention of nominally setting the poem back in the distant past while clearly commenting on the present offers Joyce the perfect excuse to introduce anachronisms to draw out the poem's contemporary relevance. Often, Joyce introduces these modernisms at points where the Chinese text deploys allusions that cannot be meaningfully translated literally without explanatory footnotes. Obviously, Joyce could have found other solutions without breaking the historical illusionism, as with the already mentioned example of the courtesan's missing eye and arm, but in others he takes the opportunity to introduce satiric logopoetic effects. As Joyce's title indicates the majority of these relate directly or indirectly to the capitalist circulation of money as the primary principle of social relations. Someone closer to home will have to explain whether there are more specific references to the heady days of the Celtic Tiger when Joyce worked on this translation.

We might usefully look more closely at the concluding two sections where Lu Zhaolin effects his moral turn. I give Joyce's version alongside a scholarly translation by Hans Frankel:

In the cycle	In the cycle of seasons, scenes change
of the seasons	without delay;
change comes	
instantaneous,	
or	In a twinkling a mulberry orchard
chard	becomes an emerald green sea.
ocean	
switch,	
gold steps	Where once there were golden steps
and white jade halls	and white jade halls
become	Today there are only green pines
green pine.	
•	———
Silent	Quiet and austere is Master Yang's life,
in the emptiness	Year in and year out a couch full of books.
he dwells,	
attentive.	
Nothing	There are only the cassia flowers
is happening	blooming on South Mountain,
but flowers	
on the mountain:	
falling always	Flying to and fro they invade his robes.
falling through	(134)
his reach	
they fall. (Joyce 266)	

Although not indicative of how Joyce usually works, the first section above appears largely produced through condensation of Frankel's version. It is the second line that is particularly striking, a somewhat oblique minimalism that stands out to highlight its pivotal function. The line in the original involves a conventional allusion, although a literal translation hardly requires a gloss to understand the point: the image of a mulberry orchard abruptly giving way to a changeable sea. This in turn is echoed as the seeming solidity of the city is replaced by pines, a symbol of longevity or constancy which were traditionally planted at gravesites – here an indication of the principle of nature as both transformation and permanence. Joyce's rendition of the second line ingeniously enacts visually and aurally the sense already given in the sibilant first stanza: the single count lines suggesting a pivot and the intricate play of sounds is like one of those musical segues in a sound track. The "or" sets up this turn before we realise it combines to become "orchard", and I cannot help but read the "chard" as suggesting the colours of both mulberry fruit and the green of the ocean. Joyce has managed to creatively vary what is likely to strike the modern reader as the redundant moralism of this section. Related difficulties appear in the final section, which introduces as a contrast to the earlier courtesan and arrogant officials a model Confucian, specifically the Han court poet and philosopher Yang Xiong (53BC-18AD). Usually this scholarly figure, who remains solitary because of his refusal to participate in the decadent commotion of Changan, is understood as remaining in tune with the natural patterns of the final two lines, a constancy of acceptance among the changes of nature. Joyce chooses to get rid of all references to austerity and bookishness for a more inwardly contemplative, Taoist or possibly Zen figure whose oneness with nature is more ambiguous as he seemingly continues to reach after what inevitably eludes. This is certainly Joyce's deliberate reworking and is enforced by the somewhat Heideggerian first stanza of the section (possibly suggested by Stephen Owen's translation: "silent there in the emptiness, the dwelling of Yang Xiong"). The quite lovely lyrical conclusion is at the same time certainly cliché Oriental – the old falling petals motif – eschewing the Confucian moral rectitude that has appealed to few modern Westerners other than Pound for the suggestion of a more outsider hermit figure.

'Outcry' from Ruan Ji

Joyce's renditions from Ruan Ji represent a selection from a sequence of 82 lyrical poems that is usually given the title *Songs of the Heart*. While this indicates the expressiveness for which these poems are noted, Ruan Ji's vexed feelings are born out of a quintessentially Chinese situation: the conflict between the Confucian obligation to serve society and a Taoist desire for personal transcendence. Living during the early decades of the tumultuous Six Dynasties period, Ruan Ji (210-263) was born into a family loyal to the Cao Wei dynasty, whose Emperor had been reduced to a figurehead at the hands of the ruthless Sima clan. Offending the de facto rulers by openly refusing to serve them would risk not only his own head but those of his entire family. Presumably by his own choice, Ruan Ji held only minor posts and developed a reputation as an eccentric and a drunk as strategies to fend off further demands of government service. Along with a group of like-minded artists and writers, known as the Seven Sages of the Bamboo Grove, Ruan Ji cultivated an interest in Taoism, although it is evident that this did not entirely compensate for his despair at the dismal state of social affairs. While Ruan Ji's lyrics clearly enough express his sense of frustration, dissatisfaction and desire for spiritual escape, they are also considered unusually obscure, presumably because they could not state too explicitly the circumstances of his anguish. Traditional commentators assume a good deal of oblique satirical allegory about which they never weary of speculating on the identity of his targets. This does not much concern Joyce, and only one of the poems he chooses to translate refers explicitly to the dangers of the time. Nevertheless this characteristic tension between a sense of social responsibility and Taoist other worldliness is at the heart of Ruan Ji's fretful expressiveness. Since *What's in Store* encourages the reader to consider poems in relation, it is not difficult to imagine Ruan Ji as a subjective version of the isolate figure at the end of 'Capital Accounts' reaching for those petals that always slip out of his grasp.

Joyce presents two sets of nine poems each; the final poem in both sets is a different version of the same poem. In some cases it is plausible to pair poems from each set but more important is how Joyce's selection and juxtapositions draw out the patterns of imagery and allusion so characteristic of classical Chinese poetry, where all that nature imagery – every plant, flower, bird, mountain and so on – carries bundles of allusive and symbolic resonance available to a readership raised on a well-defined canon. There is hardly an image or significant word that is not echoed at least once within the two sets of Joyce's translations. In the third stanza of the first poem the antithetical images of a single wild goose and the swooping throngs would traditionally be recognised as representing the solitary man of integrity (the poet himself) as opposed to those who follow the crowd and bend their principles to the prevailing winds – a general opposition we have already seen in 'Capital Accounts'. While the reader might not be expected to pick up this allegorical meaning immediately, this bird complex reappears in quite a few of the subsequent poems, with cranes and phoenixes in the same category as the wild goose – lofty symbols of integrity – as opposed to the more gregarious and obsequious swallows and wrens (see 124, 125, 161, 165, 166, 168). A number of these instances make it clear that this high flying is also associated with Taoist transcendence. Similarly the poet repeatedly speaks of climbing or setting off for the mountains, the favourite haunt of Taoist recluses, which stands in opposition to the "level" and often frozen plains or wilderness below (119, 120, 124, 163, 166). However, the poet's identification with solitary integrity is somewhat undermined by the reiterated desire for companions, albeit these are often figured as high-minded Taoists (122, 162, 167, 169). Compared with 'Capital Accounts' there is little intrusion of modern registers, as Joyce is less interested in drawing satiric parallels with the present or at least allows them to remain implicit. A humorous note from American Westerns is sounded in the second poem, as the poet tells himself to set off for the "high sierras", where, in the original, Ruan Ji suggests he is going off to the western Mountains (119). One of the relatively few words that jars the primary register of these renditions is "jetstream", which appears in the last poem of the first set and then is echoed in the first poem of the second (127, 161). In both cases this jetstream represents a higher and thus more permanent state than the antithetical "eddies", and of course it is in this more ethereal sphere where the phoenixes and their kin fly. This link suggests the tilt towards a greater emphasis on Taoist motifs in the second set, but the very choice of "jetstream" may also indicate how compromised this alternative is for Joyce's Ruan Ji. Particularly the first two stanzas of this first poem of the second set introduce quasi-technical vocabulary – "seriatim", "cosmography", "tilt of pinion", "jetstream" (161) – to project a rarefied strata where the phoenixes fly that suggests space or at least jet travel, but in the final two stanzas everything is brought closer to earth in the form of questions. The antithesis of the high-flying men of integrity versus the lowly squabblers becomes so strained in the effort to reach a suitable altitude that it generates debilitating doubts about becoming entangled in nets, consorting with "primitives" and "trading coarse tags". This pattern of hopeful assertions set against undermining questions appears in virtually all the poems of this second set, with the final poem fittingly concluding in a pair of questions.

Within the interpretive ambiguities characteristic of most classical Chinese poetry, Joyce's translations remain quite faithful to the semantic level of the original and to their structural organisation. Each stanza represents a couplet of the original, although there is local condensing or splitting of couplets for particular emphasis, and antithetical parallelism is evident throughout. Joyce's use of a stepped or hanging line functions both to mark, in most cases, the lines of the couplets, as well as to allow for more opportunities to emphasise and suggest parallels between words and phrases. Compared with 'Capital Accounts', Joyce uses more of the elliptical condensation the modernist lyrical tradition allows him and the juxtapositions between lines are more abrupt:

> In the small hours
> > far too highstrung,
> make the zither
> > twang. (118)

The use of a flexible short line allows for play between longer and shorter units, which has some analogy to the Chinese, which in this case uses a five character/syllable line that tends to be naturally subdivided into a 2 + 3 structure. The combination of even and odd syllable units is yet another antithetical pairing with potentially cosmological significance.

The thematic development of classical Chinese poems is often described as more spatial than linear. The movement between couplets can be quite abrupt and initially seem disconnected, although, once one is habituated to the antithetical mode, the reader can recognise the dialectical development. We might look at an example, and I will give for comparison the functional scholarly version of Donald Holzman:

A month
    to go
inside this summer
    furnace.
	This summer's blazing heat
	    Will be about to leave in one month's
	                      time.

Young leaves wilt,
    sweet resins sweat,
cool clouds stream
    across the sky.
	Green leaves hang on the fragrant trees;
	    Blue clouds move themselves
	        sinuously through the sky.

Seasons no sooner
    in than gone,
moon and the hunting sun
    run on.
	The four seasons alternate again and
	                      again,
	As the sun and the moon rush
	        headlong, one after the other.

Pacing, pacing	I pace back and forth in my empty
desolate halls,	room,
grief knowing	Pained to the heart that I have no
no friends	friend!
can yet desire	How I should like to look upon
true company	everlasting happiness (with him)
could cancel	And see the sorrow of parting
want.	nevermore!
(122)	(132)

In the original this is a ten-line/five-couplet poem, which we can see neatly etched in Joyce's version. The sense of being trapped in the mid-summer heat is compounded by the images of the first line of the second stanza/couplet, which obviously enough stand in for the wilted sweaty state of the poet. While maintaining the basic sense, Joyce has taken some liberties with this stanza, and it is notable that he draws out the antithesis more clearly than does a literal rendition, so that the second half of the stanza introduces an image of relief that is out of reach. The voicing of this stanza is particularly fine, with alliterative "s" sounds throughout and into the following stanza, but the "w" and vowel sounds slow down the first half, while the second half runs quickly and crisply with its "c/k" sounds. The image of cool passing clouds, however, generates the thought of the third stanza, the sense of inexorable transience in contrast to that of barely moving suffocation in the opening stanza, and so the desired relief, even when it comes, is illusionary. The last two stanzas turn from this projection onto nature to the specific situation of the poet and in doing so rewrite or expand the significance of the preceding stanzas. In contrast to the static opening, the poet now paces fretfully in his "desolate halls", desiring yet despairing of finding friends to overcome his sense of isolation. Although it is easiest to read this if we put a full stop at the end of the fourth stanza, by keeping the ending open Joyce introduces a more ambiguous and syntactically vexed reading. The Taoist suggestions in the conclusion of this poem may not be immediately obvious, and particularly in the phrase "true company" Joyce has introduced a complex pun. This can mean simply friends who would dissipate the poet's sense of loneliness, or men of integrity in a politically corrupt and degraded world. But also this "true company" looks ahead to the poem in the second set, beginning "At noon / I dress / to greet / most honoured guests" (167),

Jeffrey Twitchell-Waas

where the guests are Taoist immortals, who tend to abruptly pop up and just as quickly disappear all across Chinese literature. In this sense "true company" would enable the poet to "cancel / want" and transcend earthly desire, which is really the only hope to overcome the poet's anxieties and sense of frustration, or for that matter the summer heat. Joyce has nicely emphasised in the final stanza both "desire" and "want", thus drawing out the poet's hopeless contradiction: desiring to cancel desire, so that he ends up where he began, stuck in the heat of his desire. The poem Joyce places immediately following opens with the relief of fall's arrival, but as we would expect this proves no real solution. That poem ends with the poet abruptly calling for his carriage to take him home, which is unexpected since there had been no indication that he was ever anywhere else. Again, "home" is ambiguous as the poet feels at home nowhere, certainly not in his "desolate halls", and therefore can indicate that Taoist state he longs for but never manages to fully realise. Indeed, the next poem in the set opens with the poet climbing mountains in an effort to achieve that transcendent perspective on the messy world below. But by now we already know the outcome. The antithetical structure that both formally and thematically pervades Ruan Ji's poetry assures that he will remain within the transient sphere.

"there is nothing either finished or not yet begun": Other Poems
'Spring Comes'
This poem appears in *What's in Store* in a section of free adaptations from other works, although in this case Joyce gives no specific indication of a source. The poem clearly describes a painting, in fact a work by the early eighteenth-century painter Yuan Jiang, who was particularly known for his large-scale landscapes with elaborate architecture. However, the poet informs me that actually he is not describing a painting directly but is working from a description in somewhat awkward English that accompanied a reproduction of the scroll bought in China. The bulk of the images and phrases of the poem are taken more or less directly from this prose description. Joyce has predominately versed his source into identifiable couplets, although there is no attempt to make them pervasively parallel. The antithesis that in large measure organises the poem is that of one and many, the composition as a whole and the diversity and individuality of its detail. The leisurely long lines and the overall tone gives a disingenuous assurance of an idealised world, all the more so for its luxurious exoticness, except for a few disrupting details. The

poem certainly has a family resemblance to 'Capital Accounts' and, as we look more closely at this picture, the satiric shadows accumulate. Most obviously as the poem reaches a descriptive climax with the appearance of the imperial concubines in the fourth stanza, things turn suddenly dark, and the pivot is one of those odd verbal incongruities that the predominately flat description meanders into: "the imperial concubines / In bright peaceful and happy deluxe like we like" (72). Although different in style, this is essentially the same logopoetic technique we saw in 'Capital Accounts', where intrusive modern colloquialisms indicate that all is not what it seems. The light and luxury in "deluxe" turns into night (de- = reverse, remove) in the following couplet: "Luminosity so intense night will plunder, / Awkward dark stranger, uncouth invader. Mercy!". In the first instance we would take this "dark stranger" as an allegorical figure of mortality (perhaps we can hear an echo of "Darth Vader" as well); however, we will consider another more literal possibility in a moment. The poem moves on as if nothing has happened, culminating in an assurance that the "composition" is harmoniously knit. But once one becomes aware of the taint of darkness, the picture is more difficult to take at face value, so that the reiterated assurances of the conclusion sound somewhat strained and the peculiar use of "monstrates" in the final line can easily morph into less pleasant senses.

Not just at the end but also at the beginning, the descriptive picture is framed by meta-commentary, thus destabilising the illusion of the central description. The end of the first stanza follows a catalogue of architectural details with the comment that they "cancel curious eyes", inviting our curiosity as to what is hidden, what are those deep "implied meanings" mentioned towards the end of the poem. The end of the third stanza suddenly introduces generals with "reign in their hearts", another incongruous phrase that puns on "rain" and "reins" to go along with the "harness and armour" of the same line (71). We know from 'Capital Accounts' that generals are not good news, and here, where they are a detail Joyce has added in, they become figures of control: the rule of the empire, of the society depicted, of the artwork or poem itself, which aspires to keep everything on the level of the decorative and in the light.[6] Joyce has made a few further interpolations into the original description of the painting, one of which is the mention in the fifth stanza of camel-humps in green glaze – an image exotic even to a Chinese reader. The allusion is to a well-known poem by Du Fu, 'Ballad of the Lovely Women', which describes an elaborate springtime picnic by ladies of the court in Changan and includes these simmering camel-humps among other decadent delicacies. Du Fu's poem is coolly descriptive, but contemporary readers would have recognised the specific individuals he depicts and the poem's implicit satire against the growing power and extravagance of the Emperor's favourite consort and her family. The Emperor's infatuation, it was commonly believed, caused the neglect of good rule, and two years after Du Fu composed the poem the catastrophic An Lushan rebellion had broken out (755), abruptly ending China's most glorious age and precipitating the long painful decline of the Tang dynasty. A similar fate threatens the world of this painting.

So we have more dark shadows, which in old China particularly came from the nomadic peoples on the northern and western edges of the Empire – a perspective expressed in the 36-line poem, "barbarians / are bad / at walls" (*What's in Store* 133). Joyce's epigraph obliquely refers to this other side, the "stirrup and bow" and the desert sands beyond the Great Wall, "past" the silk (recalling the mulberry orchard near the end of Lu Zhaolin's poem) produced by a settled, cultivated people and worn by their rulers – or, perhaps more to the point here, used as "canvas", as is the case for Yuan Jiang's painting. The elliptical, oblique manner of the epigraph contrasts sharply with that of the main poem and puts in play "refinement", "incoherence" and "regulates". In the imaginary of the Chinese these nomadic peoples represent all senses of the middle term, and often they were quite literally the plunderers and uncouth invaders of the fourth stanza. An Lushan himself was from these foreign people, although supposedly serving the interests of the Chinese, order and civilisation. In several instances, the nomads went further and took over China outright, but, as is so often pointed out, the conquerors invariably became the conquered, adopting Chinese refinement, regulations and settledness. There was seepage in both directions: we might recall the "blood-sweating horses" Ruan Ji mentions (120) or 'Tocharian Music' from *stone floods* about another culture of the sands on the central Asian edges of the Empire, which rebelled, was suppressed but whose music continued to exist within the conquering culture.[7] So Joyce's poem activates the antithesis of order and others, with the main body of the poem presenting or embodying an image of refined order, like those Chinese paintings seemingly without shadows, yet curious eyes will discern dark corners like Lu Zhaolin's back streets.

'Lines in Fall'

This double poem from *stone floods* works with the first two from a sequence of fifteen poems by Meng Jiao (Meng Chiao, 751–814), a late Tang poet who developed a difficult and startling style. The wind combing bones in the second of Joyce's poems is a famous example of Meng Jiao's disturbing imagery and emblematic of his dark and bitter perspective. Joyce's poem might be described as writing over Meng Jiao. He maintains the basic structure of Meng Jiao's poems, with each of his stanzas representing a couplet of the original, and in each stanza one can discern a key image or a derivative sense from the Chinese.[8] But otherwise Joyce has freely reworked and added a wash of conceits suggested by Meng Jiao but given a ghostly pervasiveness by Joyce. The bones in the opening of the first poem come from Meng Jiao, but the appearance of related terms in the subsequent stanzas suggesting a decaying body is Joyce: head, bone / bare ribs / form breaks down / old tissue. Similarly, the image of un / weaving and loose ends in the third and fourth stanzas is in Meng Jiao, but Joyce augments this in the last three stanzas and throughout most of the second poem: fabric all washed up, thread bare, un / weaves / loose ends ravel, raw material / old tissue / / fret to bits / shreds / warp, dressed frame / yarns spun, tenters / weaves new cloth, shuttle. So we have the suggestion of a decomposing body and disintegrating fabric. We have already encountered this clothing imagery in 'A Peacock's Tale', with its implications of the poetic body simultaneously weaving and unravelling. Alongside this in the first poem, Meng Jiao's autumn dew in the second stanza become Joyce's "fall rains", which then develops into full-scale "resurgent courses" and "flood", followed by further related suggestions: washed up, wave, sand / cataract – and some of this is continued into the second poem: hard rain / sand sifts, silts up. Taken all together this might suggest a decomposing body and cloth washed up on the bank of a river, or perhaps it is more plausible to take the water / river as an antithetical image to the disintegrating body-fabric, implying continuity in change.

If the emphasis in these poems is on falling apart, in Chinese thinking the antithesis is always implicitly present, and perhaps this idea is best caught in the un / weaving imagery with which Joyce chooses to end the pair of poems and which suggests a more positive note. Admittedly this is ambiguous, since the Shakespearean echo of "bare ruined wires", which in Meng Jiao is a leafless tree, evokes the "bag of bones" with which we began and antithetically the "dressed frame", so that the "weav[ing] of new cloth" by the night and the moon may be "beyond" humankind rather

Jeffrey Twitchell-Waas

than their hope. If night and the moon work together to produce new textures beyond the lines of this poem/life, the transient moon seems nevertheless to weave as night's shuttle. The dense metaphysical manner of Joyce's poem is a wonderful interpretation of Meng Jiao's notoriously compressed, somewhat surreal style, and the latter's bleak poems of ageing fit comfortably with the dominant motifs of *stone floods*.

'Chimaera'

Joyce notes that the three animal parts of 'Chimaera' from *stone floods* are Richard Lovelace, Aloysius Bertrand and *Liezi* – the latter is the third classic work of Chinese Taoism after the *Dao De Jing* and *Zhuangzi*. Joyce states that the structure of this poem is indebted to Japanese renga, and generally one can detect the linking manner in which one stanza picks up an image or motif from the preceding. However, the linking within this poem seems as much a matter of Joyce's penchant for symmetrical forms. The stanzas of the poem divide into 5-5-5-1 groups, with the three sources used in sequence then reversed; the source that is only used once in the group starts the next group and the pattern is repeated. So, if we number the sources, which appear in the order I have listed above, we come up with the following: 12321/31213/23132/1. On the level of source content, each group circles around to where it began, as does the poem as a whole. In addition there is an alteration of two-, three- and five-line stanzas: if we skip the first group for the moment, each group begins with a five-line stanza and then alternates two- and three-line stanzas, so that each group is 52323. The seeming irregularity of the opening stanza is solved when we notice that if it is added to the extra final stanza we have five lines, so the pattern is consistent throughout while at the same time being circular. Knowing Joyce, there may be further numerical complications but this is enough for me, and whether any of this relates to renga, I cannot say.

Invariably these rigorously symmetrical and numerically generated poems, which particularly preoccupy Joyce after *stone floods*, contain materials that put in motion and dissolve the implications of such enclosed forms. In "Chimaera" the three found voices all graphically speak of mortality and change, and it is plausible to suggest that the *Liezi* passages (all those that are double indented) summarise the essential interrelated themes: a naturalistic conception of human nature and the natural law of transmutation.[9] Joyce draws on two passages from *Liezi* which he lightly edits, with the first two and second three going together.[10] Joyce could of course have found similar materials for this poem anywhere, but it seems especially apt that he chose to use a Taoist classic as expressing the characteristic Chinese principle that antitheses generate the fluctuating tension and mutual possibilities of forms and their dissolution, as well as an unsentimental naturalistic perspective on such transmutations.

'Data Shadows'

'Data Shadows', from the later short poems in *first dream of fire*, is a type of noise poem with which we have become familiar: a deliberately self-interfering text, or here actually two texts, which is then made more self-interfering by being doubled through systematic rearrangement. We are offered three potential clues as to how we might read the result: the title and the epigraphs to each half. Joyce's note explains "data shadow" as all those electronic traces we leave every time we use computers, cards and mobile phones, now greatly expanded even since this poem was written, which can be farmed, reassembled and used by others in entirely unanticipated and not necessarily beneficial ways.[11] The first epigraph is from 'Summons of the Soul' from *Songs of the South*, which is the other great foundational anthology of Chinese literature along with the Confucian *Book of Songs* (or *Odes*).[12] While the northern *Book of Songs* consists of anonymous folksongs and ceremonial poems, the poems of *Songs of the South* (or, more literally, *Songs of Chu*), traditionally ascribed to Qu Yuan, include lush descriptive detail and allegorical journeys, springing from the luxuriant landscape of the south and a culture pervaded by shamanism. 'Summons of the Soul' is presumably in the voice of a shaman attempting to lure back the soul of a just deceased king. The main body of the poem has two neat halves which deploy antithetical rhetorical strategies: first the shaman attempts to frighten the soul to return by describing the horrors the soul will encounter in every direction, a quasi-surrealist tour of the barbarian fringes, then switching to a more seductive tack he describes in lavish terms all the enticements of the home palace, complete with beautiful women and culminating in an orgiastic party. As Joyce notes, some of the imagery in the first half is taken from the first part of the 'Summons': ants, wasps, gourds, blazing sands, bloody thumbs. Also presumably the two-part structure of the 'Summons' is mirrored in the two parts of Joyce's poem: the first sounding rather ominous and the latter half sounding more positive and expansive once we get past the first stanza, although it does not incorporate any specific details from the Chinese poem. 'Data Shadows' opens with a parallel couplet and, as I read it, the first line looks forward to the second half, where order and systems take over, while the first half of the poem follows from the second line with images of pre-order. The second half begins with a survey of this unordered geography but in a tone of sizing up the situation preparatory to implementing the systems of order and clarity that predominate in the rest of the half. The epigraph to the second half is from Stanislaw Lem's *One Human Minute*, which also supplies quite a few of the lines and images of the second half of Joyce's poem. Lem's piece is a darkly hilarious fake review of a book that purports to depict all of humanity in a single minute in the form of a compendium of statistical tables on every imaginable aspect of human life. If we put these two epigraphs and their sources together, we have two images of control, archaic and hyper-modern, with control's implicit complements: the refusal of mortality and change. As Lem's reviewer points out, the effort to capture a snapshot of humankind in the form of statistics leads to all manner of absurdities concerning just what we believe to be the object of our knowledge as the welter of human experience constantly eludes the order of numbers. The shaman of course is a figure of the poet, now reduced or enhanced, depending on how you look at it, to a group of statisticians.

'Data Shadows' and its siblings, 'Approach of Bodies Falling in Time of Plague' and 'Proceeds of a Black Swap', are doubly arbitrary: on the one hand they are pieced together from found materials that might be chosen or arranged differently, and on the other the lines are systematically rearranged, which suggests that they might be rearranged in any number of yet other ways. Such works so self-consciously situated in the thick of the textual world seem to have neither identifiable beginnings nor ends, identifiable authors nor ideal readers. In this sense the poem perhaps represents the dispersed or lost traces that potentially can be regathered and rearranged in infinitely unpredictable ways. Data shadows are simply an image of textual iterability, of the soul lost because it was never entirely here. This would be consistent with Joyce's often expressed interest in process, in form as less a container than a conduit. These poems immediately raise questions about the relationship between their doubling, and in the case of 'Data Shadows' of doubled doubling. Does the rearrangement of lines constitute a new poem to be set alongside its progenitor and therefore suggest a potential serial text of various permutations – a happy image of textual play and creativity? Or are the rearranged lines set against their progenitor, a dissolving action that would refuse the containment and grammaticalisation of that original noise, as we know it always can and will be? Joyce himself has spoken of how in rereading such poems he discovers over time more meanings and linkages, but logically at some point this risks becoming too determined. In that case the textual doublings function to guarantee the operation of counter-mining, creating static and short circuits within the poem as well as outside it relative to the vast systems of data control and therefore are an image of a degree of anarchic freedom in distress. As mentioned at the outset, it does not seem to me that the poem offers a perch from which to definitely decide between these alternative readings, as the principle of parallelism and antithesis, of substitution and contradiction, perpetuates this doubling as process and flux.

Notes

[1] On the cover of *Take Over* is a collage of Irish and Chinese texts relevant to Joyce's translations. For those curious about the Chinese texts, down along the right-hand side is the first poem by Ruan Ji that Joyce renders in *What's in Store* (118); upper left is part of the entry from Robert H. Mathews' classic Chinese–English dictionary (also used by Pound) for the character *xin* (or *hsin*), meaning heart, and which is the last character of the Ruan Ji poem; lower left are the last eleven lines of the Lu Zhaolin poem that Joyce translates as 'Capital Accounts'. It is worth noting that *xin* incorporates the senses of both heart and mind or thought.

[2] In part, this paragraph is an apology for not directly comparing Joyce's translations with the Chinese originals, which in any case would stretch my competence and probably the patience of the reader as well. While I imagine that Joyce has some proficiency in Chinese, in his various notes he consistently refers to authoritative sources in English, and the occasional quotations he uses as epigraphs to poems invariably come from such sources.

[3] As one would expect, there are exceptions where Joyce allows a contemporary voice to entirely take over the translation. This is the case with "I'm not gonna die", the second version of a twice-rendered poem in the "Anonymous Love Songs from the Irish" group (*What's in Store* 95), and there is an as yet uncollected Chinese example, a version of a famous poem by Tao Qian, which as far as I know has only been published in an event pamphlet for the Cambridge Reading Series (2010), online at <http://crs0hq.tumblr.com/post/1498082774>. Tao Qian is mentioned as one of the authors on the poet's bookshelf in "93/4' (*first dream of fire* 121).

[4] The cover of the chapbook *Undone, Say*, in which 'The Peacock's Tale' was first published, gives a complete listing of the various word strings or "rhyme chains" Joyce incorporates into the lyric half of the poem, as well as those for 'De Iron Trote'. It is noticeable that aural rhyme chains are far more prominent in 'De Iron Trote' than in 'The Peacock's Tale'.

[5] Joyce's substitution of the one-arm image for the mandarin ducks is almost

certainly suggested by a synonymous allusion found frequently in Chinese poetry of one-winged birds who therefore need a mate in order to fly.

6   Joyce pointed out the triple pun on "reign" to me and indicated that this was in fact the seed of the entire poem (personal communication 27 November 2012).

7   These horses, literally designated as "Heavenly horses", were considered the finest breed available in ancient China, and a war was fought during the Han dynasty (circa 100 BC) to compel a central Asian kingdom to send them to the Chinese as yearly tribute. It is believed a parasite caused them to "sweat blood" when in a lather. The source for 'Tocharian Music' is Grousset, including the epigraph from Wu K'ung, who is relating the legendary source of the Tocharian melodies (54, 248).

8   Joyce only notes that he is working from the first two of Meng Jiao's 'Autumn Meditations' sequence in 'Lines in Fall'. There are numerous translations of selections but particularly useful is Owen (1975), who translates the full sequence with scholarly commentary (162–184).

9   Joyce apparently mentioned to Goodby that for him *Liezi* is the "strongest" voice in the poem (306).

10 Joyce's source is Graham (21, 53).

11 Joyce of course worked in the IT industry, but one source he draws on is Bernstein's article on the misuse of electronic data, which supplies several lines and phrases in the second half of the poem as well as part of Joyce's note.

12 From the quotation that Joyce gives as his epigraph, it is evident that he is using the complete and authoritative version of Qu Yuan by Hawkes, who also provides extensive commentary.

Works Cited

Bernstein, Nina. 'Personal Files Via Computer Offer Money and Pose Threat.' *New York Times* 12 June 1997. Web. 12 Dec. 2012. <https://www.nytimes.com/1997/06/12/us/personal-files-via-computer-offer-money-and-pose-threat.html?src=pm>.

Frankel, Hans H. *The Flowering Plum and the Palace Lady: Interpretations of Chinese Poetry*. New Haven, CT: Yale University Press, 1976. Print.

Goodby, John. *Irish Poetry Since 1950: From Stillness into History*. Manchester: Manchester University Press, 2000. Print.

Graham, A.C. *The Book of Lieh-tzu: A Classic of the Tao*. New York, NY: Columbia University Press, 1990. Print.

Grousset, René. *In the Footsteps of the Buddha*. Trans. Mariette Leon. London: Routledge, 1932. Print.

Holzman, Donald. *Poetry and Politics: The Life and Works of Juan Chi (A.D. 210–263)*. Cambridge: Cambridge University Press, 1976. Print.

Joyce, Trevor. 'Interrogate the Thrush: Another Name for Something Else'. *Vectors: New Poetics*. Ed. Robert Archambeau. Lincoln, NE: Writers Club Press, 2001. 136–169. Print.

——. 'The Structure of "The Peacock's Tale"'. *The Drunken Boat* 8. 2006. Web. 12 Dec. 2012.

——. *Take Over*. Willowdale, ON: The Gig, 2003. Print.

——. *Undone, Say*. Willowdale, ON: The Gig, 2003. Print.

——. *What's in Store: Poems 2000–2007*. Dublin: New Writers' Press; Willowdale, ON: The Gig, 2007. Print.

——. *with the first dream of fire they hunt the cold: A Body of Work 1966–2000*. 2nd ed. Dublin: New Writers' Press; Exeter: Shearsman Books, 2003. Print.

——. 'Why I Write Narrative'. *Narrativity* 1. The Poetry Centre, San Francisco State University, Mar. 2000. Web. 12 Dec. 2012. <http://www.sfsu.edu/~poetry/narrativity/issue_one/joyce.html>.

Lem, Stanisław. *One Human Minute*. Trans. Catherine S. Leach. New York, NY: Harcourt, 1986. Print.

Owen, Stephen. *The Poetry of the Early T'ang*. New Haven, CT: Yale University Press, 1977. Print.

——. *The Poetry of Meng Chiao and Han Yu*. New Haven, CT: Yale University Press, 1975. Print.

Qu Yuan, et. al. *The Songs of the South: An Ancient Chinese Anthology of Poems*. Trans. David Hawkes. Harmondsworth: Penguin, 1985. Print.

Jeffrey Twitchell-Waas

Bibliography

EDITOR'S NOTE: There are several points to note and editorial decisions to explain that will make the bibliography more useful. All of the sections from "Poetry: Books and pamphlets" to "Video/Sound Recordings" are organised chronologically from earliest to most recent. The critical writing on Joyce which follows – "Secondary criticism," "Reviews" and "Notes/Introductions" – is organised alphabetically, with "Dictionary entries" arranged chronologically. The references are broadly consistent with Chicago documentation style; however, further information regarding publishers' names, place of publication, dates and reprints is also included intermittently. The references to Joyce's poetry collections include information on the number of pages, which is followed by the print run of each collection in parentheses, e.g. (150). For *with the first dream of fire they hunt the cold* and *Courts of Air and Earth*, I use the acronym "POD" to indicate print-on-demand, which means that there is no print run in the traditional sense. Joyce's essay 'New Writers' Press: The History of a Project' includes an extensive bibliography of the NWP books in which he is credited for cover art on five of his own poetry collections, as well as several other NWP publications; these include Jorge Luis Borges' *Poems*, Michael Smith's *Homage to James Thomson (B. V.) at Portobello*, and Michael Hartnett's *Tao: A Version of the Chinese Classic of the Sixth Century*. There is a drawing by Joyce of the Man in the Moon modelled on that of Sabine Baring-Gould's *Curious Myths of the Middle Ages* included in the New Writers' Press Archive at the National Library of Ireland. That image was used for the cover of *Sole Glum Trek* (1967), and would later become the logo of Melmoth Press. Joyce also created the cover image for *Without Asylum*.

The bibliography is not exhaustive; there are a number of publications and references that still elude me, and of course Joyce is still writing and publishing. That said, many people helped in compiling this bibliography, and I would like to acknowledge some of them here: my thanks to James Cummins, Alex Davis, Nate Dorward, Marcella Edwards, Harry Gilonis, John Goodby, Trevor Joyce, Justin Katko, David Lloyd, Jim Mays, and Keith Tuma.

POETRY: BOOKS AND PAMPHLETS

Sole Glum Trek: New Irish Poets. Dublin: New Writers' Press, 1967. 30 pp. (500).
Watches. Dublin: New Writers' Press, 1969. 16 pp. (150).
Pentahedron. Dublin: Zozimus–New Writers' Press, 1972. 53 pp. (1,000 pb; 250 hb).
The Poems of Sweeny, Peregrine: A Working of the Corrupt Irish Text. Dublin: New Writers' Press, 1976. 48 pp. (500).
stone floods. Dublin: New Writers' Press, 1995. 52 pp. (400).
Syzygy. Bray, Co. Wicklow: Wild Honey Press, 1998. 16 pp. (228).

Hellbox. London: Form Books, 1998. 3 pp. (50).

Without Asylum. Bray, Co. Wicklow: Wild Honey Press, 1998. 13 pp. (98).

with the first dream of fire they hunt the cold. A Body of Work. Dublin: New Writers' Press; Exeter: Shearsman Books, 2001. 241 pp. (600). 2nd ed. 2003. (POD).

Take Over. Willowdale, ON: The Gig, 2003. 52 pp. (150).

Undone, Say. Willowdale, ON: The Gig, 2003. 48 pp. (150).

Dwory Powietrza i Ziemi. Edited and translated by John Comber and Lidia Nowicka-Comber. Poznań: Motivex; Dublin: New Writers' Press, 2004. 137 pp. Dual-language publication of *Courts of Air and Earth*.

What's in Store: Poems, 2000–2007. Dublin: New Writers' Press; Willowdale, ON: The Gig, 2007. 322 pp. (800).

Courts of Air and Earth. Foreword by Fanny Howe; afterword by Máire Herbert. Exeter: Shearsman Books, 2008. 95 pp. (POD).

Poems of Aregemia. Edited by Mark Mallon. Translated by Seija Kerttula and Trevor Joyce. Helsinki: Ntamo, 2012. 80 pp.

The Immediate Future. Cork: Runamok Press, 2013. 36 pp. (100).

Rome's Wreck: Translated from the English of Edmund Spenser's Ruines of Rome. Los Angeles, CA: Cusp Books, 2014. Print.

Selected Poems, 1967-2014. Bristol: Shearsman Books, 2014. 144 pp. (POD).

POETRY: PERIODICALS AND ANTHOLOGIES

'Time Piece. Clocks Err Through Anger of the Watcher'. *The Lace Curtain*, no. 1 (Autumn 1969): 20–21. Edited by Michael Smith and Trevor Joyce. Dublin: New Writers' Press.

'I Know These Streets'. *The Lace Curtain*, no. 2 (Spring 1970): 18. Edited by Michael Smith and Trevor Joyce. Dublin: New Writers' Press.

'Elegy of the Shut Mirror' and 'Surd Blab'. *The Lace Curtain*, no. 3 (Summer 1970): 30–33. Edited by Michael Smith and Trevor Joyce. Dublin: New Writers' Press.

'Engravure'. *The Kilkenny Magazine*, no. 18 (Autumn–Winter 1970): 117. Edited by James Delahunty.

'Death Is Conventional (Song, Probably Evasive)' and 'Bronze Through Seagrowth'. *St Stephen's* 2, no. 19. (Hilary Term, 1971): 12–14, 24–25. Guest-edited by Trevor Joyce.

'The Fall'. 'Ecrivains irlandais d'aujourd'hui', Special issue, *Les Lettres Nouvelles* 3, no. 1 (March 1973): 208. Guest-edited by Serge Fauchereau.

'Fulgurite'. *Icarus*, no. 67 (Winter 1974): np. Edited by Edward Brazil. Dublin: Trinity College.

'Mirror: Of Glazier Velázquez'. 'Irish Poetry'. Special issue, *The Niagara Magazine*, no. 3 (Summer 1975): 31–32. Guest-edited by Michael Smith and Augustus Young.

'One' and 'Mirror: Of Glazier Velázquez'. *The Lace Curtain*, no. 6 (Autumn 1978): 8–9. Edited by Michael Smith. Dublin: New Writers' Press.

'Poem X,' from *Sweeny*. *Granta* (Autumn 1976). Edited David Lloyd. Cambridge.

'Two Poems from *Magazine*: A Work in Progress'. *The Irish Review*, no. 8 (1990): 12–13. Edited by Kevin Barry et al. Retitled 'Cold Snap' and 'Cold Course' in *stone floods*.

'The Turlough' and 'Cry Help'. 'Autobiography as Criticism'. Special issue, *The Irish Review*, no. 13 (1992): 143–145. Edited by Kevin Barry et al.

'Coumeenole'. In *Pathfinder: Skills in Language and Literature*, edited by Michael Smith, 166. Dublin: Educational Company, 1994.

'Cold Course'. *Irish Times*, 9 December 1995, A8. Edited by Conor Brady.

'"in three quarters now you lie", a stanza from his forthcoming *Syzygy*'. *FormCard: Irish Modernism Series*, no. 4 (April 1997): np. Edited by Harry Gilonis. London: Form Books.

'Verses with a Refrain from a Solicitor's Letter,' 'Lines in Fall,' 'Chimaera,' 'Tohubohu.' 'Lewis Marsh Issue: Five Irish Poets'. Special issue, *Talisman: A Journal of Contemporary Poetry and Poetics*, no. 18 (Fall 1998): 130–137. Guest-edited by Keith Tuma and William Walsh.

'Hopeful Monsters'. *The Gig*, no. 1 (November 1998): 30–39. Edited by Nate Dorward. Willowdale, Ontario.

'A Father of the Useful Arts (1738)', 'Capital Accounts, From OBEX (work in progress)' and 'Trem Neul'. *Sub Voicive Poetry*, no. 2 (1999): 5–8. Edited by Lawrence Upton.

'Approach of Bodies Falling in Time of Plague', 'Proceeds of a Black Swap' and explanatory notes on both poems. *Shearsman*, no. 38 (February 1999): 5–9. Edited by Tony Frazer.

'Trem Neul'. *Masthead*, no. 4 (January 2000): 18–22. Edited by Alison Croggon. In 2000, *Masthead* became an online journal with issue 4 as the first digital issue.

'Data Shadows', 'Joinery', 'Let Happen' and 'DARK SENSES PARALLEL STREETS'. *Alterran Poetry Assemblage*, no. 5 (December 2000). Edited by David Dowker.

'STILLSMAN'. In *Vectors: New Poetics*, edited by Robert Archambeau, 170–181. San Jose: Writers Club Press, 2001.

from 'Saws'. *Poetry Ireland Review*, no. 71 (Winter 2001): 62–64. Edited by Maurice Harmon.

from 'Saws'. *The Gig*, no. 9 (September 2001): 3–6. Edited by Nate Dorward. Willowdale, ON: The Gig.

'The Fishers Fished', 'Concentration' and 'Incidents at Cloghroe, Co. Cork'. *Southword* 2, no. 3 (2000): 10–11. Edited by Patrick Galvin and Mary Johnson.

'Watch'. *Southword* 3, no. 1 (2001): 16. Edited by Patrick Galvin.

'The Turlough', 'Cry Help' and 'Tohu-bohu'. In *Anthology of Twentieth-Century British and Irish Poetry*, edited by Keith Tuma, 742–747. New York, NY: Oxford University Press, 2001.

'from Love Songs from a Dead Tongue'. *Masthead*, no. 5 (February 2002). Online. Edited by Alison Croggon.

'from Love Songs from a Dead Tongue'. *Poetry Ireland Review*, no. 74 (Autumn 2002): 42–59. Edited by Michael Smith.

'A Father of the Useful Arts (1738)', 'Dánta Grádha 18', 'Watch', 'Without Asylum', 'Approach of Bodies Falling in a Time of Plague', 'Proceeds of a Black Swap' and 'behaviour self!' *A Chide's Alphabet: Second Chiding*, May 2001. Edited by David Bircumshaw.

'To Lily Bloom', 'The Peacock's Tale', and 'De Iron Trote'. 'Remembering Alaric Sumner: A Retrospective'. Special issue, *Masthead*, no. 8 (February 2004). Edited by Alison Croggon.

'4 Poems from the Chinese of Ruan Ji' and 'STILLSMAN'. *Shearsman*, no. 58 (Spring 2004): 2–6. Edited by Tony Frazer.

Some poems. In *Onsets: A Breviary (Synopticon?) of Poems 13 Lines or Under*, edited by Nate Dorward, np. Willowdale, ON: The Gig, 2001.

'DARK SENSES PARALLEL STREETS. With and for Tom Raworth'. *Jacket*, no. 26 (October 2004). Edited by John Tranter.

'from Saws.' *Free Verse*, no. 7 (Winter 2004). Edited by Jon Thompson.

'Coumeenole'. In *New Writers' Press Anthology*, edited by Martin Dolan and Michael Smith with an introduction by Declan Kiberd, 93–95. Poznán: Motivex, 2004.

'From a work in progress'. *Masthead*, no. 9 (March 2005). Edited by Alison Croggon.

'STILLSMAN'. In *Vinyl: Material Location Placement*, edited by Simon Cutts, np. Tipperary: Coracle, 2005. In this book, Cutts records the exhibition of Joyce's poem 'STILLSMAN' as an installation as part of the *vinyl: project for installation* held in Cork city during July and August 2005.

'The Peacock's Tale'. In *Cork Caucus: On Art, Possibility, and Democracy*, edited by Trevor Joyce and Shep Steiner, 375–377. Cork: National Sculpture Factory and Revolver, 2006.

'*From Ana*'. *Masthead*, no. 10 (March 2006). Edited by Alison Croggon.

'The Drift' from *Syzygy*', 'The Net' from *Syzygy*', and 'The Peacock's Tale'. 'Towards OuLiPo'. Special feature, *Drunken Boat*, no. 8 (Spring 2006). Guest-edited by Jean-Jacques Poucel.

'from Outcry'. *Masthead*, no. 11 (September 2008). Guest-edited by Andrew Burke and Candice Ward.

'from Rome's Wreck.' *Poetry Salzburg Review*, no. 15 (Spring 2009): 137–139. Guest-edited by James Cummins, Fergal Gaynor and Trevor Joyce.

'from Rome's Wreck.' *past simple*, no. 6 (March 2009). Edited by Jim Goar and Marcus Slease.

'Fragmentos'. *RevistAtlántica de poesía*, no. 34 (2010): 71–80. Edited by Márius Torres. Translated by Luis Ingelmo. With an introduction in Spanish by Michael Smith. Cádiz: Diputación de Cádiz.

['granted...'] and 'Sixth Month, Year 408: Fire'. *Cambridge Reading Series: Nour Mobarak and Trevor Joyce*, April 2010, 5–6.

'*from* Ruan Ji'. In *Invisibly Tight Institutional Outer Flanks Dub (Verb) Glorious National Hi-Violence Response Dream*, edited by Ryan Dobran, Justin Katko and Sara Wintz, 18–19. New York and Providence, RI: Life Gang Documents, 2008.

'all that is the case' and 'now then'. In *The Penguin Book of Irish Poetry*, edited by Patrick Crotty, 794–795. London: Penguin, 2010.

'Wretched to me... (from the late Middle Irish)'. *MATERIALpoetry*. Edited by Simon Cutts, np. Tipperary: Coracle, 2010.

Five extracts from *The Immediate Future*. *Chicago Review* 56.2 (2011): 89–93. Edited by Joel Calahan and Michael Hansen.

Five extracts from *The Immediate Future*. *Truck*, Feb. 2013. Edited by Mark Weiss.

Two extracts from *The Immediate Future* and 'when I died...' *Return to Default*, June 2013. Edited by James Cummins, Sarah Hayden and Rachel Warriner.

PROSE

'Ideologist of Love: The Poetry of James Liddy'. *The Lace Curtain*, no. 1 (1969): 44–48. Edited by Michael Smith and Trevor Joyce. Dublin: New Writers' Press.

'The Young Poets, 12: Michael Smith'. *Hibernia* 33, no. 18 (1969): 15. Edited by John Mulcahy.

'New Writers' Press: The History of a Project'. In *Modernism and Ireland: The Poetry of the 1930s*, edited by Patricia Coughlan and Alex Davis, 276–306. Cork: Cork University Press, 1995.

'The Point of Innovation in Irish Poetry'. In *For the Birds: Proceedings of the First Cork Conference on New and Experimental Irish Poetry*, edited by Harry Gilonis, 18–24. Sutton: Mainstream; Dublin: hardPressed Poetry, 1998. Reprinted in 'Six Poets: Views and Interviews'. Special issue, *The Gig*, no. 2 (2001): 45–50. Edited by Nate Dorward. Willowdale, ON: The Gig, 2001. Also reprinted in *New Writers' Press Anthology*, edited by Martin Dolan and Michael Smith, with an introduction by Declan Kiberd, 16–22, 23–30. Poznan: Motivex, 2004.

'Why I Write Narrative'. *Narrativity* 1. The Poetry Centre, San Francisco State University, Mar. 2000. Web. 3 Aug. 2013. Reprinted in *The Recorder* 13, no. 2 (2000): 57–63. Edited by Christopher Cahill.

'Interrogate the Thrush: Another Name for Something Else'. In *Vectors: New Poetics*, edited by Robert Archambeau, 136–169. Lincoln, NE: Writers Club Press, 2001.

'Irish Terrain: Alternative Planes of Cleavage'. In *Assembling Alternatives: Reading Postmodern Poetries Transnationally*, edited by Romana Huk, 156–168. Middletown, CT: Wesleyan University Press, 2003.

'On *stone floods*: A Commentary from a Letter to Michael Smith'. 'The Fly on the Page'. Special issue, *The Gig*, no. 3 (2004): 3–15. Edited by Nate Dorward. Willowdale, ON: The Gig.

'On 'Without Asylum': An Email Exchange'. 'The Fly on the Page'. Special issue, *The Gig*, no. 3 (2004): 16. Edited by Nate Dorward. Willowdale, ON: The Gig.

'Approach of Bodies Falling in Time of Plague' and 'Proceeds of a Black Swap': Some Explanatory Notes'. 'The Fly on the Page'. Special issue, *The Gig*, no. 3 (2004): 17–18. Edited by Nate Dorward. Willowdale, ON: The Gig.

'Introduction: On This Book'. In *Cork Caucus: On Art, Possibility, and Democracy*, edited by Trevor Joyce and Shep Steiner, 17–18. Cork: National Sculpture Factory and Revolver, 2006.

'On "The Peacock's Tale".' In *Cork Caucus: On Art, Possibility, and Democracy*, edited by Trevor Joyce and Shep Steiner, 371–74. Cork: National Sculpture Factory and Revolver, 2006.

'The Construction of *Syzygy*', 'The Structure of 'The Peacock's Tale," and 'Some Notes'. 'Towards OuLiPo'. Special feature, *Drunken Boat*, no. 8 (Spring 2006). Guest edited by Jean-Jacques Poucel.

Introduction to 'SoundEye 12: Festival of the Arts of the Word. 3–6 July 2008'. *Poetry Salzburg Review*, no. 15 (Spring 2009): 82–84. Guest-edited by James Cummins, Fergal Gaynor and Trevor Joyce.

'The Phantom Quarry: Translating a Renaissance Painting into Modern Poetry'. *Enclave Review*, no. 8 (September 2013): 5–8. Edited by Fergal Gaynor and Ed Krčma.

UNPUBLISHED TALKS

'The Role of Poetry in Chinese Cultural Life'. Europe–China Association Annual Conference, University of Oxford, 1982.

'New Writers? Some Irish'. 'Assembling Alternatives', Wesleyan University, Middletown, CT, 1996.

'Irish Practice Imperfect'. Third Sub Voicive Poetry Colloquium, University of London, 1999.

Editorial work

Brian Coffey. *Versheet*, vol. 1. Edited by Trevor Joyce. Dublin: New Writers' Press, 1971. 6 pp.

Cork Caucus: On Art, Possibility, and Democracy. Edited by Trevor Joyce and Shep Steiner. Cork: National Sculpture Factory and Revolver, 2006.

The Lace Curtain, no. 1. Edited by Michael Smith and Trevor Joyce. Dublin: New Writers' Press, 1969.

The Lace Curtain, no. 2. Edited by Michael Smith and Trevor Joyce. Dublin: New Writers' Press, 1970.

The Lace Curtain, no. 3. Edited by Michael Smith; associate editor Trevor Joyce. Dublin: New Writers' Press, 1970.

Pawlowski, Robert. *Versheet*, vol. 2. Edited by Trevor Joyce. Dublin: New Writers' Press, 1971. 6 pp.

Redshaw, Thomas Dillon. *Such a Heart Dances Out. Versheet*, vol. 4. Edited by Trevor Joyce. Dublin: New Writers' Press, 1971. 6 pp.

'SoundEye 12: Festival of the Arts of the Word. 3–6 July 2008'. *Poetry Salzburg Review*, no. 15 (Spring 2009): 82–194. Guest-edited by James Cummins, Fergal Gaynor and Trevor Joyce.

Reviews

Review of *When She Was Good*, by Philip Roth, *The Far Side of the Sky*, by Maslyn Williams, and *Satori in Paris*, by Jack Kerouac. *Hibernia* 32, no. 2 (February 1968): 20. Edited by John Mulcahy.

Review of *The Hard Hours,* by Anthony Hecht, and *Just Like the Resurrection*, by Patricia Beer. *The Dublin Magazine* 7, nos. 2–4 (Autumn/Winter 1968): 107–108. Edited by Rivers Carew and Timothy Brownlow. Formerly *The Dubliner.*

'Nazi Aftermath'. Review of *Camp 7 Last Stop*, by Hans Hellmut Kirst, and *The Hour of the Unicorn*, by James Parish. *Hibernia* 33, no. 10 (May 1969): 16. Edited by John Mulcahy.

'Reading the Metre Before Moving On'. Review of *An Introduction to English Poetry*, by James Fenton. *Irish Times*, 20 July 2002, B9. Edited by Conor Brady.

Interviews

Interview by Michael S. Begnal. *The Burning Bush*, no. 7 (Spring 2002): 44–48. Edited by Michael S. Begnal.

Interview by Leonard Schwartz. *Cross-Cultural Poetics*, episode 62 (Fall 2004). Olympia, Washington: KAOS-FM.

'Partly for the Shiver'. Interview by G. Keohane. *Karnival*, no. 5 (October 2005): 9–10. Edited by Dan Finn.

'Poetry, Form, Meaning'. Interview by Keith Tuma in *Cork Caucus: On Art, Possibility, and Democracy*, edited by Trevor Joyce and Shep Steiner, 377–378. Cork: National Sculpture Factory and Revolver, 2006.

'Finding a Language Use: Trevor Joyce in 2011'. Interview by Niamh O'Mahony. *Jacket2*, 2013. Edited by Julia Bloch and Michael S. Hennessey.

Interview by Marthine Satris. *Journal of British and Irish Innovative Poetry* 5, no. 1 (2013). Edited by James Cummins and Rachel Warriner. 13-35. Print.

Video/Sound recordings

Red Noise of Bones. Dublin: Coelacanth; Bray, Co. Wicklow: Wild Honey Press, 2001. Compact disc.

SoundEye Festival Readings, Cork, Ireland, July 4, 2005. Posted at *Meshworks: the Miami University Archive of Writing in Performance*.

Question and answer session after a reading at Test Reading Series, Mercer Union, Toronto. Oct. 2007. Mercer Union, Toronto. Available at archive.org.

Reading with Cai Tianxin at SoundEye. July 2007. Posted to YouTube, Sept. 7, 2007.

Reading at Miami University, Ohio, October 2007. Posted at *Meshworks: the Miami University Archive of Writing in Performance*.

Reading with Fergal and Marja Gaynor, SoundEye Festival, July 2009. Posted September 17 2009.

Reading, SoundEye Workshops, March 2010. Posted to YouTube, Mar. 2010.

Secondary criticism

Archambeau, Robert. 'Another Ireland'. Part 1, *Notre Dame Review*, no. 4 (Summer 1997): 133–144; part 2, *Notre Dame Review*, no. 5 (Winter 1998): 135–146. Edited by William O'Rourke. Reprinted as *Another Ireland: An Essay*. Bray, Co. Wicklow: Wild Honey Press, 1998.

Begnal, Michael S. 'The Ancients Have Returned Among Us: Polaroids of 21st-Century Irish Poetry'. In *Avant Post the Avant*, edited by Louis Armand, 307–324. Prague: Litteraria Pragensia, 2006.

——. 'Beyond Tradition: The Wild Honey Poets'. *The Burning Bush*, no. 5 (Spring 2001): 14–17. Edited by Michael S. Begnal.

Butler, David. 'Where to Look for the Wild Honey'. *Poetry Ireland Review*, no. 79 (2004): 57–60. Edited by Peter Sirr.

Davis, Alex. *A Broken Line: Denis Devlin and Irish Poetic Modernism*. Dublin: University College Dublin Press, 2000. Joyce discussed on 135–148, 161–164.

——. 'Deferred Action: Irish Neo-Avant-Garde Poetry'. *Angelaki* 5, no. 1 (2000): 81–94.

——. 'The Irish Modernists and Their Legacy'. In *The Cambridge Companion to Contemporary Irish Poetry*, edited by Matthew Campbell, 88–91. Cambridge: Cambridge University Press, 2003.

——. 'Is it Really a Revolution Though?: Paul Muldoon and Linguistically Innovative Poetry'. *Masthead* 10 (2006). Edited by Alison Croggon.

——. '"No Narrative Easy in the Mind": Modernism, the Avant-Garde and Irish Poetry'. In *For the Birds: Proceedings of the First Cork Conference on New and Experimental Irish Poetry*, edited by Harry Gilonis, 37–49. Dublin: hardPressed Poetry; Surrey: Mainstream Poetry Press, 1998.

Dorward, Nate. 'On Trevor Joyce'. *Chicago Review* 48, no. 4 (Winter 2002–2003): 82–96. Edited by Eirik Steinhoff.

Edwards, Marcella. '"A Scheme of Echoes": Trevor Joyce, Poetry and Publishing in Ireland in the 1960s'. *Critical Survey* 15, no. 1 (2003): 3–17. Guest-edited by Eibhlín Evans.

——. 'Poetry and the Politics of Publishing in Ireland: Authority in the Writings of Trevor Joyce, 1967–1995'. PhD diss., University of Strathclyde, UK, 2003.

Falci, Eric. *Continuity and Change in Irish Poetry, 1966–2010*. Cambridge: Cambridge University Press, 2012. Joyce discussed on 31–35.

Fauchereau, Serge. 'Écrivains irlandais d'aujourd'hui'. Special issue, *Les Lettres Nouvelles* 3, no. 1 (March 1973): 185. Guest-edited by Serge Fauchereau.

Gilonis, Harry. 'Good Fruit and Sour: Trevor Joyce, Seamus Heaney and the Buile Suibhne Geilt'. 'Colonies of Belief: Ireland's Modernists'. Special issue, *Suitear na n-Aingeal/Angel Exhaust*, no. 17 (Spring 1999): 107–116. Edited by Maurice Scully and John Goodby.

Goodby, John. '"Comes the Experiment": Irish Poetry and the Avant-Garde'. In *The Oxford Handbook of Modern Irish Poetry*, edited by Fran Brearton and Alan Gillis, 214–236. Oxford: Oxford University Press, 2012.

——. '"Current, Historical, Mythical or Spook?": Irish Modernist and Experimental Poetry'. Introduction to 'Colonies of Belief: Ireland's Modernists'. Special issue, *Suitear na n-Aingeal/Angel Exhaust*, no. 17 (Spring 1999): 51–60. Edited by John Goodby and Maurice Scully.

——. *Irish Poetry from 1950: From Stillness into History*. Manchester: Manchester University Press, 2000. Joyce discussed on 303–307.

——. '"Through My Dream": Trevor Joyce's Translations'. *Études Irlandaises* 35, no. 2 (Autumn 2010): 149–164. Edited by Sylvie Mikowski et al.

Goodby, John, and Marcella Edwards. '"Glittering Silt": The Poetry of Trevor Joyce and the Myth of Irishness'. *Hungarian Journal of English and American Studies* 8, no. 1 (Spring 2002): 173–198. Edited by Kalman Matolcsy.

Howe, Fanny. Foreword to *Courts of Air and Earth*, by Trevor Joyce, 7. Exeter: Shearsman Books, 2008.

Kersnowski, Frank L. *The Outsiders: Poets of Contemporary Ireland*. Texas: Texas Christian University Press, 1975. Joyce discussed on 164–165.

Longley, Edna. 'Irish Poetry and 'Internationalism': Variations on a Critical Theme'. *The Irish Review*, no. 30 (Spring–Summer 2003): 48–61. Edited by Kevin Barry et al.

Mays, J.C.C. 'Flourishing and Foul, Six Poets and the Irish Building Industry'. *The Irish Review*, no. 8 (Spring 1990): 6–11. Edited by Kevin Barry et al.

——. *N11: A Musing*. Dublin: Coelacanth, 2003. Reprinted in *Little Critic*, no. 18 (Autumn 2006).

O'Mahony, Niamh. *Essays on the Poetry of Trevor Joyce*. Bristol: Shearsman Books, 2014.

Pehnt, Annette. 'Rewritings of Buile Shuibhne in the Twentieth Century'. PhD diss., University of Freiburg, Germany, 1997. Published in summary form in *Harvard Celtic Colloquium*, no. 15 (1995).

Quinn, Justin. *The Cambridge Introduction to Modern Irish Poetry: 1800–2000*. Cambridge: Cambridge University Press, 2008. Joyce discussed on 108–111.

Ryan, Catriona. *Border States in the Work of Tom Mac Intyre: A Paleo-postmodern Perspective*. Newcastle: Cambridge Scholars Publishing, 2012. Joyce discussed on 188-189.

Sealy, Douglas. 'The End of Tribalism: Irish Poetry During the Last Decade'. 'James Joyce and the Arts in Ireland'. Special issue, *The Crane Bag* 6, no. 1 (1982): 74–84. Edited by Richard Kearney.

Sirr, Peter. 'The Cat Flap'. *Poetry Ireland Review*, no. 78 (2004): 110–114. Edited by Peter Sirr.

Smith, Michael. 'The Contemporary Situation in Irish Poetry'. In *Two Decades in Irish Writing: A Critical Survey*, edited by Douglas Dunn, 154–165. Cheadle: Carcarnet, 1975.

——. 'Irish Poetry Since Yeats: Notes Towards a Corrected History'. *Denver Quarterly* 5, no. 4 (Winter 1971): 24.

Steinhoff, Eirik. 'Who Needs a Hundred Million Lilly Dollars?' *Chicago Review*, no. 49 (Summer 2003): 190–196.

Tuma, Keith. 'Collaborating with *Dark Senses*'. *Removed for Further Study: The Poetry of Tom Raworth*. Ed. Nate Dorward. Special issue, *The Gig* nos. 13/14 (2003): 207–16. Willowdale, ON: The Gig.

——. 'Introduction to the Poetry of Trevor Joyce'. In *Anthology of Twentieth Century British and Irish Poetry*, edited by Keith Tuma, 741–742. New York, NY: Oxford University Press, 2001.

——. *On Leave: A Book of Anecdotes*. Cambridge: Salt Publishing, 2011. Joyce discussed on 93–98.

——. 'Whatever Irish Poetry: Some Musings'. *The Journal*, no. 2. Limerick: hardPressed Poetry, 1999. np. Edited by Billy Mills and Catherine Smith.

Williams, Nerys. *Contemporary Poetry.* Edinburgh: Edinburgh University Press, 2001. Joyce discussed on 216–217.

REVIEWS: PERIODICALS AND NEWSPAPERS

Begnal, Michael S. 'Polar / cold / marks terminus'. Review of *What's in Store: Poems 2000–2007. Free Verse*, no. 14 (Summer 2008). Edited by Jon Thompson.

Boland, Eavan. 'Evening of Poetry'. *Irish Times*, 31 August 1967, 6. Edited by Douglas Gageby.

Bukowska, Joanna. 'Irish Topography of a Disturbed Mind in Seamus Heaney's *Sweeney Astray* and Trevor Joyce's *The Poems of Sweeny Peregrine'.* In *Ironies of Art/Tragedies of Life: Essays on Irish Literature*, edited by Liliana Sikorska, 239–264. Frankfurt: Peter Lang, 2005.

Caleshu, Anthony. 'On Radu Andriescu, Trevor Joyce, Leanne O'Sullivan, Laurie Duggan, Giles Goodland, Lisa Dart, and Mark Halliday'. 'This Time It's Personal'. Special issue, *Poetry Review* 99, no. 4 (Winter 2009): 111–114. Edited by Fiona Sampson.

Davis, Alex. 'Purity and Dirt: Review of *Syzygy'. The Irish Review*, no. 22 (Summer 1998): 114–116. Edited by Kevin Barry et al.

Donnelly, Paul. 'Demanding Voices: Review of *with the first dream of fire they hunt the cold* by Trevor Joyce and *In the Aviary of Voices* by Karin Lessing'. *Stride Magazine*, May 2002. Edited by Rupert Loydell.

Donnelly, Peter. 'Voices from the Past'. Review of *The Poems of Sweeny, Peregrine. Irish Independent*, 11 September 1976, 8. Edited by Michael Hand.

Dorward, Nate. 'In the Net: Review of Robert Archambeau, Randolph Healy, Trevor Joyce, Billy Mills, and Maurice Scully'. Review of *Syzygy. The Gig*, no. 1 (1998): 57–59. Willowdale, ON: The Gig.

Duncan, Andrew. 'Pale Angel Exuvial Who Can Mix It with the Chicken'. Review of *with the first dream of fire they hunt the cold: a body of work, 1966–2000. Jacket* 20 (December 2002). Edited by John Tranter. Web. 3 Jan. 2014. <http://jacketmagazine.com/20/dunc-r-joyc.html>

Frazer, Tony. 'Letter from England'. *Poetry Ireland Review*, no. 79 (2004): 72–77. Edited by Peter Sirr.

———. Review of *stone floods. Shearsman*, no. 36 (1998). Edited by Tony Frazer.

———. Review of *Without Asylum. Shearsman*, no. 42 (1999). Edited by Tony Frazer.

Fryatt, Kit. 'Process, Product and a Peacock'. Review of *What's in Store. Irish Times*, 19 April 2008, B10. Edited by Geraldine Kennedy.

Glavin, Anthony. 'Review of *Sole Glum Trek* by Trevor Joyce, *Endsville* by Brian Lynch and Paul Durcan, and *The Rebel Bloom* by Rudi Holzapfel'. *Hibernia* 31, no. 10 (October 1967): 17. Edited by John Mulcahy.

Higgins, Kevin. 'Review of *with the first dream of fire they hunt the cold* by Trevor Joyce'. *Poetry Quarterly Review*, no. 20 (Summer 2003): 23. Edited by Derrick Woolf and Tilla Brading.

Johnston, Fred. 'Surprised by Familiarity'. Review of *stone floods*, et al. *Books Ireland, no. 191* (December 1995): 323–324.

Jordan, John. 'Finding Poetry in Suburbia'. Review of *Versheets*, edited by Trevor Joyce (New Writers' Press). *Irish Independent*, 29 May 1971, 5. Edited by Conor O'Brien.

———. 'Five Voices'. Review of *Pentahedron*. *Irish Independent*, 6 September 1969, 6. Edited by Hector Legge.

———. 'I Knew These Streets'. Review of *Pentahedron*. *Irish Independent*, 17 June 1972, 10. Edited by Conor O'Brien.

Keery, James. 'Barbed Wire'. Review of *with the first dream of fire they hunt the cold*. *Poetry Review* 92, no. 4 (Winter 2002–2003): 107. Edited by David Herd and Robert Potts.

Kellogg, David. Reviews of Wild Honey Press titles. *Samizdat*, no. 3 (Summer 1999). Edited by Robert Archambeau.

Kiley, Frederick S. 'Review of *Selected Poems* by Brian Coffey and *Pentahedron* by Trevor Joyce'. *Éire-Ireland: A Journal of Irish Studies* 8, no. 3 (1973): 148–150. Edited by Eóin McKiernan.

Latta, John. 'Review of *What's In Store* by Trevor Joyce'. *Isola di Rifiuti*, 13 December 2007. Reprinted at *Third Factory*.

Lloyd, David. 'Review of *The Poems of Sweeny, Peregrine*'. *Granta*, probably Autumn 1976. Cambridge.

———. 'An Impressive Collection'. Review of *with the first dream of fire they hunt the cold*. *Irish Times*, 8 September 2001, 10. Edited by Conor Brady.

Longley, Edna. 'Recent Irish Poetry'. Review of *The Poems of Sweeny Peregrine*. *Irish Times*, 21 August 1976, 8. Edited by Fergus Pyle.

Marshall, T.C. "Review of Books by Trevor Joyce and Jack Collom." *Galatea Resurrects: A Poetry Engagement* 21. Ed. Eileen Tabios.

Martin, Augustine. 'A Worthy Enterprise'. Review of *Sole Glum Trek*, by Trevor Joyce, and *Endsville*, by Brian Lynch and Paul Durcan. *Irish Press*, 5 August 1967, 10. Edited by Tim Pat Coogan.

Mays, J.C.C. 'Drift into Net Back to Drift'. Review of *Syzygy*. *The Journal*, no. 1 (1998): 58–60. Edited by Billy Mills and Catherine Walsh.

———. 'Trevor Joyce's *Syzygy*'. *The Recorder* 13, no. 2 (Fall 2000): 73–76. Edited by Christopher Cahill.

———. 'Scriptor Ignotus, with the Fire in Him Now'. Review of *with the first dream of fire they hunt the cold*. *Dublin Review*, no. 6 (March 2002): 42–65. Edited by Brendan Barrington.

McCarthy, Dan. 'Book of the Day'. Review of *with the first dream of fire they hunt the cold*. *Irish Examiner*, 8 February 2002. 20. Edited by Brian Looney.

McCarthy, Thomas. Review of *stone floods*, by Trevor Joyce, et al. *Poetry Ireland Review*, no. 48 (Winter 1996): 90–91. Edited by Moya Cannon.

McFadden, Hugh. 'Richness of the Many Poetries'. Review of *stone floods*, et al. *Irish Times*, 9 December 1995, A8. Edited by Conor Brady.

McGurk, Tom. 'Tame Beer and Old Brandy'. Review of *The Poems of Sweeny Peregrine*, et al. *Hibernia* 41, no. 1 (21 January 1977): 22. Edited by John Mulcahy.

O'Brien, Treasa. 'Niamh Lawlor and Partners Based on a True Story: A Seminar on Mis-Information, University College Cork, 27 January 2007'. Review of 'Based on a True Story: A Seminar on Mis-information', Cork, Ireland, 27 January 2007. *Circa*, no. 119 (Spring 2007): 95–97. Edited by Peter Fitzgerald.

Packer, Matt. Review of *Cork Caucus: On Art, Possibility, and Democracy*, edited by Trevor Joyce and Shep Steiner. *Irish Arts Review* 26, no. 1. (Spring 2009): 135–136.

Quidnunc. 'An Irishman's Diary'. Review of *The Lace Curtain*. *Irish Times*, 19 July 1967, 9. Edited by Douglas Gageby.

Ramsell, Billy. Review of *What's in Store*. *Southword*, no. 13 (2007): 140–142. Edited by Patrick Cotter. Cork: Southword Editions.

Ryan, James. 'Readers Choice: *Stone Fields.*' *Irish Times*, 23 May 1995, 14. Edited by Conor Brady.

Review of *stone floods*. *Books Ireland*, no. 237 (February 2001): 260.

Review of *with the first dream of fire they hunt the cold*. *Books Ireland: First Flush*, no. 243 (October 2001): 275.

Review of *stone floods*. *Books Ireland: First Flush*, no. 189 (October 1995): 260.

Sirr, Peter. 'Ways of Making'. Review of *with the first dream of fire they hunt the cold*, by Trevor Joyce, and *Collected Poems*, by Pearse Hutchinson. *Poetry Ireland Review*, no. 73 (Summer 2002): 145–151.

Smith, Mandy. Review of *with the first dream of fire they hunt the cold*. *New Hope International Review*, December 2007.

Smith, Michael. 'A Modernist Eye'. Review of *Syzygy*. *Irish Times*, 26 July 1998, B9. Edited by Conor Brady.

———. 'The Young Poets: Trevor Joyce'. Review of *Sole Glum Trek*. *Hibernia* 33, no. 9 (April–May 1969): 15. Edited by John Mulcahy.

Vincent, Stephen. Review of *What's in Store*. *Galatea Resurrects*, no. 9 (March 31, 2008). Edited by Eileen Tabios.

Weir, Anthony. 'Review of *The Poems of Sweeny, Peregrine*'. *Fortnight*, no. 135 (22 October 1976): 10. Edited by Ciaran McKeown.

Wheatley, David. 'Not So Easy Options'. Review of *stone floods*. *The Irish Review*, nos. 17/18 (1995): 191–195. Edited by Kevin Barry et al.

———. 'Trevor Joyce's *Courts of Air and Earth*'. *Times Literary Supplement*, no. 5584 (9 April 2010): 24. Edited by Peter Stothard.

Zinnes, Harriet. Review of *with the first dream of fire they hunt the cold*. *Rain Taxi*, Winter 2001/2002. Edited by Eric Lorberer.

Notes/Introductions

Brancaleone, David. 'The Avant, Cork City, July 2009'. *Circa*, no. 130 (Winter 2009): 51–52.

Gilonis, Harry. Introduction to Trevor Joyce at SubVoicive Poetry. 29 January 1999.

O'Mahony, Niamh. 'Trevor Joyce'. Poets and Poems. *Poetry International*. 2013.

'Trevor Joyce'. *Prague Literary Review* 2, no. 3 (May 2004): 13–14. Edited by Louis Armand.

Dictionary entries

'Trevor Joyce'. In *Contemporary Poets*, 578. Edited by Rosalie Murphy and James Vinson. London: St James Press; New York, NY: St Martin's Press, 1970. Reprinted in 1973.

'Trevor Joyce'. In *The MacMillan Dictionary of Irish Literature*, 339. Edited by Robert Hogan. Dublin: Gill & Macmillan, 1979.

'Trevor Joyce'. In *A Biographical Dictionary of Irish Writers*, 116. Edited by Brian Cleeve and Anne Brady. Dublin: Lilliput, 1985.

'Trevor Joyce'. In *British and Irish Poets: A Biographical Dictionary, 449–2006*, 209. Edited by William Stewart. Jefferson, NC: McFarland, 2007.

Contributors to this Volume

Lucy Collins is a lecturer in English Literature at University College Dublin, Ireland. Educated at Trinity College Dublin and at Harvard University, where she spent a year as a Fulbright Scholar, she teaches and researches in the area of modern poetry and poetics. She has published widely on modern and contemporary Irish and British poetry. Recent publications include *Poetry by Women in Ireland: A Critical Anthology 1870–1970* (Liverpool) and an edition of the poems of Sheila Wingfield (Liberties). A co-edited volume, *The Irish Poet and the Natural World: An Anthology of Verse in English from the Tudors to the Romantics* appeared from Cork University Press in 2014.

Eric Falci is an Associate Professor of English at the University of California, Berkeley, where he teaches courses on twentieth-century British and Irish literature. He is the author of *Continuity and Change in Irish Poetry, 1966-2010* and is currently completing the *Cambridge Introduction to British Poetry, 1945-2010*.

Fergal Gaynor (b. 1969) is author of *VIII Stepping Poems & Other Pieces* (Miami University Press, 2011) and co-editor of the art critical journal *Enclave Review*, to which he regularly contributes reviews and essays. Since 2000 he has initiated and organised a number of mainly avant-garde cultural events, exhibitions and festivals in his native city, Cork, at whose university he currently teaches a course on the history of Irish art. His PhD, on literary and other modernisms, centred on the work of Lawrence, Cézanne and Heidegger.

John Goodby has taught at Leeds University, UCC, and since 1994 at Swansea University, where he holds a personal chair. He is the author of *Irish poetry since 1950: from stillness into history* (2000) and several works on the work of Dylan Thomas, including *The poetry of Dylan Thomas: under the spelling wall* (2013) and a new annotated centenary edition of the *Collected Poems* (2014). As a poet and translator he is the author of *Illennium* (2010) and translations of Heine, Adel Guemar, Pasolini and Reverdy.

Fanny Howe has written numerous books of fiction and poetry and has won a Guggenheim, a Lenore Marshall Award and the Ruth Lilly Lifetime Achievement Award. Her most recent collection of poetry *Second Childhood* was published by Graywolf Press. She lives and teaches in New England.

David Lloyd is a writer and critic, born in Ireland and currently living in Los Angeles and teaching at the University of California, Riverside. *Arc & Sill: Poems 1979-2009*, (Shearsman Books and New Writers' Press, 2012) collects his five previous books of poetry: *Taropatch* (Oakland: Jimmy's House of Knowledge,

1985), *Coupures* (Dublin: hardPressed Poetry, 1987), *Change of State* (Berkeley: Cusp Books, 1993), *Sill,* (Los Angeles: Cusp Books, 2006), and *Vega* (Los Angeles: Mind Made Books, 2009). His play, *The Press*, premiered at Liverpool Hope University in 2010. *Kodalith*, a sequence of poems, is available from Smithereens Press, http://www.smithereenspress.com/. As a critic, he works on Irish literature and culture and on poetry and aesthetics. His most recent critical book is *Irish Culture and Colonial Modernity, 1800-2000: The Transformation of Oral Space* (Cambridge, 2011). He is the editor of Cusp Books, a chap-book press based in Los Angeles.

PETER MANSON lives in Glasgow. His books include *Poems of Frank Rupture* (Sancho Panza Press), *Adjunct: an Undigest* and *For the Good of Liars* (both from Barque Press) and *Between Cup and Lip* (Miami University Press, Ohio). Miami UP also published his book of translations, *Stéphane Mallarmé: The Poems in Verse.* http://petermanson.wordpress.com/ for more information.

NIAMH O'MAHONY is completing a PhD on poetic appropriation in the writings of Trevor Joyce, Alan Halsey and Susan Howe at University College Cork, Ireland where her research is supported by the Irish Research Council. She spent 2012-2013 as a Fulbright Student at Miami University, Ohio. Niamh O'Mahony published a special feature on Trevor Joyce in *Jacket2* in February 2014 and has essays forthcoming on Joyce and Halsey in 2015.

MARTHINE SATRIS is the Associate Editor of Two Lines Press, the publishing arm of the San Francisco-based Center for the Art of Translation. She received her doctorate in English from UC Santa Barbara, writing her dissertation on contemporary avant-garde Irish poetry. Her interviews with Irish poets Maurice Scully and Trevor Joyce have appeared in *Contemporary Literature* and *The Journal of British and Irish Innovative Poetry,* respectively. She writes about books and culture for a variety of online and print publications, including *Golden Handcuffs Review* and the online magazine *The Rumpus* (www.therumpus.net). Marthine Satris also teaches English at UC Berkeley's Fall Program for Freshmen.

GEOFFREY SQUIRES (b.1942) grew up in Co. Donegal. After reading English at Cambridge he lived and worked in Iran, France, the US and England and is now retired. His poetry is collected in *Untitled and other poems* (2004) and *Abstract Lyrics and other poems* (2012) both published by Wild Honey Press, Bray. Two of his books have been translated into French, as *Sans Titre* (2013) and *Paysages et Silences*(2014) published by Editions Unes, Nice. His ground-breaking *Hafez: translations and interpretations of the ghazals* was published by Miami University Press in 2014. He is currently working on translations of medieval Irish poetry.

KEITH TUMA is the author of *Fishing by Obstinate Isles: Modern and Postmodern British Poetry and American Readers* (Northwestern UP, 1998), *The Paris Hilton* (Critical Documents, 2009), and *On Leave: A Book of Anecdotes* (Salt, 2011), among other works, and the editor of books including *Mina Loy: Woman and Poet* (National Poetry Foundation, 1998, with Maeera Shreiber) and *Anthology of Twentieth-Century British and Irish Poetry* (Oxford UP, 2001). He is Professor of English at Miami University in Ohio, where he directs the Miami University Press.

JEFFREY TWITCHELL-WAAS currently resides in Malta and edits the Z-site on the work of Louis Zukofsky (www.z-site.net).

INDEX